P9-CAG-683

i am
am 2
m 2

santa monica 2000⁺

millennium collection
Santa Monica Public Library

Ecology, Community and Delight

Landscape architecture is a key profession for a world facing an uncertain environmental future. Yet it is hindered by a chronic identity crisis. Is it primarily concerned with making beautiful places, helping people or saving the planet from ecological catastrophe? This book examines the three principal value systems which influence landscape architectural practice – the aesthetic, the social and the environmental – and seeks to discover the role that the profession should be playing now and for the future.

Ecology, Community and Delight combines a close analysis of important theoretical texts with an interview-based investigation into the values of many prominent landscape architects. A number of case studies of contemporary projects are included. Questions explored include: should landscape architecture aspire to the status of an art form? What is the relationship between aesthetics and ecology? Does landscape architecture have a social mission? How must landscape design adapt to the challenges of environmental sustainability?

The book presents a tripartite framework for understanding the values and motivations of landscape architects. It denies that any one value – beauty or usefulness or ecological integrity – can be elevated above the others but suggests that the richest and most successful designs occur when all three of the main value fields are simultaneously addressed.

Ian H. Thompson is a Lecturer in Landscape Architecture at the University of Newcastle. Originally trained as a philosopher, he practised as a landscape architect for thirteen years before returning to research and teaching.

Ecology, Community and Delight

Sources of values in landscape architecture

Ian H. Thompson

London and New York

First published 2000 by E & FN Spon
11 New Fetter Lane, London EC4P 4EE

Simultaneously published in the USA and Canada
by Routledge
29 West 35th Street, New York, NY 10001

E & FN Spon is an imprint of the Taylor & Francis Group

Typeset in Frutiger by Solidus (Bristol) Limited
Printed in the United Kingdom at the University Press, Cambridge

British Library Cataloguing in Publication Data
A catalogue record for this book is available from the British Library

Library of Congress Cataloging in Publication Data
Thompson, Ian H., 1955–
    Ecology, community and delight : sources of values in landscape
  architecture / Ian H. Thompson.
        p.   cm.
    'Published simultaneously in the USA and Canada.'
    Includes bibliographical references and index.
      1. Landscape architecture   2. Landscape architecture—Philosophy.
3. Environment (Aesthetics)   4. Landscape assessment   I. Title.
SB472.T48   1999
712'.01—dc21   99-22290
                                                    CIP

ISBN 0-419-25150-2 (hbk)
ISBN 0-419-23610-4 (pbk)

To my mother,
Christine Middleton Thompson (1925–98)

Contents

Preface and acknowledgements

More than twenty years ago, during a year out from a philosophy course, I found employment with the Planning Department of Cumbria County Council. At the County Hall in Kendal, I was met by an administrator. 'Ah, Mr Thompson,' he said, 'Geography, isn't it?' 'No,' I admitted, 'I'm a philosopher.' Scratching his head for a moment, he came to a quick decision – 'We'll put you with the landscape architects then.' I was shown into a small room where three amiable men worked at drawing boards, deciding which parts of the county were to benefit from tree-planting. It seemed like a pleasant way to make a living. People often seem surprised that a landscape architect should have started out as a philosopher, but it must have seemed natural to that administrator to place an oddity like me among this esoteric little group. He has my gratitude though, for he opened the way to a career which has never been less than interesting.

After meeting many landscape architects, and interviewing twenty-six of them for this book, I realise that it is not so unusual for people to tumble into landscape architecture as a career, rather as I did. As a small profession, it may still be overlooked by careers advisers, but it can exert a powerful attraction for those who discover it, for it offers a way to combine scientific knowledge with artistic endeavour, in an enterprise which, for the most part, is clearly on the side of the angels.

Landscape architecture deserves a higher public profile than it enjoys. Why this may be so is one of the minor themes of this book. Considering that the profession has existed since 1858, when Frederick Law Olmsted, the designer of Central Park, coined the term, practitioners still find that when they reveal their occupation to strangers a typical response is an invitation to 'come round for dinner and give us some advice about the garden'. For those of us tutored in the grand visions of Ian McHarg or Sir Geoffrey Jellicoe the gulf between the public perception and the professional aspiration can seem unbridgeable.

Yet for those who do learn about the true scope of the profession – its involvement in the reclamation of derelict land, for example, or its role in the renewal of decaying urban districts, or in the creation of city parks, squares and boulevards – it can exert a fascination. There is no doubt that landscape architecture is a powerfully vocational profession. Certainly the idea that there were people dedicated to improving places appealed strongly, twenty years ago, to this tyro philosopher, on both aesthetic and ethical grounds. One feels that there is a landscape architectural bandwagon garaged somewhere which only needs a hefty shove to get it rolling. Surely a population with a seemingly unquenchable appetite for programmes and books about the environment, travel, interior design and gardening could discover a similar interest in the condition and quality of the exterior environments of the towns and cities wherein they live and work.

For me, landscape architecture offered not only a job but also a way of reconnecting with the world after too much abstract speculation. Landscape architecture brought me literally and metaphorically back down to earth, though sometimes, when clutching soggy plans and staring into waterlogged planting pits, I had to remind myself to be grateful for this blessing. The philosophical impulse was only dormant however, for once one has the habit of asking large general questions about ultimate justifications it is difficult to stop. This book is centred on just such questions.

While it has always seemed self-evident that landscape architecture is 'a good thing', for a long time I was nagged by an uncertainty about its purposes. What was it really *for*? Much has been written about *how* to do landscape architecture. Very little seemed to be written about *why* it was worth doing, and what there was often seemed woolly or contradictory. Is landscape architecture about making places beautiful? And, if so, what is to count as beauty? Is it about making useful places? Is it about restoring some balance between mankind and nature? Are those who are drawn to the profession driven by artistic aspirations, by a sense of social injustice, by environmental anxieties, or by some mixture of all three? How indeed can such motivations be combined and how can they be expressed in designed landscapes? These are the sorts of questions which I have set out to explore in the chapters which follow. The possible answers suggested will, I hope, be of interest not only to academics and students but also to any landscape architects who have asked similar questions about their own practice.

The book began as research for a Ph.D. and my first debt of gratitude is to my supervisor, Ali Madani Pour, for guiding me safely out of the harbour. Many other Newcastle colleagues have come aboard as pilots from time to time, and I am particularly grateful to Patsy Healey for steering me towards some excellent books on interview methods and to John Benson for his hand on the tiller through the whirlpools of ecological theory. Emma Reynolds helped significantly by volunteering to assist in the transcription of interview tapes. My thanks also go to Peter Aspinall of Heriot Watt University, Edinburgh, for his help with the research methodology.

Next I must thank all twenty-six of my interviewees, who gave freely of their time and, I am relieved to say, of their opinions. I am also grateful for the hospitality that they extended towards an itinerant academic. Their names appear often in the text and also in the appendix, so I will save words by not listing everyone again here. It is customary in prefaces to take responsibility for all the opinions and errors the reader will encounter in the text. In this case, I hope that where I have represented the opinions of others I have done so honestly and accurately.

Another small band of landscape architects and related professionals have helped me since the formal round of interviews was completed. I would like to thank Louise French and her colleagues at Groundwork Black Country for an informative and enjoyable afternoon beside the Ridgacre Canal, and Petula Neilson from Groundwork St Helens, Knowsley and Sefton for a similarly instructive trip over Bold Moss Urban Common. Andrew Grant was kind enough to tell me about his designs for the Earth Centre, Doncaster, and Peter Chmiel gave me an interesting tour around the work in progress.

Many artists, landscape architects and photographers have given me permission to use their images. They have been credited in the captions, but I also mention them here because without their help this book would have been considerably less enjoyable to look at.

In its latter stages a book is a team effort. I would like to extend my thanks to everyone at E & FN Spon who has played a part in bringing this project to fruition, particularly Caroline Mallinder, Rebecca Casey, Geraldine Lyons, Sarah Daniels, Jill Freshney and Alan Fidler, the copy-editor.

Every effort has been made to contact copyright holders for their permission to reprint material in this book. The publisher would be grateful to hear from any copyright holder who is not acknowledged here and will undertake to rectify any errors or omissions in future editions of this book.

1 What this book is about

Many books about landscape architecture ask 'how-to?' questions: how can we reclaim this site?; how can we get trees to grow here?; how can I be sure that this wall will stand up in a force ten gale? This book, on the other hand, is more concerned with questions of 'why?': why is ecology important?; why does community consultation matter?; why is proposal A so much better than proposal B? It also poses the biggest 'why?' question of all – why be a landscape architect in the first place? Another way of putting this is to say that the book is concerned with the reasons why landscape architects do what they do, the values that they hold, and the underlying justifications for such values. To put this into academic jargon, it is a book of normative theory.

In writing it I have used two main sources. As one might have expected from an academic, I have buried myself in the landscape architectural literature, mining it for value statements, both explicit and implicit. But recognising that what is written in books might bear little relation to the profession as practised, I also sought out twenty-six landscape architects and interviewed them in depth in an attempt to understand their beliefs and motivations. During the period when I was writing the book I also talked to several landscape architects who had not been part of my original interview sample, but their ideas have been included where appropriate. Finally I sought to ground these investigations by looking at a number of case studies of actual projects, some – but not all – of which were undertaken by the interviewees. These are included as boxes at appropriate places in the text.

Theory: something to be done

When scientists use the word 'theory' they are generally referring to explanatory systems of ideas that have been established by observation or tested by experiment, but there is another sense of the word. The *Oxford English Dictionary* defines theory as 'a conception or mental scheme of something to be done, or of the method of doing it; a systematic statement of rules or principles to be followed'. A profession which seeks to bring about positive changes in the environment has to be based upon the conception that there is 'something to be done' and must propose preferred methods of doing it.

While recognising the narrowness of most attempted definitions of design, Bryan Lawson (1980) suggests some near universal characteristics of the design process, three of which are particularly pertinent to this inquiry. First, design takes place in the context of a need for action; second, it is prescriptive in that it deals with questions of what ought to be; and, third, it involves the designer in making subjective value judgements. This book is concerned with these inescapable value judgements. How can landscape design theory, as a 'systematic statement of rules or principles to be followed', offer the designer any guidance about the ends that are to be pursued or the manner in which they can be realised?

The condition of landscape architectural theory

The impetus behind this book came from an article in *Landscape Journal* (1992) entitled 'Most Important Questions'. The editors had written to twenty prominent people connected with the discipline of landscape design, asking for their responses to the question 'What do you consider the most important question(s) in landscape architecture today?' Far from asking for more technical knowledge, the majority of the published replies were concerned with values. R. Burton Little of the University of California, for example, wrote; 'How do aesthetics and ecology relate to one another? What are the aesthetic values that may reside within ecological design?' Taken as a whole, the responses suggested that there is much confusion about what landscape architecture is, and what objectives landscape architects should be pursuing. The editors concluded that landscape architecture is 'a discipline seeking knowledge, and an art seeking meaning through form, and an applied service profession seeking health, equity, even salvation from extinction'. Can landscape architecture be all of these things without falling into inconsistency and confusion?

What is landscape architecture?

If you are reading this, there is a high probability that you are already a landscape practitioner, academic or student, or work in a closely related field such as architecture or planning. If so, you may think that you already know the answer to this question, but it is not as straightforward as it seems. Even those within the profession get puzzled about the differences between *landscape architecture* and *landscape design*, and the picture gets even cloudier once we include terms such as *landscape planning, landscape management, landscape science,* and that hangover from pre-professional days, *landscape gardening.*

Tom Turner (1990) presents historical evidence which suggests that the first use of the expression 'landscape architecture' was in a book called *The Landscape Architecture of the Great Paintings in Italy*, written by Gilbert Laing Meason in 1827. Meason thought that architects could learn much from studying the sorts of buildings that appeared in Italian landscape paintings, and coined the phrase 'landscape architecture' to describe such buildings. Writing in 1840 J.C. Loudon used the term in the same sense, using 'landscape gardening' to refer to the layout of grounds. The term seems to have acquired its modern meaning when Calvert Vaux and Frederick Law Olmsted entered and won the competition for the design of New York's Central Park in 1858, describing themselves in their entry as 'landscape architects'.

Seven years later, Olmsted was to express his misgivings about the professional title. In a letter he wrote,

> I am all the time bothered with the miserable nomenclature of L.A. Landscape is not a good word, Architecture is not: the combination is not – Gardening is worse.
>
> (letter quoted in *OED* 1976 Supplement)

The title persisted however, being taken up by Patrick Geddes in 1903 and Thomas Mawson in 1940. In Britain the Institute of Landscape Architects was founded in 1930 and the International Federation of Landscape Architects was formed in 1948. Since the Second World War the title has spread around the world and has now gained common currency. Despite this, says Turner, it has been constantly misunderstood.

Turner notes that the word 'landscape' has itself undergone a shift in meaning. In the seventeenth century it was a painter's term, derived from the Dutch, which referred to a picture which depicted inland scenery (as opposed to seascapes, portraits, etc.) The scenery depicted was usually of ideal, or idealised, places. The eighteenth-century 'landscape gardeners' took their inspiration from painting, particularly the works of Poussin, Salvator Rosa and Claude Lorrain, but sought to realise these ideal landscapes through the tangible manipulation of earth, water and vegetation. Things started to go wrong, as far as the meaning of 'landscape architecture' was concerned, when a second sense of the word 'landscape', which Turner calls the Geographers' Sense, gained ascendancy over the original meaning. In this sense 'landscape' has come to mean 'a tract of land with its distinguishing characteristics and features, esp. considered as a product of modifying or shaping processes and agents (usually natural)'.

As Turner sees it, the problem with 'landscape architect', if 'landscape' is used in the Geographers' Sense, is that it implies God-like powers 'to raise mountains, to direct the course of rivers, to control the climate and to dictate the pattern of human settlement'. This aspiration to omnipotence is, he says, 'as preposterous as it is sacrilegious as it is tyrannical'. We could call this the Slartibartfast

Syndrome, after the alien terra-former in Douglas Adams's *Hitch-hikers' Guide to the Galaxy* who was so proud of having created the 'twiddly bits around Norway'. Perhaps some landscape designers would like that kind of power, but it is hard to imagine anything further from the realities of practice.

On one hand we have the Slartibartfast Syndrome; on the other we have an equally damaging confusion, as far as public conceptions of the profession are concerned, which springs from the use of the word 'architect'. Inevitably there is the misconception that landscape architects are a specialised species of (building) architect. The most common complaint voiced by landscape architects is that they are seen, by clients and by other professions, as subordinate members of the design team who are brought in late in the process to supply the 'soft landscaping'.

Turner makes the interesting suggestion that the word 'landscape' can be given a Designers' Sense, in which it means 'a good place'. The following definitions then become available:

Landscape design is the art of making good outdoor places.

Landscape architecture is the art of making good places by the preparation and supervision of contracts.

Landscape management is the art of managing places to make them better.

Landscape science is concerned with seeking knowledge about good places.

Landscape planning is the art of planning good places.

As Turner himself acknowledges, this leaves open what is to count as good – 'It is the task of every age to reconsider the criteria for goodness.' This is one of the aims of this book.

Turner concludes that the choice of landscape architecture as the professional title was an eccentric one, and that the profession would be better served by the title 'landscape design', as this would more accurately describe what landscape professionals do, and would make explicit the commonalities between landscape design and other design fields.

Richard Stiles (1994) notes that the debate about the profession's title and definition is now international. He points out that when the Institute of

Landscape Architects reorganised itself as the Landscape Institute in 1978,[1] establishing three classes of professional membership (landscape architects, landscape managers and landscape scientists), it had to make an uneasy choice between a number of possibilities, and many in the profession remain in doubt about the appropriateness of the option chosen. While landscape architects (or designers) and landscape managers are actively involved in manipulating the landscape, landscape scientists, in contrast, are primarily concerned with passive description, understanding and explanation of the processes which underlie landscape change.

Moreover, the 1978 reorganisation did not create a separate class of membership for landscape planners, yet 'landscape planning' would seem the best description for the sorts of strategic exercises in which landscape professionals have increasingly become engaged. If it has proved difficult to arrive at satisfactory job titles and definitions in Britain, how much more difficult it will be to do it internationally – in part because the profession has developed in different ways in different cultures, but also because of the nuances of languages and the difficulties of direct translation.

Stiles believes that 'landscape architecture' is likely to remain the overarching term for the profession, simply because it has already become established in use. He offers the following definitions for areas of sub-activity:

Landscape planning is concerned with the conservation and enhancement of landscape resources for the benefit of current and future generations *at a strategic level and usually over a long time scale*;

Landscape design is concerned with the conservation and enhancement of landscape resources for the benefit of current and future generations *at the site level and usually with a specific end state in view*; and

Landscape management is concerned with the conservation and enhancement of landscape resources for the benefit of current and future generations *as an ongoing process, usually at the level of one or many sites*.

Each of these definitions refers to the conservation and enhancement of landscape resources, which does, from the point of view of this investigation, beg certain questions about the ultimate ends of landscape practice. On the other hand, the portions of the definitions that Stiles has placed in italic type can be taken as acceptable working definitions of the differences in scope between the activities mentioned.

We may agree with Turner that 'landscape architecture' was a historical mistake, but it does not seem that a revision is imminent or likely. Stiles's usage is more consonant with the way that the terms are currently applied, so in this book the term 'landscape architect' will be regarded as the accepted title for the profession, and as the umbrella under which design, management, planning and science may be found.

However, the focus of the book is upon landscape design, i.e. that part of landscape architecture which is concerned with the design of sites. As Stiles's definitions illustrate, however, this activity merges spatially and temporally with landscape planning and landscape management, and reference will be made to these where appropriate. In most contexts the terms 'landscape architecture' and 'landscape design' can be used interchangeably without too much confusion, and many of the authors and practitioners cited do not draw much distinction between them.

Thinking about values

While we are clearing up slippery language, some clarification of 'value' seems necessary. This is another word with a range of meanings. There are hard, narrow uses prescribed for mathematics, economics or natural science, and a number of broader, more general uses. Taking 'value' as a noun, we find that the *Oxford English Dictionary*'s first four definitions all involve some reference to material or monetary worth or to equivalence in exchange. The fifth talks about worth or worthiness, but only in relation to persons. The sixth definition is closer to the sense in which it will be used in this book: 'the relative status of a thing, or the estimate in which it is held, according to its real or supposed worth, usefulness, or importance'.

People have all sorts of reasons for valuing things. The residents of Much Muttering value the village post office, not only for the postal services it provides but because it is one of the social centres of the community. They value the war memorial because it

looks rather fine upon the village green, and because it provides a tangible link with the past. They value the local reservoir, not just as a water resource but also as a beauty spot and for the recreational possibilities it offers. The local children value the woods just outside the village as a playground and a source of conkers in the autumn. The local landowner values the same wood as a fine stand of timber, while the field naturalists prize it for its badger sets. So the list goes on – we could characterise some of the values we have already discovered as utilitarian, social, aesthetic, historical and environmental.

Non-monetary and monetary values

Note that only the landowner in our fictional village is concerned with the exchange value of a commodity. When we talk about values we are often not talking about monetary values. Indeed it might be argued that some sorts of value cannot be translated into economic terms. A family might regard great-grandfather's pocket watch as a unique, irreplaceable item. Its value at the pawn shop or antique dealer's might be low, but to the family it has great worth. Perhaps it could be argued that even this sort of value could be given a monetary equivalent. If the watch were stolen, there would be a maximum amount that the family would pay to get it back. Equally, suppose that the Department of Transport wanted to drive a motorway through the very heart of Much Muttering. There would perhaps be some level of payment that would function as an effective inducement for the residents to leave, and this could be taken to represent the monetary value of the non-monetary values inherent in the place.

However, the fact that some monetary translation can often be found for other sorts of values does not mean that it *always* can be, nor does it mean that in those cases when such a translation is possible the non-monetary value has been *reduced* to the monetary. Money can be used as the medium of exchanging values, but far from this making it the most significant or fundamental kind of value, it reveals its secondary, dependent status. Money only works because there are other sorts of value which are worth having in their own right. Another way of putting this is to say that money is a proxy for some sorts of values.

Recent research into the recreational value of countryside has looked at the amounts users would be willing to pay in order to continue enjoying it. For example, environmental economists have carried out a study of the use and passive use values of the British canal network, by asking respondents how much they would contribute towards a programme that maintained boating, towpath and heritage features along canals. The researchers estimated the value of these aspects to be £145 million per annum, a sum far in excess of the income of the revenue of British Waterways and government grant in aid (Adamowicz *et al.*, 1995).

In this way, argue the economists, goods and services not exchanged on markets can be brought into the economic calculus, opening the way to greatly improved forms of cost–benefit analysis.

When one first reads of the moves economists have made to put financial values on intangibles like scenery or recreation one may be surprised or even affronted, for it is not apparent prima facie that this exercise is valid. It seems odd or inappropriate to stick a price tag on the Lake District or the Rocky Mountains. We are used to paying to see paintings in a gallery, but we do not confuse the price of the ticket with the worth of the paintings. No doubt galleries could increase their entrance prices to the level where none but the very rich would be willing to pay for entry, but this would in no way alter the (non-monetary) value of the artworks.

The philosopher, Arne Naess (whose 'Deep Ecology' will be discussed in Chapter 8), reacts against the economists' approach arguing that 'you cannot slap a price tag on nature' (Naess, 1989: 124).

He cites an argument put forward by Paul Hofseth: if somebody asks a person, B, what he or she will pay in order that A does not break B's arm, the amount suggested by B cannot be taken as the price or the value of the arm. It is not permitted to break human arms. Analogously, access to free nature is a right. Similarly if a government, A, asks a population, B, what price it will pay for protecting a part of nature, the price is not the price of that part of nature as $10,000 is the price of a certain car.

The economists can respond to such criticisms by saying that the lack of quantitative data in support of protection functions as if data actually were offered; namely, the price zero. Thus the economists may claim that what they try to prevent is the price zero from being used in the decision-making process. This is an expedient move which skirts around some

serious philosophical difficulties, but even Naess is pragmatic about what environmental economics can offer. Perhaps it is better that such evaluations are carried out than not carried out, but ultimately our value system is not, and should not be, a monetary one.

Values as principles

There is another commonly used sense of the word 'value'. When we talk about someone having a 'well-developed sense of values', or say that they have a particular 'set of values' or a 'value system', we are using the word 'values' to refer to the moral principles or accepted standards of a person or social group. Once we enter the moral sphere, value is commonly attached to abstract concepts like *freedom* or *dignity* rather than concrete objects like pocket-watches. It is an easy slide from saying 'I value my freedom' to talking about freedom as a value. Similarly, in aesthetics, we can move from 'I value that painting for its beauty' to 'beauty is the value I am seeking'.

Abstract nouns like the French revolutionary mob's cry of 'Liberty, Equality, Fraternity!' are generally as vague as they are emotive. There are rallying cries in architecture too. While conducting the interviews for this book I learnt of Henry Wotton's 'Commodity, Firmness and Delight'.[2] My version of this – 'Ecology, Community and Delight' – is a sort of battle-cry too. But just as political theorists, attempting to understand concepts like *liberty* and *equality* soon run into difficulties, so may we when we look at landscape architectural values more closely. Liberty and equality both seem like ends worth pursuing, but it is soon becomes evident that absolute liberty (if such a thing is possible) is incompatible with absolute equality, so which is to prevail? The normative questions become even more difficult as other values – such as justice, for example – are brought into the equation. The search for a better life demands that there should be guidelines for action, but the formulation of goals and the elaboration of utopias is fraught with difficulties.

None the less, unless landscape architecture is about making life in some sense better, it is hardly worth pursuing. To the extent that it is concerned with social matters it must take account of some of the goals which have exercised the minds of political thinkers, but it also pursues aesthetic goals, and general concepts like beauty are as problematic as liberty or fraternity. Furthermore, both traditional politics and landscape architecture are now having to work out the place of new, ecologically derived goals like *sustainability*.

Personal and professional ethics

Woolley and Whittaker (1995) usefully distinguished between four varieties of ethics which have a bearing upon the landscape practitioner.

The first is 'personal ethics' which might also be called private morality. This consists of a person's moral beliefs and values which will have developed over a lifetime and which will have been influenced by the societal and family milieux in which that person has developed. To the extent that an individual may identify closely with a professional role, they may assimilate beliefs which are widely held within their profession into their personal morality, but it was interesting to discover through the interviews undertaken during the empirical phase of my research that people could often distinguish what they believed personally from what they believed in their roles as professional landscape architects.

Woolley and Whittaker's next two ethical fields are 'business ethics' and 'professional ethics'. Business ethics covers such matters as trust, honesty and fair trading, without which the business world would soon collapse into chaos. To the extent that landscape architects, particularly those who operate in the private sector, have business dealings they are bound by codes of business ethics. Professional ethics, on the other hand, covers questions of propriety and reputation. Matthews (1991) suggests that professions are restrictive cartels which justify themselves to the public by guaranteeing high levels of expertise. Professional codes lay down duties and standards of conduct towards clients and towards other members of the profession. Above all a professional must not bring his or her profession into disrepute. It may be simpler to regard both business ethics and professional ethics (in the sense just described) as aspects of professional propriety. They have little to say about what landscape architects should be seeking to promote. They are more concerned with things that landscape architects should not be doing – like lying, cheating or stealing.

When we come to the more positive aspects of the landscape architect's role, Woolley and Whittaker's

analysis is not complete. They identify 'environmental ethics' as an important source of values for the profession and make a casual linkage between the rise of landscape architecture as a profession with the first emergence of environmentalism during the nineteenth century.[3] However, their diagram (Figure 1.1) makes no mention of the two other most significant sources of positive values for landscape practice – the social and the aesthetic. I would suggest a revision of their diagram (Figure 1.2).

The main thrust of Woolley and Whittaker's paper was to criticise the Landscape Institute in Britain for backing off from a commitment to environmental ethics. It was clear from their reported interviews with the then President and the then Registrar of the Institute that a political decision had been taken to restrict the professional body's ethical guidance to matters of professional propriety. In accordance with this some aspirational statements about the Institute's aims have now been dropped from its code of conduct. This statement, for instance, is no longer to be found:

> It is the aim of the Institute to preserve and enhance the national landscape and members must bear this purpose in mind when advising clients.[4]
>
> (L.I. Code of Conduct, 1970)

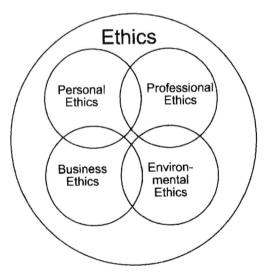

Figure 1.1 Ethical elements: concerns for the landscape professional.
(After Woolley and Whittaker, 1995.)

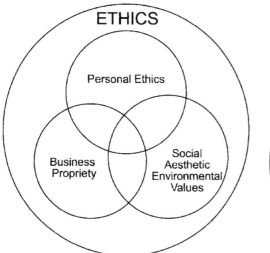

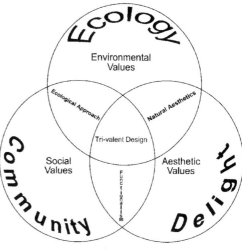

Figure 1.2 Ethical elements in landscape architecture: a suggested revision.

Figure 1.3 Overlapping value fields in landscape architecture.

Woolley and Whittaker (1995) conclude, rightly in my view, that a professional code of ethics should be about more than just propriety and should seek to set out the profession's core values for public evaluation. If these values are able to withstand such scrutiny, then the profession's standing can only be enhanced. However, their analysis of what those core values are does not go deep enough. Indeed, they take references to the preservation of fine landscape to be evidence of environmental values when it could be argued that such references say more about certain aesthetic ideals. A more complete analysis needs to take account of plural sources of values in landscape architecture.

Three value areas

The research upon which this book is based began with the hypothesis that the main sources of positive values in landscape architecture were to be found in three areas – the aesthetic, the social and the ecological (Figure 1.3). This hypothesis was suggested by my own reflections upon practice, but gained credibility from a close reading of seminal texts like Ian McHarg's *Design with Nature* (1969), Brenda Colvin's *Land and Landscape* (1970), and Garrett Eckbo's *Landscape for Living* (1950) as well as more contemporary contributions to the literature like Robert Thayer's *Gray World, Green Heart* (1994). My

confidence in the broad outline of this schema was strengthened further by conversations with colleagues and has been largely confirmed by the interviews conducted with landscape architects undertaken during 1997.

The task of identifying value systems in the landscape architectural literature had both historical and philosophical dimensions. A historical perspective could seek to explain the origins and development of significant strands of value, while a philosophical perspective would seek to find the ultimate justifications for value positions and would also attempt to relate values from different areas.

At the outset of the research I had hoped to discover some overarching value which might bring the disparate triad of aesthetic, social and environmental concerns together. During the course of the investigation it became clear that this was a mistake. This was partly because, in both the reading and in the interviews, a multitude of divergent values was appearing, and it became apparent that to force them into some artificial structure or rigid hierarchy was going to do violence to some of them.

From the beginning there was a parallel between this investigation into landscape architectural values and the sorts of questions that are almost routinely asked in political theory, questions about aspirational concepts such as liberty, equality and justice and how these values might relate to one another. During the course of this parallel study, I came across John Gray's very readable summary of the political theory of the late Sir Isaiah Berlin, which contained some ideas which made me rethink my project (Gray, 1995).

Central to Berlin's philosophy is the idea that there may be different kinds of goods or values, some of which are rivalrous and conflictual:

> Within our own liberal morality, for example, liberty and equality, fairness and welfare are recognised as intrinsic goods. Berlin maintains that these goods often collide in practice, that they are inherently rivalrous by nature, and that their conflicts cannot be arbitrated by any over-arching standard.
>
> (Gray, 1995: 43)

To make matters even more difficult, some of these goods will be internally complex and contain conflicting elements. Liberties of information conflict with liberties of privacy, for example, or equality of opportunity conflicts with equality of outcome. In our present investigation we will see how the aesthetic values of artistic creation may conflict with aesthetic values of scenic preservation.

Berlin's doctrine of value-pluralism has a third level which recognises that different cultural forms will generate different values (an observation that applies as much to aesthetics as it does to ethics) and that although these may overlap to a greater or lesser extent there is always the possibility that values from different cultures will be found to be incommensurable.

To say of two values that they are incommensurable is to say that they cannot be weighed against one another. Gray uses examples from outside ethics to drive home this point:

> We can recognise great cathedrals that are Gothic or Baroque in style, but, because their styles are so different and have so little in common, we cannot rank a great Gothic cathedral against a great Baroque church. Still less can we rank either against the Taj Mahal or the Zen rock garden at Ryoanji.
>
> (Gray, 1995: 51)

For Berlin this value-pluralism does not lead to scepticism, relativism or subjectivism, for he has no doubt in the objectivity of the values he discusses. It leads instead to what he calls 'agonistic liberalism', for human beings must often choose between con-

flicting values without recourse to any overarching standard which might help them.

As Figure 1.3 shows, the ecological, social and aesthetic missions of landscape architecture are overlapping. Notice that there are segments where two value fields converge. Functionalism, for example (which is discussed in Chapter 6), is a social ideal which also has an aesthetic dimension. The 'Ecological Approach' (described in Chapter 8) embodies both ecological and social values, but tended to demote aesthetic concerns. Tantalisingly there is an area in the centre of this diagram where all three value fields overlap, thus recognising the theoretical possibility of work which is socially valuable, ecologically sound and aesthetically interesting. In practice there have been few projects which have manage to unite all three value areas in this way, though Chapter 10 looks at some contemporary work which strives towards this goal.

The additive nature of the overlapping value systems should be clear from these diagrams. Any project may succeed in creating value in one, two or all three areas. Conversely, a scheme may have great merit when judged on its artistic merits but may make no contribution whatsoever to social welfare or to ecological sustainability. Indeed, it is conceivable that a scheme might have great merit in one area, but a *negative* value in one of the others. Building a large formal garden for an African dictator may have aesthetic merits, but socially and environmentally it could be entirely detrimental.[5]

This conceptual analysis can provide a framework for the critical appraisal of works of landscape architecture. It also has a normative force in that in general landscape practitioners should be seeking to maximise positive values in their work, and this would seem to require the attempt to maximise values in each of the value fields – ecological, social and aesthetic.

Values in practice

While the sort of historical/philosophical approach described above can tell us much about the conceptual interrelationship between value systems, and can even provide us with a normative theory, all of this is worthless unless the values that landscape architects espouse in practice and seek to embody in their designs bear some resemblance to the values to be found in the literature.

The second strand of my research sought to discover the values held by practitioners. To this end I interviewed twenty-five British mid-to-late-career landscape architects. The interviews generally took place in their offices and lasted between 1 and 1½ hours. They took the form of guided conversations, in which I encouraged my interviewees to examine their motivations and their satisfactions and dissatisfactions, and to talk about the kinds of projects, either their own or by other people, which they regarded as successful or exemplary.[6]

The interviewees were chosen to represent a reasonable geographical spread – the main areas in which interviews were conducted were London, Oxfordshire, Manchester and Liverpool, North-East England and Central Scotland/Edinburgh – and a variety of types of practice, ranging from large multi-disciplinary private practices such as the Building Design Partnership, through smaller regionally based practices such as Randall Thorp in Manchester, to public authorities such as Salford City Council and the London Boroughs of Westminster and Newham, and voluntary sector organisations like the East Durham Groundwork Trust.

As one might have expected, the range of opinions and value statements elicited from this sample was very wide, confirming the impression that the landscape profession is a 'broad church'. At times the goals of landscape practitioners are very close to those expressed in the literature; at times they depart from them markedly. Again, as one might have expected, there is a pragmatism about practice which can be a long way from the idealism of theory.

The structure of this book

The way this book is arranged reflects both the conceptual schema represented in Figure 1.3, and the two research perspectives, theoretical and empirical. The book is divided into three main sections, dealing with ecological values, community or social values and aesthetic values, respectively. The choice of the word 'delight' to embrace the aesthetic values is intended to cover both the kinds of aesthetic pleasures to be found in the experience of beautiful scenery and the perhaps more cerebral satisfactions of contemplating designed landscapes. The section on Delight therefore contains four chapters while the others have only two and three respectively.

The even-numbered chapters are based upon the historical and philosophical aspect of the research and seek to relate landscape architectural theory to other areas of thought, such as philosophical aesthetics, social and political theory and environmental ethics. The odd-numbered chapters approach the same subjects from an empirical direction and are based upon the interviews. Odd and even chapters are intended to complement one another, but readers who are mostly interested in an overview of the British landscape profession as it enters a new millennium could read the odd-numbered chapters first, while those mainly interested in theory could follow the thread of the even-numbered chapters.

The odd and evenly numbered chapters, drawing as they do on very different types of source material, are also different in style, tone and content. It would have astonished me if practitioners had talked in the same kind of polished prose that is found in academic textbooks. The quotations from the interview transcripts used in the odd-numbered chapters are as near to verbatim as possible, with only minor tinkering to improve intelligibility. Most of the landscape architects interviewed did not regurgitate the theories they had heard as students, but told me about their experiences in practice. That there are gaps between theory and practice will be evident to anyone reading this book. This, in itself, is quite interesting for these openings reveal directions in which practice might develop. My own interest in pursuing theoretical matters beyond the bounds of the sort of matters usually taught on landscape architectural programmes has perhaps exaggerated these gaps, but it seemed necessary to locate landscape architectural theory within wider fields of enquiry, and my hope is that this book will be read by both theoreticians and practitioners and that theory and practice can thus be brought closer together.

The concluding chapter seeks to draw together the various strands developed in each of the main sections, by suggesting a critical framework for landscape architecture. It seeks to reveal the implications of the research for contemporary practice, and to point the way towards new areas for both design innovation and further research.

Notes

1 These names refer to the professional institute for landscape architects in the United Kingdom.

2 Henry Wotton (1568–1639) described these three values in *The Principles of Architecture*, published in 1624.

'Commodity' is a synonym for usefulness or functionality. 'Firmness' is a reference to sound construction. 'Delight' should be self-explanatory.

3   The first person to use the title 'landscape architect' was Frederick Law Olmsted, the designer of New York's Central Park.

4   As Woolley and Whittaker note, a similar reference to preserving fine landscape was removed after 1978.

5   As one of my colleagues pointed out, the gardens might be used by the poor after the overthrow of the dictator! Of course this social benefit would be accidental, and would not have formed any part of the briefing or design process. However, it does illustrate the point that the connection between values that underlie a design, the form it takes, and the way it is eventually used is loose rather than deterministic.

6   These interviews were then transcribed and analysed using NUD.IST software (Non-numerical Unstructured Data. Indexing, Searching and Theory-building).

Bibliography

Adamowicz, W.L., Garrod, G.D. and Willis, K.G. (1995) *Estimating the Passive Use Benefits of Britain's Inland Waterways,* Research Report 95/2, Centre for Rural Economy, University of Newcastle upon Tyne.

Colvin, B. (1970) *Land and Landscape,* J. Murray, London.

Eckbo, G. (1950) *Landscape for Living,* F.W. Dodge, USA.

Eckbo, G. (1969) *The Landscape We See,* McGraw-Hill, New York.

Gray, J. (1995) *Berlin,* Fontana Press, London.

Hackett, B. (1971) *Landscape Planning: an Introduction to Theory and Practice,* Oriel Press, Newcastle upon Tyne.

Harvey, S. (1987) *Reflections on Landscape: the lives and work of six British landscape architects,* Gower Technical, Aldershot.

Jellicoe, G.A. (1960, 1966, 1970) *Studies in Landscape Design,* Volumes I, II and III, Oxford University Press, Oxford.

Jellicoe. G.A. and Jellicoe, S. (revised edition 1987) *The Landscape of Man,* Thames and Hudson, London.

Lawson, B. (1980) *How Designers Think,* Butterworth Architecture, London.

Lyle, J.T. (1994) *Regenerative Design for Sustainable Development,* Wiley, New York.

McHarg, I. (1969) *Design with Nature,* The Natural History Press, Garden City, New York.

Matthews, R. (1991) 'The Economics of Professional Ethics: Should the Professions be More Like Business?', *The Economic Journal,* 101: 737–750.

Naess, A. (1989) *Ecology, Community and Lifestyle: outline of an ecosophy,* Cambridge University Press, Cambridge.

Stiles, R. (1994) 'In Search of a Definition', *Landscape Design,* No. 234 (Oct): 44-48.

Thayer, R.L. (1994) *Gray World, Green Heart: technology, nature and the sustainable landscape,* John Wiley & Sons, New York.

Turner, T. (1990) 'Was "Landscape Architecture" a Good Idea?', *Landscape Design,* No. 191 (June): 28–29.

Woolley, H. and Whittaker, C. (1995) 'Ethical Practices in the Landscape Profession: a research note' *Landscape Research,* 20 (3): 147–151.

PART I
DELIGHT

Detail from Robert Camlin's design for Uppermill Cemetery, Saddleworth, Greater Manchester, pp. 68–69 (overleaf).

2 Natural aesthetics

The problem of beauty

Landscape architects are much concerned with beauty, both the contrived beauty of gardens and the natural beauties of the countryside, but what is it that makes a scene beautiful? Are there any underlying principles of aesthetics that will help us to recognise or create beautiful places? For landscape architects this is not an idle question, for they may often be called upon to defend their ideas of beauty, sometimes in the quasi-legal surroundings of a public planning inquiry.

The concept of beauty has had a chequered career in the history of aesthetics. For centuries after Plato it remained central, and for several eighteenth-century British philosophers scenic beauty was an important concern. In the nineteenth century, however, interest in natural beauty lost ground to an interest in art. It became clear that the possession of beauty was not a sufficient condition for the existence of a work of art. A real landscape or human face (as opposed to ones on canvas) could be called beautiful, but this did not make it a work of art. Nor was beauty a necessary condition for art. We can all think of paintings – Piccasso's *Guernica*, perhaps, or Bacon's *Screaming Pope*[1] – which we would wish to call works of art but would find it difficult to think of as beautiful. Once beauty had been abandoned as a potentially defining property of art, other ways to define art and to recognise good art were sought, with ideas of meaning or significance taking centre stage. The focus of twentieth-century aesthetics moved away from beauty altogether. This attitude is summed up by Stolnitz, who wrote 'on the whole, nature is deficient in psychological and symbolic interest, compared to art' (Stolnitz, 1960: 51).

Before the dethronement of natural beauty, landscape gardening enjoyed the status of a sister art to painting, sculpture or poetry. The relentless waves of avante-gardism which swept through the fine arts left gardening marooned. Social and economic factors also played their part. Few people today have the leisure, money or land to create the sorts of gardens made by eighteenth-century aristocrats. Though gardening is still enormously popular as a pastime, as an art it hardly exists. There are those, notably the late Sir Geoffrey Jellicoe, who have striven on behalf of landscape architecture (as the professional descendant of landscape gardening) to bring it back alongside the other fine arts. In Chapter 4 we must judge how successful this attempt has been, and in Chapter 5 we will consider whether the idea that landscape architecture is, or can be, an art form is central to the value structure of the profession.

In this chapter, however, the object will be to give some account of natural beauty, and, in doing so, to place the aesthetic values which contemporary landscape architects may espouse into the context of a centuries-old discussion. What qualities, according to the theorists, must a landscape have before we are to call it beautiful? How do we recognise beautiful landscapes? How might we go about creating places that give delight?

Plato and the transcendental

Sometimes the landscape designer is faced with a dilemma which may seem childishly simple – am I going to use straight lines here, or free-flowing curves? The question may appear naive, but it cuts straight to the heart of the Western cultural dichotomy. Classicism faces up to Romanticism. Reason confronts Empiricism. Rationality takes on Emotion. We have to start to grapple with this somewhere, so let us make it somewhere near the beginning.

A.N. Whitehead once described the history of Western philosophy as 'a series of footnotes to Plato' (Lovejoy, 1965: 24), an observation which certainly holds true for Western aesthetics, so it will be worth while considering Platonic theories in some detail.

Unfortunately there is little to be found in the Platonic dialogues to suggest that either he, or his mentor Socrates, was particularly interested in the beauty of nature. For Plato the world is imperfect and in some sense shadowy and less than real. There is, he maintains, a metaphysical realm of ideal Forms. These Forms are universal and unchanging rather than particular and malleable, which is to say that they comprise the meanings or definitions of things. There are Forms of everything – of vase or horse or flower, but also (problematically) of dung beetle or dustbin. Abstract universals like Justice or Beauty also exist. A flower is a flower because it partakes of the Form of flower, but it is beautiful because it partakes of the Form of Beauty. The Form of Beauty exists in a non-empirical realm where it has the same sort of being as ethical ideals, and mathematical entities like numbers or the idea of perfect equality.

In Plato's system the beauties are hierarchically arranged. Beauty of mind is considered superior to beauty of body. The beauty of laws or institutions is superior to that of individual minds, while at the summit is the essential Form of Beauty itself. Works of art occupy a lowly position in this system because Plato propounds an 'imitation theory' whereby whatever beauty a painting or a statue might possess it has by virtue of its less than perfect resemblance to a physical object or person, which itself is but a shadowy copy of an ideal Form.

We can also find currents of functionalism in Plato's aesthetics. Household knives may vary in size and shape but they share in common the essential function of cutting. They do this to the extent that they resemble the ideal Form of knife. Modernist aesthetics owe much to Plato. Le Corbusier famously (or infamously) described a house as a machine for living in. Designed objects which are functional, the modernists asserted, will also be aesthetically satisfy-

ing; but this is easier to say of a household utensil or a building than it is of a garden or a landscape, for what is the function of a garden? This is a matter to which we will return in Chapter 6.

In general the higher Forms are those which are closest to the unalloyed purity of mathematical concepts. In the *Philebus* Plato discusses the essential properties that beautiful things have in common. He distinguishes between complex beautiful things and simple beautiful things. Complex beautiful things are likely to have certain ideal proportions, and a balance which creates a dynamic stillness and self-completeness. These qualities can be further distilled, for Plato writes that 'the qualities of measure and proportion invariably constitute beauty and excellence'.[2] Monroe Beardsley (1975) notes that the Greek word which has been translated as 'proportion' is *symmetron,* and that for Plato there is a close association between beauty and symmetry.

In the case of what Plato calls simple things, we appreciate sounds that are smooth and clear and notes that form a single series; also colours that are pure, white being the purest; and shapes that are simple geometrical forms. The three qualities that these things share are unity, regularity and simplicity.

The Forms are not directly accessible to the senses but must be approached through the rational activity of the mind. In the *Timaeus,* (35, 36) Plato, under the influence of Pythagorean number theory, suggests that the harmony of the world can be expressed in two geometrical progressions (based upon the squares and cubes beginning at unity), 1, 2, 4, 8 and 1, 3, 9, 27, which can be combined into the seven-number sequence 1, 2, 3, 4, 8, 9, 27. He believed that the ratios between these numbers could account not only for all musical consonancies but for the visual harmonies of architecture and indeed the order of creation and the perfection of the soul. Wittkower (1973) has demonstrated the influence of the Pythagorean–Platonic theory of harmony upon Renaissance architects.

In a variety of reformulations the Platonic conception of aesthetics, with its emphasis on mimesis in art and a theory of beauty based upon rational concepts of order, symmetry and proportion, was to remain dominant until the advent of empiricism during the Enlightenment. Plato's influence upon Aristotle can be seen in the latter's *Metaphysics*: 'the chief forms of beauty are order and symmetry and definiteness'.[3]

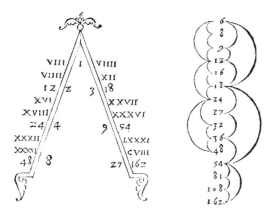

Figure 2.1 Diagram by Francesco Giorgi, 1525, which relates Pythagorean ratios to the Greek musical scale.

According to Beardsley, Aristotle's conception of order can be analysed into qualities of completeness, proportion and measure. We can summarise the qualities that Plato and Aristotle associated with beauty in the following list:

- unity
- regularity
- simplicity
- proportion
- balance
- measure
- definiteness

If one were to eavesdrop on a conversation between a landscape architecture student and her tutor, one might expect to hear many of the same concepts employed.

The perseverance of Platonic thought

Plato's philosophy continued to be taught into the first centuries of the Christian era, but its character was gradually modified into the system known as Neoplatonism, and the most notable Neoplatonist was Plotinus (AD 204/5–270).

Plotinus rejected the view, commonly held after Plato, that beauty consisted in symmetry, pattern and 'charm of colour'. Basing his arguments upon a revival of the Theory of Forms, he argued that unity is the essential characteristic of beauty because this is something that all the Forms must have. He further identified the Form of the Beautiful with the Form of the Good and equated ugliness with evil. This close identification between goodness and beauty, or between ethics and aesthetics, became a recurring theme in Western philosophy. However, as sub-sequent chapters will argue, such a position cannot be maintained once plural sources of values are recognised.

One aspect of Plotinus's thought that is particularly relevant to our inquiry is his response to Plato's denigration of art. Plato condemns art because he sees it as an imitation of an imitation. Works of art are at two removes from the world of transcendental ideal Forms. Plotinus suggests, however, that a tree and a picture of a tree share alike in the Form which bestows on each whatever beauty they may possess.

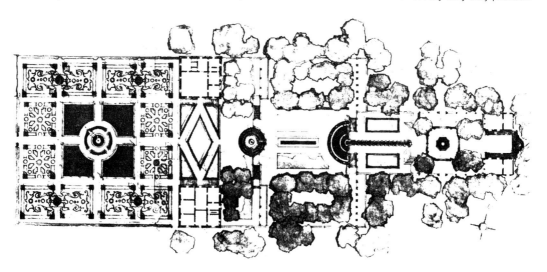

Figure 2.2 The Villa Lante at Bagnaia, designed by Vignola in 1566 – symmetry and order. (Courtesy of Academy Editions.)

A painter may be more successful in capturing the ideal Form of the tree than the imperfect specimen he is taking as his model. In other words, artists may improve upon nature. We can see in this a foreshadowing of the idea of improvement, which was to become an important influence upon the development of landscape gardening.

Renaissance Neoplatonism

It is a commonplace that Renaissance thinkers rediscovered the wisdom of the ancients, but in terms of aesthetics just what did they find and what use did they make of it?

If we consider the ideas of a leading Neoplatonist like Marcilio Ficino (1433–99), familiar themes soon emerge. Like Plato and Plotinus, Ficino finds a transcendental element in all beauty. The twist that Ficino gives to the traditional theory is that where Plotinus had emphasised unity as the essential characteristic of beautiful things, Ficino elevates harmony, and analyses this into yet another triumvirate of qualities: arrangement, proportion and adornment. In his Commentary to the *Timaeus,* Ficino discusses three types of proportion, the arithmetic, geometric and harmonic, which were to have an enormous influence upon Renaissance architects. Neoplatonic ratios lie at the heart of the theories of architecture advanced by Leon Battista Alberti (1409–72) and echoed a century later by Palladio (Andrea di Pietro da Padova, 1508–80).

Wittkower notes that for Alberti beauty is dependent upon a harmony in a building and this 'does not result from personal fancy, but from objective reasoning. Its chief characteristic is the classical idea of maintaining a uniform system of proportion throughout all parts of a building. And the key to correct proportion is Pythagoras' system of musical harmony' (Wittkower, 1973: 33).

The Pythagorean system of proportions appears again in Book I of Palladio's *Four Books of Architecture* (1570). 'Although variety and things new may please every one,' he writes, 'yet they ought not to be done contrary to the precepts of art, and contrary to that which reason dictates; whence one sees, that although the ancients did vary, yet they never departed from some universal and necessary rules of art, as shall be seen in my books of antiquities' (Book I, Ch. 20).

Neoplatonic influences upon landscape design

Writers on Italian Renaissance gardens generally stress the manner in which the geometry of the house was extended into the garden. Thus Jellicoe and Shepherd note that 'the instinct of formality considered the garden so much a part of the house, that in its simplest phase it was regarded as nothing more or less than an extra room, a salon flooded with unlimited light and air' (Jellicoe and Shepherd, [1925] 1985: 18). The same authors also suggest that 'Alberti, who . . . left little garden work, had a more immediate influence through his published treatises' ([1925] 1985: 11).

Alberti, in fact, says little directly about gardens, although some of Chapter IV in Book IX of his *Ten Books* is given to the subject. About the layout of gardens he recommends his readers to:

> Let the Ground also be here and there thrown into those Figures that are most commended in the Platforms of Houses, Circles, Semicircles, and the like, and surrounded with Laurels, Cedars, Junipers with their Branches intermixed, and twining one into the other.

If we follow this recommendation and turn to those passages which prescribe the footprints of buildings, we find guidelines concerning suitable geometrical figures, angles and proportions (Ch. VIII, Book I); and if we seek what Alberti has written upon the subject of proportion we find that he too subscribes to the Pythagorean system (Ch. VI, Book IX). Taking these passages together it is clear that Alberti was recommending a formality in gardens based upon the same series of ratios and harmonies that he advocated for the design of buildings. Alberti reiterates the Pythagorean view that the ratios which generate musical harmonies also produce visual harmonies, and his explanation of the particular ratios is much clearer than that to be found in the *Timaeus* (ratios of 2 : 1, 3 : 1, 4 : 1, 3 : 2, 4 : 3, 4 : 9, 9 : 16, and 3 : 8 are all favoured).

However, it is not readily apparent that Italian garden designers entirely submitted to the disciplines of the Neoplatonic ratios. Jellicoe and Shepherd suggest that the formality of Italian gardens was modified by the characteristics of the landscapes in which they were constructed, and that 'the lines of the gardens should grow less defined as they left the house, like water ripples spreading from a centre, to die away in their surroundings – lines always formal but less and less emphasised' (Jellicoe and Shepherd, [1925] 1985: 19). In *The Landscape of Man*, Geoffrey Jellicoe makes a similar observation: 'the interior of the house thrust itself outwards, levelled to the rising or falling site, the shapes made more by intuition than by mathematical calculation' (Jellicoe and Jellicoe, 1975: 155). Jellicoe and Shepherd also note that in the seventeenth century a passion for theatricality and ostentation led to the deliberate exaggeration of scale and form to be found in the Baroque. It would seem, therefore, that it would be easy to overstate the role that mathematical calculations of proportions played in Renaissance garden design.

The growth of empiricism

While it may be easy to see how notions of symmetry, balance and mathematically ordered relationships can be arrived at through thought, it is less easy to see why particular ratios or proportions should always be preferred, particularly if the parallelism between music and the visual arts is thrown into doubt, as it was in the eighteenth century by Hogarth. He saw no reason for assuming that because 'certain uniform and consonant divisions upon one string produce harmony to the ear . . . similar distances in lines belonging to form, would, in like manner, delight the eye' (Hogarth, [1753] 1971). It was this difficulty which would motivate empirical approaches to the problem of beauty.

Beardsley notes that there were both rationalist and empirical sides to Renaissance thought. For the

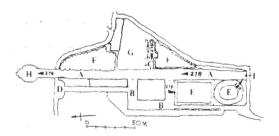

A Long alley
B Grass view terrace
C Grotto garden
D Entrance drive
E Original water garden
F Bosco
G Lemon garden
H Cypress garden
I Statue on viewpoint

Figure 2.3 Villa Gamberaia, Settignano, a classical design fitted to an awkward site – 'lines always formal but less and less emphasised'. (Courtesy of Academic Editions.)

Figure 2.4 Villa Dona dalle Rose, Valzanzibio. (Courtesy of Academic Editions.)

latter we must turn to the painters. As we have seen, the idea of mimesis or imitation was central to classical theories of art. The good painting was the painting that most closely resembled its subject. In their attempts to become better exponents of their calling, artists like Leonardo da Vinci and Albrecht Dürer had to become something akin to scientists. Alberti too, in his capacity as artist and art theorist rather than architect, was a systematic empiricist. It was not enough for him to know that, in theory, proportion, harmony or order were essential to beauty. To be a good artist he had to know what particular proportions would achieve the desired effect. To work out the canon of human proportions presented in his *Sculpture,* for example, he had to measure many real people (*Della statua,* 1435).

However, there is a logical gap between observing proportions and concluding that they are harmonious, and this explains why aesthetic interest shifted away from the examination of objects to the study of psychology. Explanations were needed for aesthetic creation, on the one hand, and for aesthetic enjoyment on the other. In particular, aestheticians were concerned about 'the problem of taste'. Shaftesbury believed there to be a faculty of taste, a sort of inward eye which was able to grasp beauty and goodness, and that judgements based upon this aesthetic sense were absolute and universal; but if taste is analysed as subjective response, we are plunged into a relativist aesthetics, in which liking or disliking are all that matter. If the faculty of taste enables us to perceive beauty, just as our eyes can see yellow or our taste buds tell us that something is

sweet, why is there so much disagreement about what is beautiful and what is not?

The Scottish philosopher, David Hume, was, however, able to view the absence of a priori principles of taste with equanimity, for he believed that there were common dispositions within human nature to be pleased or displeased. This is a profoundly empirical stance, yet Hume was no relativist. He thought that the general principles of taste were uniform in human nature, but that some people, through insensitivity, inattention, prejudice or inexperience, made erratic judgements. Something close to Hume's view has been behind the psychological investigations of landscape preferences to be described later. An interesting corollary of Hume's theory is that people can be trained to be more sensitive, more attentive and without prejudice. It is possible to educate experts in aesthetics. This has a bearing upon contemporary debates about the use of 'experts' in landscape assessments, rather than seeking the views of 'ordinary people'.

The line of beauty

As its title suggests, Hogarth's *Analysis of Beauty, Written with a View of Fixing the Fluctuating Ideas of Taste* ([1753] 1971) was a direct response to the problem of relativism, and it is of great interest to this present inquiry since it has been connected with perhaps the best known of all landscape gardeners, Lancelot 'Capability' Brown.

Hogarth opens his argument by suggesting that all questions of visual beauty are questions about lines,

Figure 2.5 Hogarth's Line of Beauty.

because all shapes and solids can be reduced to them. Then he notes six characteristics that contribute towards the beauty of a line: fitness, variety, uniformity, simplicity, intricacy and quantity (or size). The 'line of beauty' is the line in which these qualities are optimised, and it turns out to be a happy mean between lines that are too twisted or bulged, and thus judged 'gross and clumsy', and lines that lack variety and intricacy, which are therefore considered 'poor and mean'. Its three-dimensional counterpart he calls the 'line of grace'.

Hogarth illustrates his thesis with pictures of chair legs and women's corsets, but, as Tom Turner has pointed out (Turner, 1986: 97), the curves of a woman's body were directly compared with those of a Brownian landscape by contemporary commentators.

Hogarth's *Analysis of Beauty* was published in 1753, two years after Brown had left his job as head gardener at Stowe. Brown was 38 and had hardly begun his career as an improver, for most of his work was accomplished in the 1760s and 1770s. It is conceivable that he could have read Hogarth and been influenced by him, but the extent of this influence is hard to judge. Brown's work at Stowe itself and his work at Petworth were begun before Hogarth's book appeared. Dorothy Stroud is probably close to the truth when she writes:

> It is no coincidence that Brown began his astonishingly successful career as a landscape designer (1751) in the same decade that Hogarth published *The Analysis of Beauty* (1753) and Burke his *Inquiry into the Ideas of the Sublime and Beautiful* (1756). The influence of these books on Brown may have been no more than indirect and contributory; but his conception of landscape represents so exactly Burke's of 'Beauty', and made such notorious use of Hogarth's serpentine 'line of beauty', that we must regard all three as complementary exponents of the *Zeitgeist*.
>
> (Stroud, 1950: 29)

Hogarth's theory is a variety of formalism. Turner has suggested that 'serpentine curves can be conceived to occupy an intermediate place in the Neoplatonic hierarchy. They are not as perfect as the circle and square but have more generality than the random patterns and jagged lines which characterise wild forests and mountains' (Turner, 1986: 42). For the landscape gardeners this meant that random

Figure 2.6 The Line of Beauty used in landscape: the Grecian Vale at Stowe, attributed to 'Capability' Brown. (Courtesy of Michael Downing.)

nature could be taken and improved upon.

Turner has also drawn our attention to a gradual change in the meaning of the term 'nature' in the course of the eighteenth century. When Pope wrote 'all art consists in the imitation and study of nature' ('On Gardens', *The Guardian*, Sept. 1713), his idea of nature was still mathematical and Neoplatonic. By the end of the eighteenth century, the 'nature' that landscape gardeners strove to imitate was the empirical world, not the ideal world of Plato's Forms (Turner, 1986: 26–27), and Sawrey Gilpin, the nephew of William Gilpin, would take great exception to the suggestion made in Sir Henry Steuart's *Planter's Guide* that circles and ovals are 'prevalent in all the most beautiful objects in nature'. They were not to be found in the New Forest, noted Gilpin.

The beautiful and the sublime

Edmund Burke's celebrated investigation of aesthetic qualities, *A Philosophical Enquiry into the Origin of Our Ideas of the Sublime and the Beautiful*, was motivated by the same concerns that propelled *The Analysis of Beauty*. He sought to produce a 'logic of Taste' that might end disagreements over aesthetics and serve as a basis for criticism. Burke delves deeper than Hogarth, however, for he does not confine himself to describing those sensible qualities that are normally associated with aesthetic pleasure, but suggests physiological or psychological mechanisms whereby these qualities achieve their effects.

Burke's psychology does not postulate an inner aesthetic faculty but links our aesthetic reactions to our drives and emotions. He notes that our 'leading passions' consist principally of those connected with self-preservation and self-propagation. The love of female beauty, argues Burke, is mixed with lust, but if we subtract from it the element of physical desire, we are left with a response that can be taken as a paradigm for the appreciation of beauty. The qualities of objects that Burke believes can produce this effect are smallness, smoothness, gradual variation and delicacy.

Burke's analysis of sublimity follows similar lines. He notes that pain and danger produce in us the emotion of fear, yet if we subtract from this experience any genuine threat, just as we removed lust from our response to female beauty, we experience the astonishment, admiration, awe and respect which is our response to the sublime.

The significance of this development, as Beardsley tells us, 'was a recognition that other qualities than beauty, even though the latter be taken broadly, were capable of affording direct aesthetic satisfaction' (Beardsley, 1975: 197). Beauty had, in effect, been dethroned, and it was not long before a third aesthetic category, the Picturesque, was claiming its place.

The picturesque

In advocating the line of beauty, Hogarth had started to uncouple the appreciation of beauty from rationality. Burke's entirely sensuous notion of Beauty took this further; indeed, the requirement for consistency within his system led him to deny any part for the time-honoured qualities of symmetry and proportion. As Hussey has commented, the categories of the Beautiful and the Sublime sufficed for a while to explain all aesthetic pleasures, but 'in the landscape painting of Gainsborough appeared a great quantity of rough, shaggy, and summarily delineated objects, derived from the Dutch landscape, that immediately pleased connoisseurs but were obviously neither sublime nor beautiful' (1927: 13). On the other hand, as the Revd William Gilpin pointed out, there were scenes which met Burke's criteria for Beauty, yet made poor subjects for painting. It became evident that a further category was needed, and Gilpin obliged by coining the term 'Picturesque Beauty', which referred to objects that were both beautiful and suitable for pictures. Uvedale Price, a Whig squire from Herefordshire, was quick to seize upon the implications of these developments in aesthetic theory. In his *Essays on the Picturesque* (1794–95),

he suggested that there were three aesthetic categories rather than just two: the Beautiful, the Sublime and the Picturesque. As Hussey says:

> Thus 'picturesque' for Price meant far more than 'suitable for painting' – the definition that Gilpin had favoured. While the outstanding qualities of the Sublime were vastness and obscurity, and those of the Beautiful smoothness and gentleness, the characteristics of the Picturesque were 'roughness and sudden variation joined to irregularity' of form, colour, lighting and even sound.
>
> (Hussey, 1927: 14)

The categories of Beautiful and Picturesque did not overlap as different qualities were essential to each.

Initially Price found a supporter in another aesthetically inclined squire, Richard Payne Knight of Downton, Salop. Both were enthusiastically committed to the Picturesque and both took up their pens against the kind of landscape improvement carried out by Brown and his successor Repton. However, they soon found that they had radically different conceptions of the Picturesque. Price, as we have noted, thought that the Picturesque was a distinct category alongside the Beautiful and the Sublime. Knight denied that such objective categories existed; the picturesque was simply a manner of viewing things.

Knight attacked the idea of the Picturesque as a category in his *On Taste,* where he makes fun of a passage in Price's *Dialogue on the Distinct Characters of the Picturesque and the Beautiful,* in which a young woman had been praised for her Picturesque charms rather than her beauty:

> My friend Mr. Price indeed admits squinting among the irregular and picturesque charms of the parson's daughter, whom, (to illustrate the picturesque in opposition to the beautiful) he wishes to make appear lovely and attractive, though without symmetry or beauty. He has not, however, extended this want of symmetry and regularity further than to the features of the face; though to make the figure consistent, the same happy mixture of the irregular and picturesque must have prevailed throughout her limbs; and consequently must have hobbled as well as squinted; and had hips and shoulders as irregular as her teeth, cheeks and eyebrows.
>
> (Hussey, 1927: 74)

In response, Price loosened his view to admit that a particular object or scene could contain a mixture of qualities and thus partake of both Beauty and Picturesqueness. Thus for both authors something like Gilpin's Picturesque Beauty was a possibility.

To the contemporary mind these capitalised categories seem highly artificial. Nowadays we recognise that the meanings of words do not correspond to fixed categories, but are slippery things that arise from our everyday use of language. As it happens, the words *beautiful, sublime* and *picturesque* have lost most of their former nuances and are often used interchangeably. In many ways this is regrettable, as it suggests that we have become blinder or more indifferent to aesthetic qualities than were our eighteenth-century counterparts. What is important about the eighteenth-century debates for landscape designers, and for this present inquiry, is that qualities other than regularity and symmetry were seen to have aesthetic value. The Sublime and the Picturesque remain part of our cultural background; we may not use the words often, or in quite their original sense, but they continue to offer us ways of interpreting and valuing what we see.

In Price's *Dialogue* the views considered to be Picturesque, setting aside the parson's squinting daughter, included a gypsy's hovel beneath a gnarled oak of a wild and singular appearance, with bark 'full of knobs, spots and stains'; a rutted lane with shaggy banks; and a rambling parsonage, in good repair, but half smothered in vines, roses, jasmines and honeysuckles. The latter is said to be pleasing and charming; unlike the gypsy's hovel it is beautiful as well as picturesque. It does not take much imagination to place any of these views on a contemporary picture postcard or chocolate-box lid. Too much contrivance turns the Picturesque into the twee, but a case could be made to support the assertion that it has now become the dominant aesthetic, more widely appreciated than the Sublime or the Beautiful.

As an explanation of beauty in landscape, the Picturesque theory simply pushes the aesthetic problem back a stage, for who is to decide what makes a good painting? The conceptual artists Vitaly Komar and Alexander Melamid[4] recently highlighted this difficulty by producing paintings which were based upon the results of a telephone survey using the methodology of market research. One of the resulting works – *America's Most Wanted* – is an autumnal landscape including a lake, mountains, wild animals and a group of people at leisure (it also includes a bewigged George Washington). The point of Komar and Melamid's intellectual joke is that this is a laughably awful painting, compositionally dull and aesthetically unrewarding. Simply conjoining a number of things which people find pleasant does not mean that the resulting scene will make a picture.

The Picturesque has been seen, by Hussey among others, as a step along the road to abstraction. If one discounts the subject matter of a scene and any symbolic resonances, all that remains is a pattern of colours and textures that may or may not be pleasing. If the criterion of the aesthetic is whether or not a scene would make a good painting, then all sorts of (at first sight) unlikely contenders spring forward. Fearsome mountains are not the only landscapes to have been rehabilitated; De Loutherbourg's fiery painting of *Coalbrookdale by Night* (1801) extended the tradition of landscape painting to industrial scenes. In this, as in some of Turner's pictures of railway locomotives or steamboats, we are dealing with a variety of man-made sublimity, for our reactions include a sense of awe or terror at the gigantic forces released. Landscape architects are often involved in the siting of large-scale industrial structures, such as power stations, dams, or factories, in rural landscapes. They recognise the powerful formal qualities that such structures may possess. A view including cooling towers may still be Picturesque.

The Beautiful, the Sublime, the Picturesque – and the Designed

How then should the landscape designer respond to the traditional aesthetic categories? At a superficial level, it is not hard to supply answers.

One plausible line would be to argue that the designer should give the clients or the users what they prefer. If this is regularity, then a formal garden is the answer. If they admire smoothness and flowing curves, then something Beautiful and Brownian will suffice. If they are looking for something Picturesque, then perhaps a shaggy wild garden is what is required. Of course, the clients or the users may be ill-informed or blind to the existing qualities of the site. It is part of the designer's role to understand the context; a formal garden might work well in front of a mansion with a symmetrical elevation, but in a

Figure 2.7 These 'existing and proposed' sketches by T.H. Mawson, dating from 1900, illustrate the use of the Transitional Style, where a formal terrace leads to a Beautiful park with views of a Picturesque landscape beyond. The proposals sketch is also a good example of 'technocentric accommodation' (see Chapter 8). Notice how the inconveniently placed factory chimneys and workers' cottages have vanished from the scene! A Marxist might also have something to say about this!

woodland clearing could look entirely out of place. Tom Turner's representations of English Garden Styles (Figure 2.7) show some of the permutations available, including mixed or transitional styles which combine a degree of formality in association with buildings with more relaxed or naturalistic lines at a distance. This is still a very popular strategy among landscape designers.

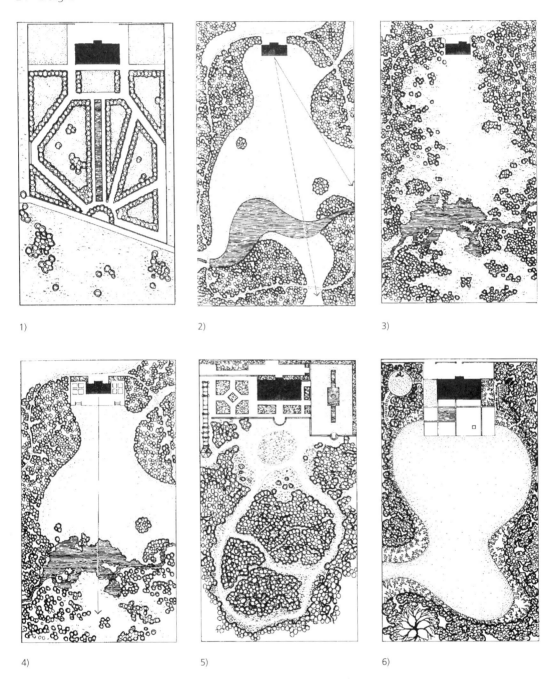

Figure 2.8 An accelerated tour through English garden history. These plans are taken from Tom Turner's *English Garden Design* with the kind permission of the author. **Top row**, left to right: 1) the French Style in England; 2) the Serpentine Style. Compare these curves with Hogarth's 'Line of Beauty'; 3) the Irregular Style. Picturesque effects were sought by making the planting wild and irregular. **Bottom row**, left to right: 4) the Transitional Style, so called because there is a transition from the ordered terrace close to the house, through the Beautiful curves of the park, to the Picturesque wildness of the landscape beyond; 5) the Arts and Crafts Style. Another mixed style, with an ordered terrace and a transition to a woodland garden planted in the Irregular fashion; 6) the Abstract Style, combining a rectiliniar geometry (reminiscent of Mondrian) with sweeping biomorphic curves (owing something to Hogarth but more to Matisse).

The spirit of the place

Although we noticed Neoplatonist tendencies in Pope's writings, his often-quoted injunction 'Consult the Genius of the Place in All' marked a turning point towards empiricism, and it has become a central tenet of landscape architectural method. Turner has called it the 'Single Agreed Law of Landscape Design' (Turner, 1996: 161). Of all the aesthetic ideas described thus far, this is the only one which all practitioners seem to remember, perhaps because their tutors once drilled into them the idea that a good design must be preceded by a good site survey and that this must include subjective as well as objective information. Perhaps too, Pope's dictum gives them the authority to trust their intuition.

Pope urges designers to respect the particularities of a place, and, as we will see in the following chapter, this issue of local distinctiveness is one which landscape architects care passionately about, perhaps because they see it being eroded on a daily basis by the commodification of experience and the internationalisation of design and construction. In architectural circles resistance to this homogenis-ation of place has been offered in the form of 'critical regionalism', the proposal that the materials used in buildings and the devices used to mediate climate should be appropriate to local circum-stances.[5] Critical regionalism is not a return to the vernacular, but seeks to combine the benefits of global advances in construction technology with the best of local traditions.

Another source of resistance, at least in Britain, has been the charity Common Ground, which has campaigned for the conservation of local distinctive-ness though imaginative initiatives like the New Milestones Project which has encouraged local com-munities to commission craftspeople and sculptors to produce site-specific works which crystallise local feelings about the places that they value.[6]

We must remind ourselves, however, that Pope's instruction was to consult the genius of the place, not to follow it slavishly. Although, as we shall see, the strategy of harmonising and blending new developments into their surroundings is still the most popular approach among contemporary landscape architects in Britain, other strategies based upon difference or contrast may be equally appropriate responses to the qualities of a site. Respect for place should not confine the landscape architect to backward-looking strategies which could easily degenerate into pastiche. Most designers would hope for more out of the design process, including the chance to achieve new insights and to generate new styles, or at least some interesting reinterpretations of old ones.

Taking the empirical project forwards

Twentieth-century approaches to landscape aesthe-tics have taken the empirical project forward by trying to identify deep-seated, biologically based preferences for certain types of landscape. Many critics and philosophers have suggested that rather than trying to classify a set of beautiful objects, it is more productive to take aesthetic experience as the starting point.[7]

Some guidance about the nature of our aesthetic experience can be obtained from the philosopher, Santayana ([1896] 1961), who distinguished between three experiential levels.

There are some pleasures, like the raw feeling of the wind on our cheeks, the sun on our faces, or the sound of tinkling water, which are direct and immed-iate. He calls this the level of 'sensory' aesthetics.

At a higher level, he says, we are able to appreciate the 'formal' qualities of objects. Many of the concepts employed by landscape architects – words such as *unity, balance, proportion, harmony* – describe such qualities. As well as being extremely useful in discussing both natural and designed land-scapes, such formal qualities have, as we have already seen, played a prominent role in the history of philosophical aesthetics, where unsuccessful attempts have been made to use them as sufficient or necessary conditions for beauty (or of art).

Above the formal level is the level that Santayana calls the 'symbolic'. At this level, objects carry mean-ings. Cultural values are ascribed to landscapes and it becomes impossible to view the landscape as if those values did not exist. The example most fre-quently quoted is the change in attitude towards mountain scenery which occurred during the eight-eenth century. Turner describes it thus:

Travellers were frightened by wild scenery at the beginning of the eighteenth century. When passing through the Alps they would shut their eyes or pull down the blinds in their coaches to hide the jagged cliffs, the torrents, and the imminent prospect of being catapulted over a precipice. By the century's end this fear had so far diminished that a positive liking for 'Salvator Rosa and Sublimity' had taken its place. Travellers sought for ever-wilder places, and garden designers responded to their new visual taste.

(Turner, 1986: 101-102)

Any landscape can be described in sensory, formal and symbolic terms. Consider the North Pennines Area of Outstanding Natural Beauty. A sensory description would mention the spring of the heather, the freshness of the wind, the clatter of a disturbed grouse as it takes flight, and so on. Formal qualities like the harmony of the moorland colours, or the subtlety of the curves on the long, low horizon might then be introduced. It could also be described in symbolic terms, but the same landscape could mean different things to different groups. To the town dweller it might represent wilderness, freedom or escape. To the local sheep farmer it might represent home or, perhaps, unrelenting toil.

Biological, cultural and personal

The Australian geographer, Stephen Bourassa, has suggested a tripartite theoretical framework for research into the aesthetics of landscape (Bourassa, 1991). His view is similar to Santayana's in that he thinks there are three levels or modes of aesthetic experience, but he produces different categories: the biological, the cultural and the personal.

At the biological level, he argues, our aesthetic reactions are governed by laws, and these may be discovered through scientific investigation. These laws operate independently of cultural or learned responses. Presumably they are often overridden by the latter, but it would also seem to follow that they could 'break through' in the manner of primitive drives or instincts. It is easy to see how our sensory aesthetics might be accounted for at this level, but, as we shall see, biological theorists have also attempted to explain formal and symbolic qualities in terms of the recognition of meaningful patterns in the environment.

At the next level, says Bourassa, our aesthetic responses are not determined by biological laws but are conditioned by cultural rules. Different groups will have different responses. This level accords with Santayana's symbolic level, but it might be argued that some formal qualities are culturally determined.

Bourassa suggests that individuals can transcend both the biological laws and the cultural rules of their society through creative personal strategies. He distinguishes between *perceptual strategies* and *design strategies*. A creative perceptual strategy is a new way of seeing. He cites Tunnard's opinion of Wordsworth as an example;

> Wordsworth made the Lake District, already a tourist resort, into what we would today call an object of cultural tourism. He and his sister Dorothy created a landscape of the mind, as those who themselves sought out the scenes of his poetry soon discovered.
>
> (Tunnard, 1978: 45)

Design strategies, on the other hand, innovate by physical modification of the landscape. Numerous examples from the history of garden and landscape design could be suggested, but a particularly salient instance might be the retention of Wray Wood and Henderskelf Lane at Castle Howard in North Yorkshire. Lord Carlisle had been advised by George London to drive a straight avenue from the north front of the house up the small hill which bore Wray Wood, a stand of mature beech trees. Carlisle, we are told by Switzer, did not wish to spoil the wood. Instead of creating a formal avenue through the wood, an ancient path which curved around the southern flank of the wood was turned into a grassy walk, linking the house to the Temple of the Four Winds. Hussey describes Wray Wood as 'historic ground, since it became the turning point of garden design not only at Castle Howard but in England', to which Turner would add 'and the world' (Turner, 1986: 86).

Personal strategies, if emulated by society, can in time come to form part of the cultural background.

Biological theories

Cultural explanations of aesthetic preferences are inherently contingent and relativistic, and many aestheticians have found this unsatisfactory. One response to this, in the field of landscape aesthetics, has been the attempt to find biological laws which will be universally applicable to all humans at all times. Obviously, if such a basis could be discovered the task of landscape architects would become much clearer. They could look to biology to tell them which landscapes were valued and why. They then

Figure 2.9 and Figure 2.10 Castle Howard, North Yorkshire. A turning point in the history of English landscape design. **Left**: the straight avenue. **Right**: the curving ride which skirts Wray Wood.

could make it their business to conserve, enhance or create such landscapes.

The Savannah Hypothesis

Perhaps the most comprehensive and determined attempt to put aesthetics upon a biological foundation has been made by the behavioural ecologist, Gordon Orians (1980, 1986). His argument is that the habit selection mechanism has been under the strong influence of natural selection for most species; choice of habitat exerts a powerful influence on survival and reproductive success. One might therefore expect that humans would have strong positive responses to those landscape features which, in evolutionary terms, had represented good habitats. A good habitat has to provide a home and supplies of food and water. Orians cites evidence which shows that birds and animals do not have the time to assess these things directly. Instead they are able to recognise promising patterns in the environment.

Orians suggests that because human evolution occurred in the savannahs of East Africa, human beings should prefer similar types of landscape, characterised by expanses of grass, dotted with isolated trees or clumps of trees.

Orians produces various kinds of evidence for this hypothesis:

1 Explorers in the North American West consistently seemed to prefer savannah-like landscapes. Orians believes that in western literature in general such landscapes are consistently described more favourably than closed forests, bare plains or deserts.
2 Properties with views of parkland and properties adjacent to water consistently yield higher prices than properties without these attractions.
3 Studies using photographs have found that 8- and 11-year-old residents in the north-eastern United States have shown preferences for savannah landscapes over the locally more common, and therefore more familiar, deciduous and coniferous forests. However, above the age of 15 this effect was not present, a finding which Orians attributes to intervening cultural influences. No age group expressed a preference for desert or rain forest.

Orians hypothesised that those environments which humans designed for their own pleasure, by manipulating topography, vegetation and water (i.e. gardens or the sorts of landscapes created by landscape architects) would resemble savannah. The strongest evidence for this is the English Landscape park which clearly does resemble savannah. Rainy season Africa, at least, bears an uncanny resemblance to Oxfordshire. However, there are clearly many gardens that look nothing like the savannah, including all the great formal gardens.

Orians tries to dismiss the counter-examples by saying that in these cases the landscape preferences have been determined by cultural factors. While this line of argument is consistent with Bourassa's tripartite framework and the idea that biological factors may be overlain by cultural ones, the very existence of the counter-examples is a great obstacle for the theory. The usefulness of the Savannah Hypothesis in explaining landscape preferences depends upon the degree to which the landscapes in question have been subject to human alteration and the degree of cultural conditioning in the subjects. Theoretically it could entirely account for the preferences of savages (using that word to mean completely uncultured individuals in Rousseau's sense), but such people nowhere exist. It might explain *some* of the preferences of cultured individuals when presented with natural habitats, or human-influenced landscapes which resemble such places, but it will be difficult, if not impossible, to say, in any particular case, whether a cultural influence is at work. One would expect a general theory of landscape aesthetics to account for cultural landscapes as well as natural landscapes. The Savannah Hypothesis can cope when the former resemble the latter, but it fails completely when they do not.

In addition to his prediction about the form of designed landscapes, Orians also thought that the shapes of trees that people preferred would tend to resemble those found in savannah, i.e. they would be broader than they were tall, with wide canopies, short trunks and small compound leaves. Orians

Figure 2.11 Zebras in Zambia: but if the animals were missing, could this be Oxfordshire?

studied Japanese gardens because these were designed to emulate and perfect nature, but his findings are less than convincing. The Japanese maples, he found, did have the characteristics of savannah trees, but the similarities were less obvious in the case of oaks. Conifers do not resemble savannah trees at all, but Orians argues that in Japanese gardens they are pruned in such a way that they do. Once again, the one-sidedness of the theory is evident. It uses naturalistic styles of gardening as evidence, but cannot draw similar support from, nor offer any explanatory account of, non-naturalistic forms of garden. The Savannah Hypothesis has nothing to say, for instance, about our apparent liking for pleached limes, lombardy poplars, topiary or monkey puzzles.

Other criticisms can be made. In general the Savannah Hypothesis offers no account of the pleasure we take in functional or organised landscapes. It ignores the satisfactions that arise from recognising patterns in the landscape. Nor does it offer an account of the attraction of apparently threatening places, such as mountains, waterfalls, gorges, etc. It does not provide an explanation of the Sublime.

Information Processing Theory

The theory put forward by Rachel and Steven Kaplan, a team of environmental psychologists, is broader than the Savannah Hypothesis, which it subsumes, but like the latter it proceeds from consideration of the survival needs of the human species in prehistoric times. Human beings, say the Kaplans, could not have succeeded as big game hunters on the African savannah by physical prowess alone; they would have had to use their wits to survive. They argue that it was the human capacity to process large amounts of information that gave them the edge over their competitors. It follows that they would have fared better in information-rich environments where this faculty could be fully employed. The Kaplans invoke natural selection, in a similar manner to Orians, to explain why, over an evolutionary span, mankind has come to prefer such landscapes.

In a series of empirical investigations spanning twenty years the Kaplans have attempted to ascertain what qualities of landscapes are rich in information. The four characteristics they identify are complexity, coherence, legibility and mystery. These characteristics are considered in terms of the amount of information that they immediately provide and the amount that they predict will be forthcoming upon further exploration. Complexity, for example, is immediately apparent and suggests that the scene deserves further study. Mystery implies that further exploration will be rewarded with further information. Coherence and legibility both contribute to the understanding of information received.

Studies of real landscapes using the four variables have produced some interesting conclusions. Landscape preferences have tended to fall into one of two categories – legible park-like scenes on the one hand, and scenes that contain an element of mystery on the other. Generally, legibility and mystery have proved to be the characteristics that correlate with landscape preferences. Regression analyses upon the four categories have suggested that 'mystery is the most consistent of the informational factors' (Kaplan and Kaplan, 1989: 66). This last finding supports the contention that human beings are information-hungry creatures, always seeking new situations and new knowledge.

What relevance do the Kaplans' findings have for landscape designers? It would seem that too much coherence may lead to boredom, but that too much complexity may tax cognitive abilities. Legibility is always a good thing, and it can be created by the provision of cues which allow subjects to orient themselves in the landscape. The importance attached to mystery suggests that designed landscapes which reveal their secrets will gradually, in general be preferred to those where everything is immediately apparent.

Unlike the Savannah Hypothesis, the Information Processing Theory can be used to explain the appeal of formal gardens as well as informal gardens or natural landscapes. Formal gardens are likely to be coherent and legible, and are often rewardingly complex. However, they are often designed to be taken in from a single viewpoint; their complex patterns are intended to be seen from an elevated terrace or walk. This may mean that they are deficient in the quality of mystery. Versailles, for example, was intended to impress by its scale, which had to be immediately apparent. However, rides cut through the great plantations which formed the main vistas provided minor opportunities for concealment, introducing an element of mystery. A garden like Stourhead in Wiltshire, on the other hand, was designed to provide a promenade circuit along which new vistas would gradually be revealed. Here we see the quality of mystery being carefully manipulated to provide a succession of satisfying aesthetic experiences.

Prospect and Refuge Theory

The Prospect and Refuge Theory, developed by Jay Appleton, formerly Professor of Geography at the University of Hull, bears some similarities to those of Orians and the Kaplans in that it seeks to explain positive feelings about present-day landscapes in terms of evolutionary survival. Appleton (1975) suggests that to the extent our aesthetic reactions to landscape are inborn, they should be universal, which implies that the same sorts of landscapes will be presented in a positive light across the full spectrum of world art and literature. We have already encountered a similar claim from Orians. Appleton, however, concentrates his attention upon the representation of landscape in painting. He argues, after the ethologist, Konrad Lorenz, that in terms of survival it is important to 'see without being seen'. A hunter-gatherer must be able to spot prey or possible predators without himself being spotted. This suggests to Appleton that the most significant features in landscapes will be prospects, which offer opportunities for viewing, and refuges, which offer opportunities for concealment.

It is important to realise that Appleton's theory is concerned with *symbolic* refuges and prospects. Features in landscapes can suggest opportunities for seeing or hiding without actually being good viewpoints or refuges. A tower on a hill in the middle distance will be regarded favourably whether or not the view from that point turns out to be good (and in considering a *painting* that includes a tower we have no way of finding out!). A third category, the hazard symbol, is introduced to explain the appeal of features like waterfalls or ravines, thus extending the scope of the theory to cover typically Sublime landscape features.

Appleton provides a detailed taxonomy of prospect, refuge and hazard symbols, providing selected examples from landscape design, painting and literature to support his theory, but it has been noted that many of his examples are ambiguous. 'Darkness', says Bunske in a review of Appleton's book, 'may not always signify a refuge, but may instead be

Figure 2.12 and Figure 2.13 The promenade circuit at Stourhead was devised to present a sequence of views. Here are two of them: view towards the Temple of Apollo; and view west to the Pantheon. (Courtesy of Michael Downing.)

Figure 2.14 Prospect & Refuge: this illustration was originally prepared by Jay Appleton for *The Experience of Landscape*. (Courtesy of Jay Appleton.)

Figure 2.15 The Victoria Falls from the security of the Zambian riverbank; perhaps the ultimate experience of sublimity.

forbidding; it is, in fact, one of the few universal environmental elements that induces fear in infants' (Bunske, 1977: 149–151).

There have been attempts to confirm Prospect and Refuge Theory experimentally, a number of which have been reviewed by Appleton himself (1984). Bourassa notes in particular Woodcock's comparison of preferences for savannah, hardwood forest and rain forest (Bourassa, 1991: 82). Woodcock concluded:

> In brief people prefer landscapes which provide good views of large expanses of territory with other promising vantage points visible in the distance. But they also prefer that their broad expanses come equipped with convenient refuges as well, they do not favour open spaces devoid of cover. And they like scenes that not

only show much but show further opportunities for exploration as well.

(Woodcock, 1982: 302)

Appleton's classification of prospects and refuges is undoubtedly too simplistic, as Bunske's observation about darkness suggests. A dark wood might offer a refuge, but it might also be threatening, and it could also be mysterious, inviting exploration. Nevertheless, the language of prospect and refuge has entered into the landscape designer's vocabulary, suggesting, at the very least, that these concepts make intuitive sense and are useful in discussing landscapes.

Jellicoe's Theory

The late Sir Geoffrey Jellicoe was not a scientist like Orians or the Kaplans. His theory was developed in the course of a lifetime's study and practice of landscape design rather than through experiment. It is largely intuitive but it draws upon the empirical findings of others, particularly Orians.

In the Introduction to his *Guelph Lectures on Landscape Design* (1983), Jellicoe suggests that landscape design is 'a projection of the psyche into its natural environment', and he provides a model of the way the mind is organised which is related to stages in human evolution.

Jellicoe suggests that the psyche has levels, which he calls 'transparencies', an analogy which suggests that the earlier and deeper levels are not entirely hidden by the shallower and more recent ones. Like Orians, the Kaplans and Appleton he believes that our emotional responses to landscape can be accounted for by our evolutionary history as a species.

Hence, at the 'scarcely perceptible' primeval level there is *Rock and Water*, 'without a known influence on the psychology of the present day'. A positivist would surely protest that if this level is undetectable and without effects, it is no more than an imaginative elaboration. Above this is the transparency that Jellicoe calls the *Forester*, which is identified with the time that our ancestors spent in the sub-tropical forest and which accounts for all that is sensuous and tactile in our appreciation of landscape, including our love of flowers.

Next is the level he calls the *Hunter*, which was formed on the African savannah and accounts for our liking of the sort of parkland created by 'Capability' Brown. This element of his theory seems to have been taken directly from the Savannah Hypothesis. On top of this we find the *Settler*, which represents our transition to an agricultural existence and accounts for our love of mathematical order. A formal garden like Versailles appeals to our instincts at this level. Plato, it seems, must have had the mind of a Settler. The Kaplans have offered an account of the appeal of such places in terms of coherence and legibility.

The *Forester*, *Hunter* and *Settler* are all straightforward enough and seem to make sense intuitively. The fifth level, which according to Jellicoe is a contemporary addition, is more problematic. He calls it the *Voyager* and suggests that mankind is currently on a journey of discovery; he is thinking not of an outward journey, but of the kind of inward exploration begun by Freud and taken further and deeper, some would say, by Jung. Surely if this is a journey into the subconscious mind it is going to involve a descent through all previous levels, right down to *Rock and Water*. Jellicoe's metaphors seem mixed here, for how can a level or a 'transparency' also be a journey? Jellicoe's interest in Jungian psychology can be put to one side, however, until we come to consider his view that landscape architecture can be considered as a fine art, where it plays a central part in his thought.

None of the biological or habitat theories are sufficient to explain all human aesthetic responses to landscape. Orians's is the most severely limited as it only seems to explain the appeal of certain kinds of landscape. Appleton's is more widely applicable, but the evidence to support it does not fully convince. If one accepts the Kaplans' view that human survival was linked to the ability to process information, the subsequent elaboration of their theory in terms of coherence, legibility, complexity and mystery does have considerable explanatory force across a wide spectrum of types of landscape. Jellicoe's theory is more in the nature of a heuristic framework for understanding our reactions to various kinds of landscape. It is useful and interesting, rather than scientific.

We may ask how these theories help designers to decide what is of value in the landscapes they design. The Savannah theory does not give much guidance, except to suggest that certain kinds of parkland landscape will be appealing. Similarly, Jellicoe's 'transparencies', considered apart from his other ideas, seem to offer very little guidance to the designer, beyond the observation that forests, savannahs and ordered agricultural landscapes all have their own kinds of appeal.

Appleton's theory promises to go deeper by discovering just what it is about landscapes which creates their appeal. He provides a taxonomy of symbolic features which will evoke aesthetic responses in the users of a landscape, but just as Komar and Melamid failed to paste together a good painting, it is arguable that a merely additive process of incorporating vistas, prospects, peepholes, secondary vantage points, refuges, etc. is no guarantee that the resulting landscape will be a satisfactory aesthetic whole. The most that can be said is that Appleton provides a toolkit both for the analysis and the creation of landscapes.

Of all the habitat theories, the Kaplans' seems to offer most to the designer, for by identifying the characteristics of aesthetically pleasing landscapes they assist in the formulation of sub-goals in the design process. The designer who wishes to produce an aesthetically satisfactory landscape will seek to produce one that is legible, appropriately complex, and coherent, with elements of mystery. Of course, the exact balance of these characteristics, and the means by which they are created, remains a matter of skill. Like Appleton, the Kaplans provide a toolkit, but it is perhaps a more flexible and appropriate one for the designer.

The place of beauty

This chapter opened by asking how we might recognise beauty. An easy answer has not emerged; indeed the whole question has become more complicated, for it is apparent that beauty has meant different things to different people at different times – for Plato it was timeless order, for Hogarth it was a gently curving line, while for Payne Knight it could be a natural shagginess. It is easy to think of a landscape to match each of these conceptions: a formal garden, a Brownian park and a wilderness.

Moreover, it appears that our initial questions were too narrow, for the range of aesthetic responses to landscape is not confined to the appreciation of beauty. We also like to be thrilled by the Sublime, and, in certain frames of mind, seem to be able to take an aesthetic pleasure in just about anything, including blast furnaces or satanic mills.

Bourassa (1991) has provided an enormously useful conceptual framework for considering our aesthetic responses to landscape. Perhaps its most interesting feature is the link between personal strategies and cultural values. This frees artists or designers from slavishly following the cultural norms, and casts them in the role of expeditionaries who bring back new treasures from their explorations.

The boundaries of the aesthetic must therefore not be seen as fixed. There should always be room for an avant-garde. Conversely, what is fresh or new need not be elevated over what is traditional. Tastes may vary over time, but it is certain that if a particular quality or style has once appealed, it has the capacity to do so again. This is the main lesson of Jellicoe's model of the mind, with its layers of psychic transparencies.

It seems that Jellicoe, Bourassa, the Kaplans, Orians and Appleton are all expressing aspects of the truth, but where does this leave the designer? Those who write about landscape aesthetics do not produce rule books or manuals to tell others how to design. On the other hand, there does seem to be a growing consensus about the underlying characteristics of our biological responses to places, and this body of knowledge will continue to grow. It leads in turn to considerations of human ecology, and away from a rationalistic aesthetics. This is not to deny that formal landscapes have their own sort of appeal, but it does suggest that this appeal is more of a cultural phenomenon than a biological one.

Landscape planning and aesthetics

The main focus of this book is upon landscape design, but a chapter on landscape aesthetics cannot ignore the very large body of research which has developed in the area of landscape planning. This became very important in Britain during the 1970s, at a time when county councils were anxious to include assessments of landscape quality in their Structure Plans.[8] It is worth noting, however, that while many of the methodologies devised recognised the essentially subjective nature of aesthetic judgements about landscape, there was a strong impetus to place landscape assessment on a more objective footing. Authorities which are responsible for the formulation of public policies and for the allocation of public resources money need to be able to demonstrate that they have reached their decisions by rationally defensible means. This led to attempts to use complicated statistical methods such as regression analysis to determine what aspects of landscape were valued by observers.

The completion of the round of structure planning coincided with a general disillusionment with complex statistical approaches to the subject, and the period following the Countryside Commission's 1988 review has seen a general retreat from questions of evaluation in favour of approaches which seek to describe, analyse and classify landscapes rather than to evaluate them.[9] At the same time there has been a fruitful convergence between those concerned with the visual aspects of landscape and those concerned with nature conservation, which has culminated in the publication of a comprehensive map.[10]

The present interest in the character of local and regional landscapes can be seen as an essential prerequisite for landscape evaluation, and there is now much interest in how this approach can be turned into a tool for managing landscapes. Most notably Warwickshire County Council (1993) has used a landscape character study as the basis for deciding between policies for conservation, enhancement, restoration and change. Of course once evaluation is back on the agenda, the genie of

subjectivity is once again out of the bottle. In Warwickshire it seems that strong landscape patterns, diversity and distinctiveness were the attributes given a positive value. There are resonances here with the much older terminology of the 'spirit of the place', tying contemporary initiatives back into the aesthetic theories of the eighteenth century. Warnock and Brown (1998) argue that the condition of a given landscape has both a visual and an ecological dimension, utilising ideas of 'ecological health', a concept which will be examined in Chapter 8.

To believe that subjectivity in assessing landscapes can be avoided is an error which ignores the fundamental philosophical distinction between facts and values. Moreover, if we are honest enough to admit that aesthetic judgements are inescapably subjective, this raises difficult questions about who is to make such judgements. Another strand in the literature criticises the use of professional assessors, such as landscape architects, arguing that it is the public's perceptions of landscape which should prevail in policy-making. The biological theories described earlier in this chapter can be used to support either view. If all human beings have much in common when it comes to landscape preferences, then who needs experts? On the other hand, if it is cheaper to

Figure 2.16 Character Map of England. 157 distinct areas of landscape character have been identified. Undertaken by Chris Blandford Associates for the Countryside Commission.

use experts, and their views are likely to be representative of widely held opinion, then why not use them? Generally the more democratic view that local people should have an active involvement in the landscape assessment process is prevailing (Swanwick, 1998). The Yorkshire Dales National Park Authority commissioned a study in which the public were asked to comment on an artist's impressions of possible future landscapes which could result in their localities from different management policies. Although this was seen as an interactive form of interpretation, the authors of the study were quick to see the potential of the technique for involving people in political debates about landscape change (O'Riordan *et al.*, 1993). The involvement of local communities in this way would seem to combine aesthetic, social and (potentially) ecological values in a worthwhile manner.

A summary of aesthetic strategies

Returning to questions of design, we must now attempt to summarise the guidance that this broad survey of historical aesthetics might provide for designers. There is no single theory which rises to trounce all-comers. Instead we find a plurality of values and strategies amongst which designers may choose. Each has value in its own right. Interesting questions arise, however, in terms of the main argument of this book, about the degree to which particular aesthetic approaches may embrace the social and ecological values identified in later chapters. Here are some possible strategies:

1 Classical/formal

This draws upon the classical conception of Nature which referred to an underlying universal order, consisting of geometrical and numerical relationships. It emphasises symmetry, regularity and proportion. As we will see in Chapter 6, it has often been associated with distinctly authoritarian trends in city planning. It can also be taken as representative of an attitude towards nature which emphasises human control.

2 'Beautiful' Improvement

This is the approach recommended by Hogarth and Burke, which may be considered a form of Neo-platonism in which figures based upon gently curving lines are to be preferred over the geometrical patterns of the Formal tradition. It is exemplified by the landscape gardens of Brown and Repton. It lies somewhere between rationalism and empiricism, in that it recognises the inherent beauties of nature, but suggests that mankind is in a position to improve upon what has been given.

3 Naturalistic/Picturesque

The origins of this approach lie in empiricism rather than rationalism. In this tradition the idea of nature comes from everyday experience rather than from contemplation of an ideal world of Forms. The sort of interventions in nature sanctioned by this approach are confined to the rearrangement of natural objects, including vegetation, to create more painterly compositions. Many landscape architects subscribe to the view that the hand of the designer should not be seen. This is the naturalistic approach taken to its limits.

4 Sublime

This approach recognises that beauty, whether conceived in terms of formal regularity, curving lines, or natural shagginess, need not be the only aesthetic goal in the creation of landscapes. Human beings can respond to scenes which display the overwhelming power or vastness of nature (or indeed of man-made industrial processes) with awe and wonder. The delight taken in such scenes is paradoxical because they are discomforting rather than reassuring. Designers may nevertheless contrive to increase these reactions through their interventions.

5 Biologically based

Such strategies are related to 3 and 4 above in that they are based upon an empirical approach to nature, but they go further by recognising that human beings have an evolutionary history which has a bearing upon contemporary responses to landscape. Designers can seek to appeal to deep-seated instincts when intervening to 'improve' nature. Moreover, it explicitly recognises that human beings are part of nature, and when they respond aesthetically they are responding as animals. The biological approaches taken by Orians, Appleton and others can be seen as a development of Burke's insight that aesthetic responses are related to instincts for self-preservation and procreation.

6 Functional

The idea that the beautiful object is the functional object (and by extension the beautiful landscape is the functional landscape) has a history which goes back at least as far as Plato. It finds a specific echo in Jellicoe's *Settler,* who loves ordered fields and rows of crops, partly for their mathematical precision but also for their practicality. This tradition came to the fore in the Modern movement, which will be explored more fully in Chapter 6.

7 Symbolic

Designers can be said to be employing a symbolic approach if they set out to make their landscapes carry meanings. In such designs the cultural associations are as important as, and may indeed override, any effects at the instinctive level. Jellicoe's Kennedy Memorial at Runnymede, which is an allegory based upon *Pilgrim's Progress* (itself an allegory), exemplifies the approach, but there is a sense in which every formal garden, even if devoid of overt symbolism, is a representation of mankind's domination and control of nature, while every wilderness garden symbolises the idea of mankind-within-nature. The idea that designed landscapes can carry symbolic meanings is closely related to the idea that they can be works of art, which will be explored more fully in Chapter 4.

This list is not meant to be exhaustive, nor the categories mutually exclusive. It is easy to see how the Naturalistic and the Biologically based could be combined. It is harder (though not impossible) to see how the Functional and the Symbolic or the Biologically based and the Classical might be united.

Aesthetic values alone are not enough

To restrict design to aesthetic concerns is to misrepresent the complexity of the activity. Aesthetic values have to be measured against functional needs and societal and ecological concerns. The rutted lane described in Price's *Dialogues* might look well on a postcard, but what would it be like to walk on? The gypsy's hovel might be worthy of a conservation order, but how does the gypsy feel about living in it?

A manicured formal garden might satisfy the client's love of rational order or gratify his sense of control, but how does it measure up against criteria for sustainability? The difficulty of disentangling biological from cultural factors, and the admission that we are all a combination of Forester, Hunter and Settler, suggests that the grounds for choosing one brand of aesthetics over another cannot come from within aesthetics itself. It is at this point that other values, social, functional, political or environmental, need to be entered into the calculus. This is the project we will pursue in later chapters.

Notes

1 Study after Velázquez's *Portrait of Pope Innocent X*.
2 *Philebus* 64e (trans. Hackforth).
3 Aristotle, *Metaphysics* (XIII [M] iii).
4 Commencing in 1993, Melamid and Komar hired telephone researchers in thirteen countries to conduct a survey of artistic preferences. Once armed with the data, they created, for each country, paintings representing the 'most wanted' and 'least wanted' attributes. The results were then posted on the website hosted by the Dia Center for the Arts, New York. Web-users were encouraged to respond to the paintings by e-mail.
5 The term 'Critical Regionalism' was coined by Alexander Tzonis and Liane Lefaivre, but has become associated with Kenneth Frampton. For further reading see Chapter 5 of Frampton's *Modern Architecture, A Critical History*, 3rd edition, 1992, Thames and Hudson, London, which is devoted to this theme.
6 The charity Common Ground was established in 1983. It has promoted three major projects – the Parish maps Project, Woods and the Green Man, and the New Milestones Project. Artists commissioned in the course of New Milestones have included Peter Randall-Page, Simon Thomas, Andy Goldsworthy, Christine Angus, John Maine and David Nash. For further information see Joanna Moreland's *New Milestones: Sculpture, Community and the Land,* 1988, Common Ground, London.
7 Urmson (1957) concluded that 'whatever the criteria of the aesthetic may be they cannot be found by trying to delimit a special class of objects', and Jerome Stolnitz suggested in his *Aesthetics and the Philosophy of Art Criticism* (1960) that the object of attention is of less importance than the aesthetic attitude with which it is approached. However, the dominant empirical tradition suggests that some objects are more suitable or fitting for aesthetic contemplation than others.
8 To attempt to review the complexity of the issues and the variety of approaches adopted within the confines of this chapter would be an impossible task and interested readers are referred to a review produced by the Landscape Research Group for the Countryside Commission (1988).
9 In America the term 'landscape inventory' is often used to

describe the procedure which describes, analyses and classifies landscapes.

10   *The Character of England: Landscape, Wildlife and Natural Features*, 1997, Countryside Commission, English Nature.

Bibliography

Appleton, J. (1975) *The Experience of Landscape*, John Wiley and Sons, London.

Appleton, J. (1984) 'Prospects and Refuges Revisited', in *Landscape Journal*, 3(2): 91–103.

Beardsley, M. (1975) *Aesthetics from Classical Greece to the Present*, University of Alabama Press, New York.

Bourassa, S.C. (1991) *The Aesthetics of Landscape*, Belhaven Press, London and New York.

Bunske E.V. (1977) Review of *The Experience of Landscape* in *Annals of the Association of American Geographers*, 67(1): 149–151.

Burke, E. ([1759] 1968) *A Philosophical Enquiry into the Origin of Our Ideas of the Sublime and the Beautiful*, edited by J.T. Boulton, University of Notre Dame Press, Notre Dame, Ind.

Hogarth, W. ([1753] 1971) *The Analysis of Beauty, Written with a View of Fixing the Fluctuating Ideas of Taste*, Scolar Press, Menston, England.

Hussey, C. (1927) *The Picturesque: Studies in a Point of View*, G.P. Putnam and Sons, New York.

Jellicoe, G.A. (1983) *Guelph Lectures on Landscape Design*, University of Guelph.

Jellicoe, G.A. and Jellicoe, S. (1975) *The Landscape of Man*, Thames and Hudson, London.

Jellicoe, G.A. and Shepherd, J.C. ([1925] 1985) *Italian Gardens of the Renaissance*, Academy Editions, London.

Kaplan, R. and Kaplan, S. (1989) *The Experience of Nature*, Cambridge University Press, New York.

Lovejoy. A.O. (1965) *The Great Chain of Being*, Harper, New York.

Orians, G.H. (1980) 'Habitat Selection: General Theory and Applications to Human Behaviour', in J.S. Lockard, ed., *The Evolution of Human Social Behaviour*, Elsevier, New York.

Orians, G.H. (1986) 'An Ecological and Evolutionary Approach to Landscape Aesthetics', in E.C. Penning-Rowsell and D. Lowenthal, eds, *Landscape Meanings and Values*, Allen and Unwin, London.

O'Riordan, T., Wood, C. and Sheldrake, A. (1993) 'Landscapes for Tomorrow', *Journal of Environmental Planning and Management*, 36(2): 123–147.

Santayana, G. ([1896] 1961), *The Sense of Beauty: Being the Outline of Aesthetic Theory*, Collier Books, New York.

Stolnitz, J. (1960) *Aesthetics and the Philosophy of Art Criticism: A Critical Introduction*, Houghton Mifflin, Boston.

Stroud, D. (1950) *Capability Brown*, Faber and Faber, London.

Swanwick, C. (1998) 'New Forces for Change: Landscape Assessment in Practice', *Landscape Design*, No. 269: 8–10.

Tunnard, C. (1978) *A World with a View*, Yale University Press, London.

Turner, T. (1986) *English Garden Design*, Antique Collectors' Club, Woodbridge, Suffolk.

Turner, T. (1996) *City as Landscape*, E & FN Spon, London.

Urmson, J.O. (1957) 'What Makes a Situation Aesthetic?', *Proceedings of the Aristotelian Society*, Supplementary Vol. XXXI: 75–92; reprinted in J. Margolis (ed.) (1962) *Philosophy Looks at the Arts*, Charles Scribner's Sons, New York.

Warnock, S. and Brown, N. (1998) 'A Vision for the Countryside', *Landscape Design*, No. 269: 22–26.

Warwickshire County Council (1993) *Warwickshire Landscape Guidelines*.

Wittkower, R. (1973) *Architectural Principles in the Age of Humanism* (4th edition), Academy Editions, London.

Woodcock, D.M. (1982) 'A Functionalist Approach to Environmental Preference', Unpublished Ph.D. dissertation, University of Michigan, Ann Arbor.

3 In practice: improving the view?

The beauties of nature

In the introductory chapter of *Design with Nature* (1969),[1] Ian McHarg describes his childhood in the soot-blackened streets of industrial Glasgow, and the way in which his experiences of the polluted city were heightened by the contrasting scenery of Loch Lomond and the Scottish Highlands which lay almost upon Glasgow's doorstep. When I first read this, it resonated because I grew up in Barrow-in-Furness in Cumbria, a town kept economically alive by a nuclear shipyard, which also boasted a steelworks and the largest slag bank in Britain. But Barrow's back garden was the English Lake District, and at least once a month as I was growing up I would go walking among hills that had been celebrated by Wordsworth and explored by generations of shipyard workers with hob-nails banged into their work boots. Though I seem, like many of my interviewees, to have stumbled upon landscape architecture as a career, I have often wondered if its appeal had something to do with those formative years, when I was regularly exposed to the contrast between an urban landscape which could be ugly and a rural landscape which was nearly always beautiful.

One of my interviewees, Nigel Marshall, the Principal Landscape Architect for East Sussex County Council, described a similar experience:

> I was 14 or 15 when I moved up to London. My father ran prison farms up till that point, and was then moved to head office in London, so we all had to trundle in there and having had the benefit of a fairly rich environment, coming to the concrete jungle made a major impression on me.

Seeking to return to a life associated with the land, Marshall had already obtained a place at agricultural college when he came across an advert for a traineeship in landscape architecture with the Greater London Council. Looking back on this he thinks he was very fortunate:

> Whilst I would have enjoyed agriculture, it would not have been as complete a job for me as landscape, which engages horticultural skills and, as it has developed over time, involves an over-view on the landscape planning side, with elements of the aesthetic. I was never a great artist. I came to it more from the sciences, with, I believe, a fairly full appreciation of landscape through that experience of rural living very much into urban living.

While many of my subjects had an active interest in art and design before training as landscape architects, for some it was the direct appreciation of 'natural' landscapes which drew them towards the profession. Simon Rendel told me:

> Although it was design that really made me enthusiastic about landscape, actually it was the aesthetic quality of non-designed landscapes that brought me into it . . . I suppose underlying it all is just a feeling that the things that I really love, in terms of nature, are things that can't really be recreated. They can with water sometimes, and they can perhaps with woodland, but at other times the idea that you can re-create the real beauty of the natural situation just doesn't wash. I think you can sort of imitate it in a design, but

once you've lost the thing that was really good, then you're trying for other things which have similar qualities.

Rendel's interest in landscape conservation led him to develop a technique known as Tranquil Areas Mapping with the support of the Council for the Protection of Rural England. These maps show the cumulative effects of intrusions upon the landscape, whether they be visual, like transmission masts for cellular phones, or audible, like the flightpaths of commercial airlines.

You've got this danger of everything joining up and nothing being left. It's amazing how unaware people can be of this. Of course, when you go to Australia or somewhere, why should they be aware? It's not really an important thing out there. But I think we are in a tight situation really, where so much change has occurred in the last thirty years and you have a situation where the younger generation is probably very used to the fact that

there have always been aeroplanes in the skies, there has always been the noise from road traffic, there will always be the sense that something's only a hundred metres away. They've got used to that, and yet, when you produce a map like I did, then you realise that all these people who are living in big cities, they psychologically depend upon the idea that there is open countryside beyond there in big swathes that they can go to.

Rebecca Hughes (Principal Landscape Advisor, Scottish Natural Heritage), like Nigel Marshall, came into landscape architecture from the sciences, but she is able to pinpoint the moment of her epiphany. She remembers that as a botany under-graduate in Durham she was undertaking a field study of changing land use patterns in the South Wales valleys:

It was one of the first places where the Forestry Commission used Sylvia Crowe's[2] skills to manipulate plantation design and diversify the species mix and I went there to do fieldwork for my dissertation . . . my favourite occupation . . . and was camping there and soil sampling, and I got to notice the forestry that had been designed by her, and it was getting to the stage where you could see what it was doing, and showing how it could reflect landform and even further the landscape characteristics by using different colours, different species.

I was most impressed by this, and I talked to the forester who lived and worked there . . . and asked him about it. 'Oh, it was done by this lady who's come down here in her tweeds, twin set and pearls to tell us all what to do.' Apparently it was most unlike the Forestry Commission to have anyone female working in such a way, and according to the local foresters she was quite wonderful to help with all these 'landscape' things, and I thought 'that's the kind of work I'd like to do'.

Significantly, both Marshall and Hughes have been drawn towards large-scale landscape planning, where there is an emphasis upon the conservation of existing landscape of high quality. Marshall explained his role thus:

Well, we are living in a county that is pretty good. We are not living in a county where there are major restoration needs, so conservation in its most

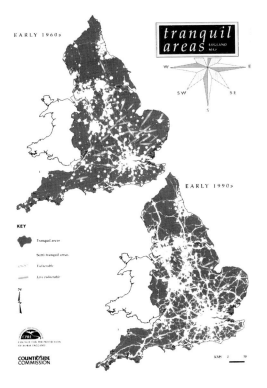

Figure 3.1 Tranquil Areas Map: a technique developed by Simon Rendel for the Council for the Protection of Rural England and the Countryside Commission.

active form is vital and is fundamental to what we are about, but whether we use the word 'creating' or the word 'enhancing' the two come together, because we are not in a preservation situation. I think very much in terms of conservation being an active pursuit.

He illustrated his philosophy by describing an on-going project in the south coast town of Eastbourne, which has already been running for fifteen years and which involves 1,300 acres of floodland in the middle of the town:

> We are creating a totally new landscape there, but within the conservation framework which is needed – wetland habitats and that sort of thing – so the two, conservation and creation, very much come together. Without the positive creative bit . . . we are talking about major earthworks, lake creation, recreational area creation, new woodlands . . . without that, you can't work with conservation.

While both Hughes and Marshall were clearly interested in nature conservation, it was evident from some of their remarks that this was not synonymous with landscape conservation. Hughes told me about a recent debate that had taken place within Scottish Natural Heritage concerning that organisation's opposition to a large-scale development proposal. Ultimately SNH objected on nature conservation grounds rather than landscape grounds:

> The landscape argument wasn't seen as being as strong as the nature conservation argument, which is, to my mind, the wrong way to run the argument. Yes, I agree that the nature conservation argument is stronger, but I don't think that's a reason to drop another part of your justification for objecting to a particular development proposal.

Behind this statement lies a concern, shared by several of the people I talked to, that planning arguments based upon aesthetic judgements are not taken very seriously, and that this is to a large degree because they are considered subjective. Arguments based upon nature conservation are easier to justify objectively. Marshall would like to see these two elements in environmental assessment move closer together:

The ecologists have got their Sites of Special Scientific Interest and their National Nature Reserves, which are very scientific, but they're only such a small part of the story. It's great that they've got those, but what influence do they have on a wider context? That's one of the reasons I'm pleased that English Nature and the Countryside Commission got together to produce the Character Map of England.

These comments reflect the existence of a division in conservation circles which was institutionalised in Britain in 1949 when two distinct agencies, the Nature Conservancy Council (now English Nature) and the Countryside Commission, were established. While the NCC was staffed by ecologists and concerned with wildlife, the Countryside Commission was staffed with rural planners who employed landscape architects to advise on the condition of the landscape.

While there is evidence that these two strands are growing closer, it would be wrong to suggest that all landscape architects, or even just those who work regularly in rural areas, are now ecological purists. For example, Dougal Thornton, who when interviewed was the Principal Landscape Architect for Stirling District Council, put people before aesthetics and aesthetics before nature conservation. He told me:

> We've got this Millennium Forest in Scotland. Now the east side of Loch Lomond is a mixture of oakwoods with big plantations of Forestry Commission conifers: larch, sitka spruce . . . you name it. Not a lot of Scots pine because it's a bit too wet for it. The Millennium Commission has got this big lump of money and these protagonists for native trees say that the whole of the east side of Loch Lomond should go back to native woodland. I have got major problems with that in terms of aesthetics. I think it will be bloody boring as sin. I think the patchwork of deciduous and coniferous plantations which we've got at the moment is quite enriching visually, and I think if you asked the punters how they feel, they'd say that as well.

Fitting in

It will be clear from the previous section that some landscape architects see themselves as the guardians of high-quality rural landscapes. They are defending them against damaging developments, but if this were the only role that landscape architects played, the profession would be very small indeed. In reality landscape architects, particularly those working in the private sector, will find that they are often brought in to assist a developer in getting a development proposal through the planning process. Tom Robinson of the Newcastle practice, Robinson Penn, has a very clear-eyed view of this role. It is very different, he told me, from the conception of landscape architecture he had when he was studying:

> I had an idea it was much more creative, arty and pure, a kind of sculpture-meets-gardening and of course it isn't. It can be, but it rarely is. And practising, I've seen that most of it is related in one form or another to development. It's either repairing the land after development, it's planning for development or it's actually physically designing something to accommodate development.

Landscape architects in the public sector might find themselves considering landscape proposals from a position on the other side of the legislative fence. It may be their job to advise a local authority planning committee on the acceptability of a particular planning proposal and the quality of any associated landscape plan.

The rules by which this game is played vary enormously from place to place. In particular, certain forms of development might be acceptable in an urban area which would not be considered suitable in a rural context. How then do landscape architects see this aspect of their work? In the rural situation it seems, at least for some, to be a matter of making developments fit in as inconspicuously as possible. Here Pauline Randall, of Randall Thorpe in Manchester, describes a landscape scheme designed by Hal Moggeridge (of Colvin Moggeridge) for a water treatment works:

> It was basically a land-forming process to sink the building, screen it and make it disappear from the landscape. It was done in a way that was totally sensitive to its surroundings. I admire that.

There is a strong school of thought which believes that landscape design, at least in the rural context, should be as self-effacing as possible. Rodney Beaumont of Gillespie's Oxford office, not

himself a natural champion of this approach, remembered having heated discussions of this philosophy with David Skinner who taught landscape architecture at Heriot-Watt University, Edinburgh:

> Away back in the 1970s I used to have some real up-and-downers with Davie. He used to say 'I get the best kick when I can't find what I did.' In other words, I've hidden it; I've camouflaged it; I've put it under the ground; I've covered it. I've designed it, but it's lost, it's lost in the wider picture.

One of the schemes which Elizabeth Banks considers to have been successful involves just such an element of camouflage. This is the landscape design for the Wellcome Trust Genome Campus at Hinxton Hall, outside Cambridge:

> I think the way we've been able to design the landscape to put the cars underground and set the little building away from the big building,[3] and you can't really see the big building from anywhere . . . It was relatively revolutionary because though the building got bigger, we were able to set it in its landscape and the landscape came first . . . and also the conceptual business of putting the cars out of sight for an office building in the country. In London it's normal, but it's not normal if you're doing a science park.

Many designed landscapes are physically unbounded. They merge into the surrounding landscape. Some practitioners see their skill lying in the ability to make seamless transitions. A successful landscape design in these terms will not be noticed by the majority of people.

Peter Fischer has undertaken a lot of work in urban fringe and semi-rural landscapes which are subject to pressures from the cities nearby. He particularly enjoys restoration work because he believes that he has the knack of blending a new landform into its surroundings:

> I got into doing landfill by chance, and that is immensely rewarding because what they want is maximum volume, but you're trying to make sure that it works in landform terms to fit the landscape that you're working in . . . You can't always do it so that it looks totally natural because you've got all this stuff to accommodate. Our lifestyle has created waste and although there are attempts at

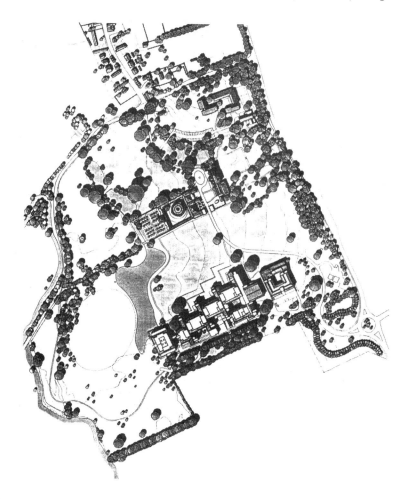

Figure 3.2 Landscape masterplan for the Wellcome Trust Genome Campus, Hinxton, Cambridgeshire. The landscape design is by Elizabeth Banks Associates. Sheppard Robson (architects) produced the drawing.

recycling and reduction it is a problem that won't go away.

I don't think putting in something artificial is right. If we can make it look as much part of what exists as possible, then I think that's the right approach. I do believe that in rural landscapes we should be building on the texture of what's there. So yes, the hand of the landscape architect should be invisible.

Ray Keeley, who at the time of the interview had a one-man practice in the North East, is the antithesis of an egotistical designer:

If my schemes look as if they've always been there, and if some people come and don't even notice that they've suddenly appeared, there's satisfaction in that. There's an aesthetic element in there.

I try not to make statements in my work that stand out. It's a temptation.

Many landscape architects recognise that there is something paradoxical and problematic about a profession which is often at its most successful when it is noticed the least, and draw an obvious contrast with architecture, which has high-profile exponents who produce very visible design statements. Tim Gale of Edwards Gale explained the problem thus:

I think part of our difficulty in getting a high profile as a profession is that some of the major contributions that we've made to the environment in this country have been on things like roads and the New Towns and so on, but they're not like a major building that you can point to and say 'X did that. Isn't it wonderful?' Our work is something

Figure 3.3 The new lake and park at the Wellcome Trust Genome Campus, Hinxton, Cambridgeshire, showing the relationship between the old and new buildings. Landscape design by Elizabeth Banks Associates. Photo by Francis Ware.

which, though it might have had a strength when it was done, after a generation or so is just part of the environment. And, of course, that's its intent! So I see that as entirely appropriate, but I see it as having within it the seeds of some difficulties.

There are two main responses to this problem. The first is simply to accept that the aesthetic values which obtain in landscape architecture are very different from those to be found in architecture, and to get on with what landscape architects have traditionally done. Some are quite hostile to the idea that the names of individual landscape architects or even practices should be attached to particular landscapes. Pauline Randall is of this persuasion:

> I don't think landscape architects should be attributed for everything they do. I don't think the public should need to know that this was a Randall

Thorp design in order to appreciate it. But I do enjoy hearing of landscape architects who have become eminent because they have done a broad base of work and have made a real contribution, rather than just because they have become known as a designer.

For some the philosophy of 'seamlessly fitting in' is as appropriate in urban areas as it is in the countryside. Peter McGuckin, of Newcastle-based Branson McGuckin, has been the consultant landscape architect for the redevelopment of the city's East Quayside, where he adopted an understated approach:

> Actually I don't think it's all that clever to be doing something that's big and strong. The cleverness is doing always, for each site, what is right. Imposing your will might be good, but it might be bad. Working with the grain might have been better.

And in the case of the Quayside, which is the most satisfying example I can think of, we worked with the grain of the vernacular in terms of materials, and really decided that there was too much going on elsewhere so it was necessary to do this almost as a foil, to show that good design was not always about big statements.

Figure 3.4 Seamless design on Newcastle's East Quayside. (Courtesy of Peter McGuckin of Insite.)

Figure 3.5 Low-key design which responds to the spirit of the place. The redevelopment of Newcastle's East Quayside. (Courtesy of Peter McGuckin of Insite.)

Figure 3.6 Andrew Burton's sculpture, reminiscent of sails and rudders, also responds to the spirit of Newcastle's East Quayside. (Courtesy of Peter McGuckin of Insite.)

McGuckin believes that the landscape architect's job is often to harmonise disharmonious elements:

> Being sympathetic to the surroundings is important. Of course you can have a cacophony of surroundings. One of our projects is to do a masterplan for Newcastle College.[4] There the campus has evolved over many years and there's a lot of 'sixties buildings, lots of different styles, architects putting their own individual stamp on it, and very often, I feel, the landscape architect is like a mediator. They're there to provide the coherent matrix to get all these oddities to somehow gel together and it's a difficult task.

Other landscape architects look towards their cousins in architecture with something almost like envy and yearn to produce dramatic new landscapes. Rodney Beaumont agreed, somewhat reluctantly, that in the countryside and the urban fringe, a restrained approach was probably necessary, but saw the urban landscape as presenting the most exciting challenges and opportunities.

Figure 3.7 A discordant note: the restraint shown by the landscape architects on Newcastle's East Quayside was not shared by the craftsman commissioned to design these railings. (Courtesy of Peter McGuckin of Insite.)

In the countryside or the edge of town . . . it's very much about landscape planning and assessment and amelioration. It's not about making statements and perhaps I have to accept that's probably correct, because we're trying to keep our countryside in balance, whereas our towns are man-made and . . . are where the bulk of people live. For me, they have to be exciting places to be. They have to have exciting life about them and have exciting spaces.

Beaumont argues strongly for a more assertive, self-confident approach to urban landscape design, and there are many who would agree with him. Perry Twigg, a senior landscape architect for Salford City Council, also made the comparison with architecture:

You get prominent architects whose work makes a real statement in terms of a building. You get famous architects whose work you recognise. That doesn't tend to happen much with landscape architects and I feel that landscape architecture does need to become a more prominent feature rather than blending in with what's there . . . if people do start coming up with quality designs and landscape architects become well-known for the quality of their design, then I think it can only do the profession good, because a lot of people do still class us as glorified gardeners.

Roger Kirk-Smith, a partner in the Liverpool office of ASH, was worried by the landscape architect's tendency to produce anonymous design. It put him in mind of an adverising slogan once used for the now vintage Bristol motor car:

'Its styling is so subtle as to be understated' I'm not sure if 'understated' was the word they used . . . 'So simple it has to be be self-effacing' . . . that's the term. 'Its style has to be so subtle as to be self-effacing.' Something like that. I think a lot of British design is self-effacing, has been self-effacing, and you can argue that this is the British sickness, a lack of confidence.

However, he predicted that the younger generation of British landscape designers would be different:

Barcelona has influenced a lot of students in their thinking. I think it has been good. It has made them more confident in the scope of their profession.

On the other hand, he cautioned against turning every design commisssion into a showpiece:

Figure 3.8 The Bristol Saloon – style so subtle as to be self-effacing?

Figure 3.9 Parc del Espanya Industrial, Barcelona – urban landscape design at its most assertive.

I think we have to be a bit careful. I do think there is a tendency . . . it's the old thing about the graduate on a year-out who gets given a small urban space and says 'This is it! Place de Concorde!' No. It's just a small urban space. People just want somewhere they can sit down . . . you've got to know where to be self-effacing, where not to make the big statements.

If there is a discernible consensus about this self-effacing/assertive division, it is to the effect that a more restrained, contextually determined aesthetic is the appropriate choice for the rural scene, whereas a more vigorous, idiosyncratic and high profile approach is acceptable, or even desirable, within the city. Tim Gale espoused this balanced philosophy:

One of the things that people always say to me is that they would love to see lots of newspaper articles in the broadsheets about what we are doing, and so would I, but it doesn't sit quite so happily with what journalists are generally

interested in, like say a major building by Richard Rogers. But I'd see that not as a problem, just as a fact.

On the other hand, I do believe that there are plenty of opportunities where we ought to be making stronger statements in some areas. I think a major contribution the profession has made has been to reclaim derelict land. I think that's a tremendous thing to have been involved in. But also in urban areas . . . I think we can be too self-effacing in urban areas. I think some bolder, stronger statements, like the ones most of us have seen now in Southern Europe, would be entirely appropriate, and I'm sure we're going to get them, because I think the new generation of landscape architects who are emerging from college are interested and excited by this.

Local distinctiveness and the spirit of the place

During the course of the interviews some ideas appeared with such regularity that I feel justified in regarding them as central to the value structure of the profession. One of these was Pope's famous dictum 'consult the genius of the place'.[5] If landscape architecture is about anything, it is about responding in a sensitive way to the existing qualities of a particular site. Peter McGuckin's response to the vernacular grain of Newcastle's East Quayside is one example of this. It would seem that this approach can be applied as readily in the town as it can be in the countryside, and it seems to offer an escape route from the self-effacing/assertive dilemma. When I asked Heather Lloyd, landscape architect for Westminster City Council, where she stood on this issue, she replied:

I think it depends where you are designing for. It's the *genius loci* again. I think the place should be telling you how to respond and also the brief obviously, but the place should be saying what sort of design you should be coming up with. There is nothing wrong with seeing something and saying 'I know a landscape architect has been involved', particularly in the urban context . . . So again, you should feel at one with the place. You know, you go on your site visit and you feel the vibes of the place coming through. That's when you should be thinking to yourself: 'Well what sort of design should I be doing?' Should it be something very low key and perhaps naturalistic and subtle or should it be assertive?

This attitude, which has a long history in landscape architectural thinking, is also reflected in contemporary architectural thought in concepts such as critical regionalism and the call for local distinctiveness. It is interesting to find that landscape architects reserve their greatest contempt for members of the environmental design professions (including fellow landscape architects) who ignore this imperative. Here are some examples:

> I just can't believe some of the things I see sometimes. You know, bonsai trees, trees with no water and never any chance of getting any water, badly sited or just very expensive materials being used totally unnecessarily – plant materials as well as hard materials – inappropriate materials used in inappropriate locations, badly done with no sense of place.
>
> (Rebecca Hughes, Scottish Natural Heritage)

> I'm worried about the Americanisation of space. I've only been to Boston and New England, so I can't really say that I've seen a lot of America, but I get the impression from the reviews and the professional press, the type of detailing that's being used, the tightness and the regimented style . . . the quality is there, the attention to detail is there, but it's lifeless somehow . . . It doesn't have the diversity. It doesn't respond in a diverse manner. It's rather like an implant rather than a resolution of location. I suppose I mean it's a bit like McDonald's. It's a McDonald's version of landscape – and that seriously worries me.
>
> (Rebecca Hughes)

> I met an architect designing travel lodges for a big service station chain on a site north of Dunblane,[6] and I was trying to get over to him that it wasn't Chipping Sodbury.[7] There were deer problems here and they couldn't just import the landscape. They might want to import the building, but they couldn't import the landscape design from somewhere down in England for this rather exposed environment, 500 ft. up in our climate, but the guy was having to do the same building, more or less, because that was the company style. I would find that really frustrating.
>
> (Dougal Thornton, Stirling District Council)

> I do wonder whether, because scales of fees have been squeezed, you see that coming through in landscape practices too. Some do very high standard work. They are meticulous in terms of supervision and the tolerances to which things are done, but if I want to criticise them, I think that they sometimes design from a pretty much predetermined palette. You know . . . they've got their components and it's very easy for them to pull out their components on the next site . . . I think local distinctiveness has been lost and there is an element of production-line designing which worries me. The *genius loci* will be away out of the window like it has for the architects on that basis.
>
> (Dougal Thornton)

Aesthetics and professional ethics

Many of the ethical dilemmas faced by landscape architects relate to their involvement in development proposals which have the potential to be aesthetically damaging. This, of course, is often the reason that they have been brought into the project in the first place, but problems arise if the landscape architect concludes that despite their best efforts at amelioration the overall effect of the scheme is going to be negative. At this point they must take a decision about whether or not to remain involved. For Rebecca Hughes it even became a resignation issue:

> I worked on one or two schemes where I was not happy professionally at all when I was with David Bellamy Associates. I actually left in the end because of the ethical basis of some of the schemes I was working on. I had to resign. I did have to resign.
>
> Land's End was one.[8] A very important landmark to most people in the UK and abroad, and it was to be made into some form of theme park, which professionally I didn't see as appropriate at all, and I wondered about the site practicalities and the logistics as well. There was a serious erosion problem there and we were actually being asked to design in a way that would encourage intensive use that would cause further erosion of an important site . . . as important as Stonehenge, possibly. So that sort of issue is difficult at times. You have to ask 'how far can I go down this route before professionalism is compromised?'

In fairness to David Bellamy, who has been a prominent ecological campaigner both in Britain and the wider world for many years, I should say that elsewhere in the interview Hughes acknowledged that he had had a very positive effect upon her thinking. He had been her tutor for two years when she had been studying botany, and he had invited her to join the new consultancy which was set up in the mid-1980s:

> He's not a landscape architect, but he's had a massive influence upon me and upon my value systems . . . What I admire the most is that he is a scientist who has not allowed science to rule everything he thinks and does. He's got a worldly-wise and fundamentally sound foundation to his viewpoints. And I said that I resigned from the consultancy that bore his name, but so did he eventually, for pretty much the same reasons as me, I think.

Elizabeth Banks, of the London-based practice, Elizabeth Banks Associates, has turned work away on aesthetic grounds:

> The issue on one of them was the fact that they were, as far as I was concerned, going against the genre of the landscape. They wanted to cut down trees and completely destroy what was really a rather magical place, in which case I'd rather not be a part of that. We just backed down.

Peter Fischer, another London-based consultant, has refused work which would conflict with his aesthetic standards:

> There are some things that I do think are intrusive and wrong and one doesn't go after that sort of work. I've turned things down because they weren't particularly what I wanted to do, not necessarily because it was a real moral concern.

However, Fischer guards against snap judgements against certain forms of development. He has worked on a number of golf course proposals and does not believe that these are necessarily damaging:

> There is a preconception, particularly in the South, that golf-courses are bad. The further north you go, the more the attitude changes, but certainly in the South East it's 'over-my-dead-body'. I worked on one in the urban fringe where we got

permission and I genuinely believe that the risk to that landscape was 'horsiculture'. One side of the valley had been dreadfully damaged by that and the planners couldn't see that there was a risk of this land going the same way. Half of the site was landfill anyway, and I felt that we would protect the essential scale and character of the landscape by putting a golf course in. The course had to be designed in the right way and not be benched. There had to be no cut-and-fill and we explained that to the developer and they were happy with that.

Describing a proposal for a golf course in Sussex, Fischer explained how he had also been able, while dealing with sensitive aesthetic issues, to enhance the ecology of the site:

> There was a lot of ancient woodland. It had been devastated by the 1987 and 1990 storms, so that was probably the main reason that the golf course was ever allowed, because there was so much devastation from the storms and there had been wholesale clearance, very severe soil erosion, but within that area there were some remarkable habitats with just stunning variety, and two or three public footpath routes through it. We worked on replanting, encouraging those habitats that were developing as a result of the loss of tree cover, such as heathland, and establishing good management of the woodland that remained.

The most significant ethical dilemmas arise when a landscape consultant is approached to work on a project which is aesthetically controversial, but which they know is likely to go ahead whether or not they become involved. Tim Gale mentioned one of the more celebrated cases:

> There was a case about fifteen or twenty years ago when the Department of Transport decided that they needed to build a by-pass around the village of Petworth and it was going to go through or under a Capability Brown landscape, and I'm not sure whether I would have wanted to be involved in a job like that at all, but I respected Geoffrey Collens'[9] view which was that it's much better that someone who's professionally skilled undertakes a job like that, if it's going to be done, rather than someone who isn't.

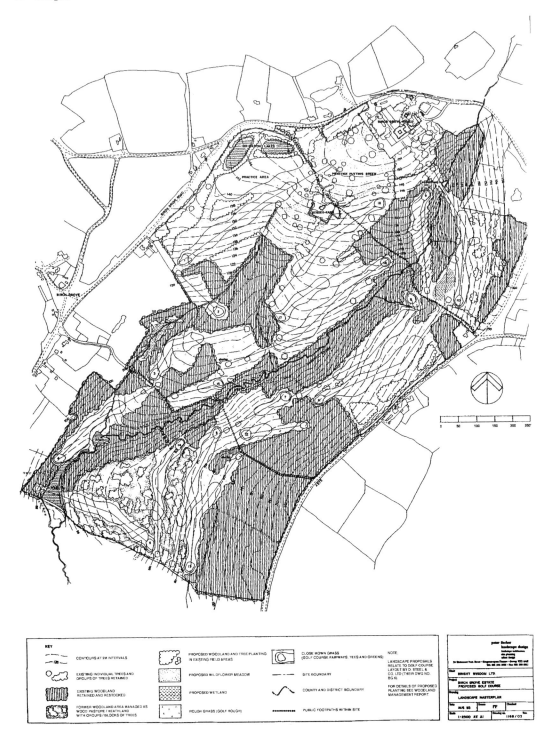

Figure 3.10 Peter Fischer's landscape masterplan for the proposed golf course at the Birch Grove Estate.

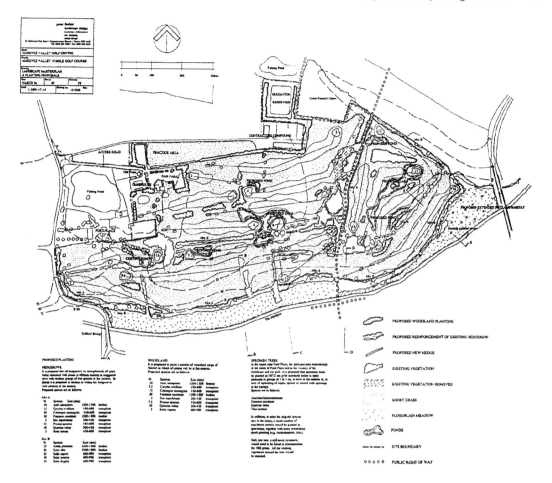

Figure 3.11 Peter Fischer's landscape masterplan for the proposed Mardyke Valley Golf Centre.

Of course other values, ecological, cultural, historical or archaeological, may be involved in such difficult cases. Gale admits that some are very problematic:

> Now you could say that at Twyford Down,[10] for example . . . but even there it seems to me that it was entirely appropriate that once a policy decision had been made that a road was going to go through there, then it needed to have a landscape architect involved in it. I wouldn't have liked to have been that person. I find that a very difficult one actually.

There is perhaps a parallel to be drawn with criminal court cases. It can be argued that every defendant is entitled to representation. Indeed, in the quasi-legal conditions of a planning inquiry it is quite usual to find that each side has its landscape experts giving evidence for and against a proposal; just as in a criminal case both the prosecution and the defence may call upon medical or forensic experts. But lawyers are not supposed to represent defendants as innocent if they know them to be guilty. Similarly, several of the landscape architects I talked to drew the line at any form of misrepresentation. Nevil Farr also mentioned the 'If I don't do it, somebody else will' argument, but he was quick to qualify his position:

> It's a moral dilemma in a sense, but also a bit of a cop out. Yes, I can make a better job of this than other people can. It's a rotten job but we will do it, and we will pressurise and we will make the very best of this that we can. If it comes to conscience or honesty or anything like that, then the answer is no. And that's a morality . . . or maybe it's just that

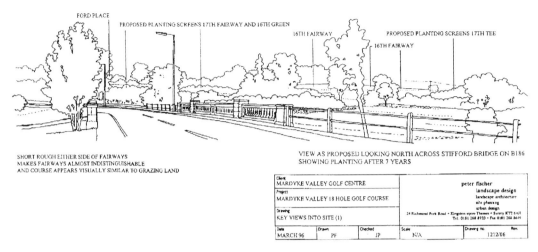

FORD PLACE
PROPOSED PLANTING SCREENS 17TH FAIRWAY AND 16TH GREEN
16TH FAIRWAY
PROPOSED PLANTING SCREENS 17TH TEE
16TH FAIRWAY

SHORT ROUGH EITHER SIDE OF FAIRWAYS
MAKES FAIRWAYS ALMOST INDISTINGUISHABLE
AND COURSE APPEARS VISUALLY SIMILAR TO GRAZING LAND

VIEW AS PROPOSED LOOKING NORTH ACROSS STIFFORD BRIDGE ON B186
SHOWING PLANTING AFTER 7 YEARS

Client MARDYKE VALLEY GOLF CENTRE	peter fischer
Project MARDYKE VALLEY 18 HOLE GOLF COURSE	landscape design landscape architecture site planning urban design
Drawing KEY VIEWS INTO SITE (1)	24 Richmond Park Road • Kingston-upon-Thames • Surrey KT2 6AH Tel: 0181 268 8923 • Fax 0181 288 8649
Date MARCH 96	Drawn PF	Checked JP	Scale N/A	Drawing no. 1212/06	Rev.

3.12

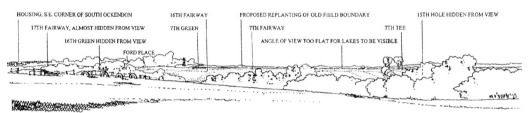

HOUSING, S.E. CORNER OF SOUTH OCKENDON
16TH FAIRWAY
PROPOSED REPLANTING OF OLD FIELD BOUNDARY
15TH HOLE HIDDEN FROM VIEW
17TH FAIRWAY, ALMOST HIDDEN FROM VIEW
7TH GREEN
7TH FAIRWAY
7TH TEE
16TH GREEN HIDDEN FROM VIEW
FORD PLACE
ANGLE OF VIEW TOO FLAT FOR LAKES TO BE VISIBLE

SHORT ROUGH EITHER SIDE OF FAIRWAYS
MAKES FAIRWAYS ALMOST INDISTINGUISHABLE
AND COURSE APPEARS VISUALLY SIMILAR TO GRAZING LAND

VIEW AS PROPOSED LOOKING NORTH FROM SITTING AREA AT BACK OF
DOG & PARTRIDGE PUB, NORTH STIFFORD SHOWING PLANTING AFTER 7 YEARS

Client MARDYKE VALLEY GOLF CENTRE	peter fischer
Project MARDYKE VALLEY 18 HOLE GOLF COURSE	landscape design landscape architecture site planning urban design
Drawing KEY VIEWS INTO SITE (2)	24 Richmond Park Road • Kingston-upon-Thames • Surrey KT2 6AH Tel: 0181 268 8923 • Fax 0181 288 8649
Date MARCH 96	Drawn PF	Checked JP	Scale N/A	Drawing no. 1212/07	Rev.

3.13

15TH TEE
10TH TEE HIDDEN FROM VIEW
PUBLIC FOOTPATH
11TH GREEN SCREENED BY PROPOSED PLANTING
10TH GREEN HIDDEN FROM VIEW
FOOTBRIDGE
10TH FAIRWAY

SHORT ROUGH EITHER SIDE OF FAIRWAYS
MAKES FAIRWAYS ALMOST INDISTINGUISHABLE
AND COURSE APPEARS VISUALLY SIMILAR TO GRAZING LAND

VIEW AS PROPOSED LOOKING NORTH FROM WHERE PUBLIC FOOTPATH FROM
THE MARDYKE ENTERS NORTH STIFFORD SHOWING PLANTING AFTER 7 YEARS

Client MARDYKE VALLEY GOLF CENTRE	peter fischer
Project MARDYKE VALLEY 18 HOLE GOLF COURSE	landscape design landscape architecture site planning urban design
Drawing KEY VIEWS INTO SITE (3)	24 Richmond Park Road • Kingston-upon-Thames • Surrey KT2 6AH Tel: 0181 268 8923 • Fax 0181 288 8649
Date MARCH 96	Drawn PF	Checked JP	Scale N/A	Drawing no. 1212/08	Rev.

3.14

Figure 3.12, Figure 3.13 and Figure 3.14 Mardyke Valley Golf Centre: sketches of proposed views. (Courtesy of Peter Fischer.)

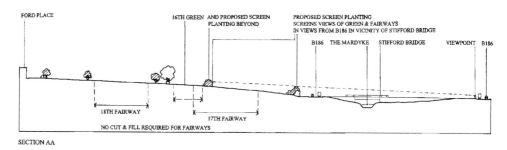

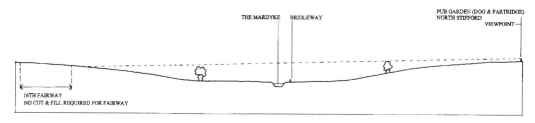

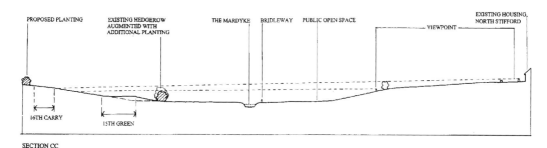

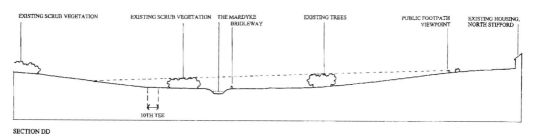

Figure 3.15 Mardyke Valley Golf Centre: typical cross sections. (Courtesy of Peter Fischer.)

you'd get crucified at the planning inquiry. I would like to think it's a morality more than anything.

Aesthetics are for people

There is no logical difficulty in regarding aesthetic values as ends in themselves; not so much 'art-for-art's sake' as 'beauty-for-beauty's sake', or conceivably 'design-for-design's sake'. In fact I did not find much evidence for this attitude among my interview

subjects. As we will see in Chapter 5, landscape architects are inclined to regard 'design' as an activity which is distinct from 'art', with its own particular kinds of excellence. One of the differences between these two activities is that artists are free (within the obvious constraints of feeding, clothing and housing themselves) to pursue personal agendas, whereas the designer is always working for some form of client in the context of some sort of need. When landscape architects talk about aesthetic matters they are usually quick to justify or qualify their statements in terms of the beneficial effects that will ensue for people once there has been an improvement in the appearance of their environment.

Ray Keeley admitted that he could derive great personal pleasure from completing a scheme to his own aesthetic satisfaction and yet he added:

> You do something for its innate aesthetic qualities perhaps, but if you were the only person that saw it . . . there would be an element of frustration if you couldn't share that. It's like writing a masterpiece that nobody else reads.

David Appleton, of The Appleton Group, went even further:

> It seems to me that at the end of the day the landscapes that we create ought themselves to be sufficiently attractive to be appreciated without wanting to know why. And this constant quest for knowledge as to why and how, and there always being a reason, a purpose why this is designed the way it is. I think it is very satisfying for designers, but the public will actually value and judge it on their own response which I think is perhaps, without wishing to be patronising at all, based on whole series of other values.

Nevil Farr has a similarly down-to-earth attitude. We discussed his beliefs in his Liverpool office, a short walk away from the city's revitalised docklands. He began by talking about the garden festivals which had been staged in Britain during the 1980s and early 1990s:

> Maybe I should have left the garden festivals being impressed by the landscape design, but actually I think a lot of it was rubbish. But actually it was rubbish that gave a lot of enjoyment. In the purest design sense I think a lot of it was very questionable and that's an elitist statement if ever I made one. I think you know what I mean . . . that actually, however careful we are with good design, it shouldn't be that precious that it can't be abused or it can't be filled with people, or there isn't room to put a flag or banner.
>
> I think there probably are these very precious schemes, whether it be a courtyard or whatever, that really are manicured, and you think as a design exercise that's fine. It fulfils the client's

requirements, it's got movement, it's got water, it sparkles, it's appealing to four or five senses perhaps. Then okay, maybe that's a measure of good design, but for me it is looking out over Albert Dock there and seeing 2,000 cars and 4,000 people milling around there. And okay, a lot of them are there to see the *Endeavour* which sailed in last week, and half of them are there because they want an ice cream, they want to go to the amusement arcade or buy fancy goods, and a lot of them are there because the Tate Gallery is there . . . and oh, by the way, we did all that, and it's survived ten years, and didn't we have some problems with it! We could have done it better, it's very mundane, but actually people are flicking chewing gum and walking all over it and abusing it horribly, but having a good day out on a scheme that we did – and I'm sure that's good design.

Dramatic transformations

Closely related to the idea that aesthetics are for people is the notion that landscape architectural interventions can radically improve people's surroundings and thus the quality of their lives. If landscape architects sometimes get depressed at being taken for gardeners, or because they are shouldered out of the way by architects or planners, they always have the solace of before-and-after photographs to show, beyond the shadow of all self-doubt, that their profession is capable of producing dramatic, life-enhancing transformations.

It was this aspect of the profession which appealed most to Rodney Beaumont at the start of his career when he was working in Glasgow:

> I've tended to be very much an urban landscape architect. It's just the way it's been. My career in the '70s and '80s has been in dirty land . . . So in a sense there was this crusading thing . . . You had to have a spirit about you to believe you could actually change things, actually create things. You could go into a site that had been mucked about with for a hundred years by industry, and you could create a new park, recreation ground, setting for housing, setting for industry . . . whatever.

There is certainly an element of vocation in landscape work, and for some this is largely a question of aesthetics. I interviewed Tom Robinson at the end of a hectic working day during which he had paid a visit to a site where he was soon to undertake some work:

> I was walking around this site this afternoon, and I'm looking at this God-forsaken town, and I'm looking at all the money that has been spent on it, all the infrastructure works that have gone in, and it's still a God-forsaken town because nobody sees the importance of making it look well. And it's striking that the parts of the country, the cities, the parts of cities, the green parks, the landscapes that everyone can recognise as being the finest ... when *they* were built and designed, how they looked was an important part of it. So I believe that external design is vitally important.

Conclusion

Having discussed aesthetics with twenty-six contemporary practitioners I feel able to say that aesthetics are still very much at the heart of the profession of landscape architecture. In analysing the interview transcripts I used a computer programme which assisted me in indexing paragraphs according to their thematic content and then allowed me to classify them further depending upon whether they were positive, impartial or negative. Although, as we shall see in later chapters, interviewees had negative things to say about landscape architecture's aspirations to be an art form, its attempts at social manipulation and its ecological credentials, hardly anyone dissented from the view that landscape architecture is about improving visual amenity. Of course, this is not *all* it is about, and in the chapters which follow we shall be investigating the manner in which aesthetic ideals interact with other sets of values, particularly the social and the environmental.

British landscape architects will talk freely about aesthetics, but rarely make express reference to the body of aesthetic theory summarised in Chapter 1. Only one person made any direct reference to the theories of formal aesthetics promulgated by the Neoplatonists and their Renaissance followers. More surprising perhaps was how little reference was made to Capability Brown or the English Landscape School, although these were mentioned several times in passing.

As we have seen, there seems to be a division within the profession between those who think the role of the landscape architect is to produce work which is inconspicuous by design, and those who would, at least in urban situations, like to adopt a more assertive stance. Generalisations are notoriously difficult, but I did form the impression that those who were more enthusiastic about high profile urban landscape design tended to be those who had come into the profession with a background in architecture or design and who, had their lives taken a slightly different course, might easily have become architects. Conversely, those who preferred the low key approach tended to come from geography or science backgrounds. It is probably also true to say that those who had a particular interest in large-scale landscape planning and in landscape conservation tended to be advocates of self-effacing landscape design. Those who worked in cities and had an interest in urban design and economic regeneration favoured a bolder approach.

I do not believe that this gap is likely to widen to the point where the profession splits. Several of my interviewees were equally happy on either side of the division, and most people showed a high level of tolerance towards members of the profession who held values quite different from their own. Above all there was a broad consensus that what would be appropriate in the city might not be appropriate in the countryside and vice versa. This view accords strongly with the values of local distinctiveness and the spirit of the place, which seem to be broadly held among all landscape designers.

Notes

1 McHarg (1969) *Design with Nature*, The Natural History Press, Garden City, New York.

2 The late Dame Sylvia Crowe (1901–97) was a consultant for the Central Electricity Generating Board (1948–68) and for the Forestry Commission (1964–68). She was president of the Institute of Landscape Architects (the professional body in the UK) from 1957–59.

3 The design problem was how to relate the Grade II Listed Hinxton Hall to the enormous new laboratory building.

4 A tertiary college whose campus is on a steeply sloping, inner-city site on the north bank of the Tyne.

5 To build, to plant, whatever you intend,
To rear the Column, or the Arch to bend,
To swell the Terras, or to sink the Grot,

In all, let Nature never be forgot.
Consult the Genius of the Place in all,
That tells the waters or to rise, or fall . . .

6   A town in central Scotland.
7   A town in Gloucestershire, SW England.
8   For a report on Peter de Savaray's development of Land's End see the articles by Cairns Boston and John Moreland in *Landscape Design*, No. 178, March 1989.
9   Geoffrey Collens was formerly a Principal of Derek Lovejoy & Partners, London and an editorial adviser to *Landsape Design* magazine.
10 The extension to the M3 motorway through downland near Winchester in Hampshire was one of the most contentious road developments of the 1980s.

4 Landscape architecture as an artform

One of the great arts?

Thus far we have been mostly concerned with natural aesthetics. In this chapter we must turn our attention to the even thornier questions that surround the aesthetics of art. In particular we will examine the contention that landscape architecture is, or should be, a form of art. As with our discussion of beauty, our inquiry will lead us into some difficult areas of philosophical aesthetics, but first let us see where this notion of landscape architecture as art has come from.

In the eighteenth century, landscape gardening, in so many ways the forerunner of landscape architecture, was considered to be an art form with similar status to painting or poetry. Sometimes the word 'art' is simply used as a synonym for 'skill', but when landscape architects (including contemporary practitioners) become lyrical about their profession it is often in terms of its lineage as an art*form*, a usage that carries with it the implication that works of landscape architecture are also works of art. Thus we find Norman Newton writing: 'Landscape architecture: a profession only a little over a century old: an art as old as human existence' (Newton, 1971: xxi).

The dominant view has been that art and science play essential and complementary roles:

> The designer's function is therefore a dual one; he must approach the subject, firstly as a scientist, examining, analysing and weighing with factual accuracy all the circumstances and conditions of the site. Secondly, the application of that other quality of good design calls for the power of judgement and the creative power of the artist.
>
> (Colvin, 1948: 75)

Pre-eminent among those who saw landscape design as an essentially artistic endeavour was the late Sir Geoffrey Jellicoe. In 'Landscape from Art' he asserted that 'landscape design has proved itself to be one of the great arts' (Jellicoe, 1966: 1). It has been suggested that Jellicoe almost single-handedly 'resurrected landscape design as a serious art form, as something to be treated on a par with painting'

Figure 4.1 The late Sir Geoffrey Jellicoe in contemplative mood on the steps of his John F. Kennedy Memorial at Runnymede. The design is an allegory based upon John Bunyan's *Pilgrim's Progress*. (L.I. Library.)

(R. Moore, 1993: 46). He did this not just through his design commissions but also through his writing in which he advanced a particular theory of landscape design. We will need to consider what he has to say in some depth, but this discussion must be post-poned until we can frame it against a background of aesthetic theory.

Before looking at some philosophical theories of art, it is worth remarking that the whole question of the role of creativity in design has been given new impetus by the work of Kathryn Moore, who teaches landscape design at the University of Central England. She has argued very strongly that the creative, divergent aspects of design have not been given enough attention, and that the profession is hamstrung by its preoccupation with convergent thinking and rational problem solving. 'Despite the campaigning of Sir Geoffrey Jellicoe and a few others,' she has written, 'there is still a lack of ambi-tion within the profession to regard itself as an art' (K. Moore, 1993: 28–31). This is heady stuff, but is she right? Should landscape architects strive to be artists?

This then is the main question we will be trying to answer, but immediately we are upon difficult terrain because we must first ask to what extent a designed landscape can be considered a work of art? To answer this we will have to examine the criteria for calling something a work of art, and this is a central purpose of philosophical aesthetics.

Other questions flood down upon us. If it turns out that it makes sense to talk about designed land-scapes as art objects, how is this possibility or aspira-tion to be accommodated within the value structure of the profession? What relationship does this goal bear to more modest aesthetic objectives like making landscapes that are pleasing, or to ecological imperatives or social purposes that may seem mun-dane by comparison?

Theories of art

Aestheticians distinguish between two senses in which the description 'work of art' may be used. The first is classificatory – the world can be divided into works of art and objects that are not works of art. It seems to follow that there should be some criterion or set of criteria that can be used to decide in any particular case whether an object is an artwork or not. As the critic Clive Bell wrote in his book, *Art*,

either we mean by 'works of art' a class of objects having some 'quality common and peculiar to all members of this class', or else 'we gibber' (Bell, [1915] 1958: 17). The search for such a criterion has occupied much philosophical energy, but the issue remains contentious. The main contenders will be examined later, to see whether they are intelligible in the case of designed landscapes.

The term 'work of art' also bears an evaluative sense. To call something a 'work of art' is to elevate it above the ruck of commonplace objects. In common parlance and most critical commentary, speakers and writers move easily and carelessly between the classi-ficatory and evaluative senses of the phrase, and this can lead to confusion. The classificatory sense admits the possibility of bad art, i.e. objects which meet the criteria for being classified as art (whatever these may be) yet (according to some other set of criteria) are not very good. The evaluative sense implies that if something is considered 'art', it has value and is to be admired. When commentators talk about designed landscapes as 'works of art' it is usually the evaluative sense that they are employing.

It will help us to get some purchase upon the unwieldy and sprawling subject of philosophical aesthetics if we adopt the classification of theories of art suggested by Oswald Hanfling.[1] There are, says Hanfling, a number of well-articulated theories about what may constitute a work of art, and these can be summarised under four headings:

1. Art consists in the representation or imitation of nature.
2. Art is whatever provides an aesthetic experience.
3. Art is a vehicle for the expression and communication of feeling.
4. Art is whatever the 'artworld' thinks it is.

We will consider each of these in turn.

Art as imitation

The idea that art is representational, that it mimics some natural state of affairs, is found in Plato's philosophy and was taken over, more or less whole-sale, by Aristotle. The artist imitates nature, which, in the context of Plato's broader metaphysics, is in any case a pale imitation of the world of ideal Forms. One consequence of this view is that the more a painting resembles its subject, the better it must be, although, as an approach to what Plato considered to be reality, painting occupies a much lower place in his esteem than mathematics.

Imitation theories seem totally inadequate as an explanation of the aesthetic merits of landscape design, for though it is true that many designed landscapes – particularly in the Chinese, Japanese and English traditions – draw their inspiration from the study of nature, none of them sets out to copy nature in every particular. Humphrey Repton makes this clear in the first of his requisites for the perfection of Landscape Gardening; 'First, it must display the natural beauties, and hide the natural defects of every situation' (Repton, [1806] 1969: 34). His purpose is to improve nature, not merely to copy it.

It is true that some contemporary landscape practice, particularly that concerned with land reclamation, habitat creation and the mitigation of the impact of development, is concerned with the simulation of naturally occurring landscapes. In such cases, landscape designers are often most successful when they leave no evidence of their involvement. Such landscapes can certainly be 'taken for nature', but more than this, they take their place *within* nature. We might wish to praise their creators for their technical skill or for their aesthetic sensibilities, but we would not be inclined to say that any of these landscapes were works of art.

Art as the provider of aesthetic experience

Having taken a look at imitation theory and found it wanting, what of those theories which suggest that art is whatever provides an aesthetic experience? Although we respond to paintings, sculptures, symphonies, great buildings, gardens, and so on, in a variety of ways, we would nevertheless wish to say that many of these experiences are aesthetic experiences, and it is natural to ask what causes them.

We often talk about being moved by the beauty of a painting, a piece of music or a view, so beauty is an obvious contender for the role of the common and defining quality of art sought by Bell ([1915] 1958). But as we observed in the previous chapter, beauty cannot be regarded as a necessary or sufficient condition for a work of art. Wilderness areas, or those managed landscapes that we call natural, can be very beautiful, but we would not generally think of them as works of art.

We also noted in the previous chapter that even when the concept of beauty occupied centre stage it had to share the billing with other concepts, particularly that of the sublime. According to Burke ([1759] 1968), Beauty and Sublimity were incompatible opposites, yet a work of art might embrace either one or the other. This alone provides sufficient grounds for saying that beauty cannot be an essential quality of a work of art. This does not mean that the word does not have its uses, but attempts to define beauty, and to define art in terms of beauty, are certain to fail. The landscape architect who wishes to become an artist will derive little assistance from the concept.

The dethronement of beauty did not spell the end of attempts to identify formal qualities in art, however. While some thinkers have taken the view that beauty consisted of form, others have put form forward as an alternative to beauty. For such authors the presence or absence of form has been used to distinguish between works of art and objects that are merely agreeable.

In Chapter 2 we considered Santayana's three levels of aesthetic experience, the sensory, the formal and the symbolic. We noted how, from Plato onwards, different thinkers had produced different lists of the formal qualities they considered essential to beauty. Though their lists may vary, many aestheticians would follow a similar line to the one taken by Kant, in saying that it is *only* formal properties that count. Mere sensory qualities, like colour, texture and so on, might be agreeable, but cannot be the objects of judgements of taste.

> In painting, and in fact all the formative arts, in architecture and horticulture, so far as fine arts, the design is what is essential. Here is not what gratifies in sensation but merely what pleases by its form, that is the fundamental prerequisite for taste.
>
> (Kant, [1790] 1952: 67)

Clive Bell amplified this thought by making 'Significant Form' the defining quality of all works of art. He wrote:

> significant form . . . lines and colours combined in a particular way, certain forms and certain relations of forms, stir our aesthetic emotions. These relations and combinations of lines and colours, these aesthetically moving forms, I call

'Significant Form'; and 'Significant Form' is the only quality common to all works of art.

(Bell, [1915] 1958: 17–18)

Bell did not, however, think that significant form was to be found in nature:

> It seems to me possible, though by no means certain, that created form moves us profoundly because it expresses the emotion of its creator. Perhaps the lines and colours of a work of art convey to us something that the artist felt. If this be so, it will explain the curious but undeniable fact . . . that what I call material beauty (e.g. the wing of a butterfly) does not move most of us in at all the same way as a work of art moves us. It is beautiful form, but it is not significant form. It moves us, but it does not move us aesthetically.
>
> (Bell, [1915] 1958: 43)

Bell goes on to argue that significant form is the expression of 'a peculiar emotion felt for reality'. An artist's only interest in things is that they provide the means to achieve this 'particular kind of emotion', but this, rather paradoxically, only occurs when the artist is able to see them as ends, as things in themselves, 'for it is only when they are perceived as ends that they become the means to this emotion' (Bell, [1915] 1958: 61).

As an art critic concerned to bolster a particular approach to painting, Bell had little to say about natural landscapes and nothing about gardens or designed landscapes, but he did discuss landscape as a subject for pictures:

> It is only when we cease to regard the objects in a landscape as means to anything that we can feel the landscape artistically. But when we do succeed in regarding the parts of a landscape as ends in themselves – as pure forms, that is to say – the landscape becomes *ipso facto* a means to a peculiar, aesthetic state of mind.
>
> (Bell, [1915] 1958: 61)

Art, according to Bell, is akin to religion because it concerns itself with 'emotional reality'. It must not concern itself with practical purposes. This single-mindedness is easier to achieve in the world of painting than in architecture or landscape architecture. Bell does not discuss design as a discipline, but to be consistent he would no doubt have to deny that its products could be considered as art, even though designers might be concerned with form as well as with function. When landscape architects manipulate landform, they may conceivably do it 'as a means to a peculiar emotion', but other practical and scientific considerations also play their part.

It is possible to stretch Bell's theory to accommodate those landscape designers who have been able to place purely aesthetic considerations ahead of all others. This presumably would set their work apart from nature, and certain landscapes, produced in this way, might then qualify as works of art. But Bell's theory has, in any case, been severely criticised as an example of vicious circularity. If the only thing that makes form significant is that it evokes a particular sort of emotion, we are entitled to ask how we recognise this aesthetic emotion. The unsatisfactory answer is by the presence of significant form! The two ideas are defined in relation to one another.

Moreover, Bell's theory oversimplifies the nature of aesthetic experience, for it is not really possible to throw a cordon around formal properties and say that they are all that matter in art. Considerations of the symbolic meaning of a work, its context, its place in the artist's canon, its whole connection with the world of human affairs, must all be given their weight.

In rejecting Bell's theory, we need not take the further step of rubbishing the notion of formal qualities, for surely we do recognise and value such things as unity, complexity, symmetry and so on, whether we find them in nature or in works of art. But to say that there is such a thing as proportion, or symmetry, or mystery, is to say nothing about why we value such things.

Art as a vehicle for feeling

Santayana's third level of aesthetic experience is concerned with the manner in which objects can express symbolic values. Bourassa (1991) argues that all values that cannot be explained by our biological origins must come into this category, and furthermore that many formal systems of aesthetics, for example the Golden Section, are best understood in this way. Geoffrey Jellicoe, whose views we will shortly consider in detail, quotes in his *The Landscape of Allegory* (*Studies in Landscape Design*, Vol. III) a passage written by Kenneth Woodbridge about Henry Hoare's creation at Stourhead in Wiltshire:

> art is a symbol making activity, giving form to inward states because only in this way can they

be experienced and assimilated. Symbolic forms, rich in associations, crystallise ideas and feelings which would otherwise escape definition; their existence enables individuals, whose own vague thoughts and feelings are otherwise unformulated, to participate in a collective ritual with others . . .

(Jellicoe, 1970: 20)

The most sophisticated theory of art based upon the notion of symbolic communication is that worked out by Susanne Langer in her book, *Feeling and Form* (Langer, 1953*)*. Langer believes that language is a poor medium for the expression of our emotional lives and that works of art function as 'non-discursive' or 'presentational' symbols – they somehow capture and articulate some aspects of our experience which cannot be expressed in words.

Langer first developed her ideas in relation to music, which she considered to be 'a tonal analogue of emotive life' (Langer, 1953: 27). Music is able to function in this way, she suggests, because there are 'certain aspects of the so-called "inner life" – physical or mental – which have formal properties similar to those of music – patterns of rest, of tension and release, of agreement and disagreement, preparation, fulfilment, excitation, sudden change' Langer, [1942] 1957: 228). 'Music shares a logical form with human feelings, therefore it "articulates forms which language cannot set forth"' (Langer, [1942] 1957: 233).

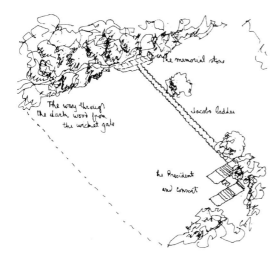

Figure 4.2 Geoffrey Jellicoe's sketch for the John F. Kennedy Memorial at Runnymede inspired by John Bunyan's *Pilgrim's Progress*.

From a particular theory about music, Langer went on to create a general theory applicable to all the arts. 'Art', she wrote 'is the creation of forms symbolic of human feeling' (Langer, 1953: 40); thus she maintained that architecture is concerned with the symbolic expression of human life – 'the image of life which is created in buildings' (Langer, 1953: 99).

Langer made no reference to landscape design as a distinct branch of the arts, but it is clear from the following passage, in which she quotes with approval from an article by Otto Baensch, that she recognised the potential for feelings to be expressed symbolically by landscape:

> The mood of a landscape appears to us to be objectively given with it as one of its attributes, belonging to it just like any other attribute we perceive it to have . . . We never think of regarding the landscape as a sentient being whose outward aspect 'expresses' the mood that it contains subjectively. The landscape does not express the mood, but has it: the mood surrounds, fills and permeates it, like the light that illumines it, or the odour it exhales; the mood belongs to our total impression of the landscape and can only be distinguished as one of its components by a process of abstraction.
>
> (Baensch, 1923, quoted in Langer, 1953: 19)

One difficulty that Langer has to address is that different people will have different feelings when confronted with the same piece of art. This can be as true of an actual landscape as it is of a painting of a landscape or a Beethoven sonata. Her way out of this is to suggest that works of art are 'unconsummated symbols' that convey something about the morphology of a feeling but do not have determinate content.[2]

Once again it is easy to see how Langer's theory could be extended to cover landscape design, for certainly designed landscapes produce emotional reactions in those who visit them; but equally certainly these are different reactions for different individuals or even different occasions. It would be an interesting project to add a chapter to *Feeling and Form* extending Langer's theories specifically to landscape architecture, working out in detail how the devices of the designer (rhythm, occult balance, framing, etc.) might be used to 'articulate what is verbally ineffable – the logic of consciousness itself' (Langer, 1957: 26).

Langer thinks that even utilitarian objects can become works of art. A craftsman produces goods, but, if those objects are also able to function as non-discursive symbols of the inner life, they can also be works of art. This is one way of explaining the appeal of many workaday agricultural landscapes.

Langer's theory has had its critics however. It has been pointed out that if an artwork gives form to a previously inconceivable element of experience, artists cannot know what they are making until they finish, but this is hardly borne out by psychological investigations into the nature of creativity. Like so many general theories in aesthetics, Langer's has ultimately been found wanting, yet it contains many insights of value to landscape design, and, as we will see, bears some strong similarities to the theory of art presented by Jellicoe.

The Institutional Theory

The Institutional Theory is a radical alternative to all the theories examined so far. Some philosophers, having rummaged in vain for a single property defining all works of art in the bran tub of qualities, feelings and experiences, yet wishing to maintain, as did Bell, that some such common property must exist, have suggested that it must be some kind of 'non-exhibited' property. George Dickie claims to have discovered such a quality. He suggests that what all artworks have in common is their acceptance by the 'artworld', by which he means the social institution that consists of the totality of artists, producers, gallery directors, critics, connoisseurs, art historians and so on. Indeed, 'every person who sees himself as a member of the artworld is thereby a member' (Dickie, 1974: 36).

Nothing could be further from the mysticism and transcendentalism of Bell or the subtle psychology of Langer. On the one hand, Institutional Theory seems to have almost cynically missed the point about art; on the other, its explanatory force can be quite seductive. It explains, for example, how new art forms, such as photography or film, can come into being, and how problematic works like Duchamp's 'ready-mades' (the urinal that became *Fountain*, for example!) can come to be considered works of art. It might also be invoked to explain how gardening, which was regarded as a fine art in the eighteenth century, is no longer thought of in that way today. Geoffrey Jellicoe's lifelong mission to re-establish landscape architecture as a fine art is easy to explain in terms of a propaganda campaign directed at the 'artworld'.

According to Institutional Theory, what makes something into a work of art is a speech-act or performance analogous to christening: 'I name this a work of art.' The very act of hanging a painting in a gallery makes it into a work of art. However, a suitable institutional setting is required before the performance can succeed. A gallery director's utterance will succeed where the lollipop lady's will not. There is no reason why a designed landscape should not be accepted as a work of art. It would help if the designer intended that it should be one, and said as much, but even this is not necessary if persons of sufficient authority can be found who regard it as such. It would seem, purely as a matter of fact, that many of the landscapes designed by Geoffrey Jellicoe in Britain, or by Dan Kiley or Lawrence Halprin in the United States, have indeed realised this level of acceptance within the artworld.

However, the inadequacies of the Institutional Theory start to appear when we consider paintings or poems which have never been exhibited or published. It does not seem to follow that these cannot be works of art simply because they have never been put forward for appreciation. On the other hand, to accept the Institutional Theory implies that one can never question the status of anything exhibited in a gallery. Yet if we consider some of the pieces that have been exhibited, whether they be Carl Andre's infamous bricks, or paintings by chimpanzees or very young children, we would not wish to say that anyone who questions whether these are art is thereby talking self-contradictory nonsense. The question of whether or not something is art is not settled simply by reference to the context it appears in.

Consider also the position of the gallery director who has to make the decisions about what to hang. The Institutional Theory will give him no guidance, because it says nothing about the traditional qualities of art. He will need reasons for selecting one piece rather than another, and all that the Institutional Theory can tell him is that once he has decided, then the chosen piece will be the work of art! We may wish to see more works of landscape architecture accepted as works of art by the artworld, but we will have to find reasons why that world should admit them. These reasons cannot be provided by the Institutional Theory.

Jellicoe's theories of art and landscape architecture

We are now in a position to discuss Geoffrey Jellicoe's theories against a background of philosophical aesthetics. Does what he has to say make sense? Do his theories imply that we should be practising landscape architecture in a particular way?

Jellicoe's main contention is that landscape architecture is, or can be, a form of art. In order to justify this he must offer an aesthetic theory which explains what art is. In terms of Hanfling's fourfold classification, the particular theory Jellicoe elaborates can be described as one which regards art as a vehicle for the expression and communication of feeling, but it differs from Langer's in that it is expressly a communication theory of art. As such it also resembles the theory offered by Tolstoy at the end of the nineteenth century and, as we shall see, is open to similar criticisms.

Jellicoe never wrote a full and direct treatise upon his theory of landscape design. We have instead the three volumes of his *Studies in Landscape Design* (1960, 1966, 1970) which collect together papers based upon various lectures and addresses given in the course of his career. The *Guelph Lectures on Landscape Design* (1983) provide another important source.

Jellicoe was more concerned with meaning than mere beautification. In 'Landscape from Art', a speech given to the Institute of Contemporary Arts in 1961,[3] he said: 'We have in this country at last reached a point when seemliness as an objective is no longer enough; we can and should make landscape as meaningful as painting.' What is it then that most painting possesses but much landscape design lacks?

Jellicoe's answer is bound up with his Modernism, which owes more to artists like Hepworth and Nicholson than to architects like Gropius or Corbusier. He is less concerned with functionalism than with the exploration of the subconscious, as a later passage from the same speech reveals. Talking about modern art he said that 'the literary or intellectual meaning of a picture as seen photographically by the eye was subdued and even eliminated in order that the instincts should predominate. This is the basis of abstract art' (Jellicoe, 1966: 4).

Figure 4.3 Geoffrey Jellicoe's proposals for the east walled garden at Sutton Place, enclosing the Paradise Garden and the Moss Garden. (Courtesy of Landscape Institute Library.)

What then are these instincts? Jellicoe's answer is not very clear. He seems to invoke both Einsteinian space-time and evolutionary palaeontology when he suggests that:

> The arts are preoccupied firstly with the new dimension of time and space that has been with us from the start of the century, and secondly with our own primitive origins in relation to these dimensions.
>
> (Jellicoe, 1966: 4)

Subsequently, in the introduction to his *Guelph Lectures on Landscape Design* (1983), he suggests that landscape design is 'a projection of the psyche into its natural environment', and he provides a model of the way the mind is organised which is related to stages in human evolution. As we saw in Chapter 2, Jellicoe suggests that the psyche has levels, which he called 'transparencies', and that our emotional responses to landscape can be accounted for by our evolutionary history as a species.

The *Forester, Hunter* and *Settler* seem to make sense intuitively, but the *Voyager* is more problematic. Contemporary humanity, Jellicoe believes, is voyaging in Jungian fashion into its own psyche. It is never very clear what Jellicoe expects to find in the unconscious, but this is not perhaps very surprising. After all, the delvings of Freud and Jung seemed to produce very different subconscious contents. It is clear from Jellicoe's references to 'analytical psychology' (a term coined by Jung and distinct from psychoanalysis) that he believes in Jung's idea of the 'collective unconscious', a storehouse of primitive symbols common to all humanity. In 'The Landscape of Symbols', in *Studies in Landscape Design* (Volume III), Jellicoe discusses the history of the cross, the circle and the spire, admitting in a footnote his debt to Jung's *Man and his Symbols* (1978).

We might feel justified in asking why this Jungian subject matter should be so important to landscape design? Jellicoe's answer comes in 'Towards a Landscape of Humanism', where he writes:

> It would seem that to project into the environment the whole and not merely part of the mind of man, individual or collective, is the highest objective in the creation of landscape as an art.
>
> (Jellicoe, 1983)

And if we need to be convinced that this is important, Jellicoe writes elsewhere that:

> this effect upon human beings is the ultimate objective of all landscape design, whether rural or urban. To obtain this impact we have already established that it is necessary to have subconscious as well as conscious appeal.
>
> (Jellicoe, 1966: 7)

Jellicoe thinks that this effect on human beings is to be therapeutic. It reconciles the unchanging tempo of our bodies to the increasing tempo of modern life. For landscape design to achieve this, the rational design process must be accompanied by a shadowy process which taps the subconscious.

According to Jellicoe this is how it works in all art, not just in landscape design that aspires to be art. The artist must somehow penetrate his or her own consciousness, then the results of this exploration must somehow be represented in the work in such a way that they can be communicated to an audience. The distinction between the individual unconscious and the collective unconscious need not detain us. In some cases, the artist will attempt to communicate something from his or her personal unconscious. At other times, the artist will succeed in reaching the deep substratum which Jung believed human beings held in common – in which case the recipient of the communication may recognise something already known at the deepest level.

Jellicoe does not merely suggest that sometimes when landscape design achieves the status of art, such communication of subconscious contents occurs. It is clear that Jellicoe thinks that in successful art it must *always* occur; in other words he regards such communication as a *necessary* condition for making landscape designs that are to be considered as art.

It is less clear whether he is saying that the occurrence of such a process provides a sufficient condition. Is it possible for an artist or a designer to effect such a communication and yet fail to make a work of art? Jellicoe is not very rigorous about the way he uses the term. Sometimes he seems to be using it in a classificatory way; often, however, he uses 'art' as a term of approbation. He does not seem to have considered the possibility that a piece of landscape design may communicate something from the subconscious, thereby (according to his own theory) qualifying as a work of art, yet still be poor or indifferent.

Though we may be in sympathy with Jellicoe's

wish to see landscape architecture included in the pantheon of the arts, in seeking to justify its inclusion by reference to a communications theory of art he has simultaneously produced a very restricted notion of what art may be.

As suggested above, there is a strong parallel between Jellicoe's theory and that advanced by Leo Tolstoy in his book *What Is Art?* (Tolstoy, [1930] 1994). Tolstoy's answer was that an object was a work of art if and only if (i.e. a necessary condition) it caused its audience to experience feelings, it was intended to by its creator, and its creator had personally lived through the experiences so aroused. In Jellicoe's case what is transmitted is not emotion but some message from the collective unconscious.

The first problem with Tolstoy's theory is that there appear to be many works of art which do not seem to embody strong feelings – for example, elegant sonnets or meticulously constructed chamber music. Tolstoy would have to say that these could not be considered works of art. If some of Jellicoe's statements are taken at face value, he seems to be regulating landscape architecture in a parallel way. If a design does not tap into the subconscious we should not call it art.

At the time Tolstoy put forward his theory he was a fervent Christian. He supplemented his theory with a second necessary condition; not only must works of art communicate emotions, these emotions have to be worthwhile ones which promote the brotherhood of man. Pride, sexual desire and world weariness will not do. If we were to accept Tolstoy's theory, many of the paintings in the world's galleries would have to be removed from the walls. Giving this sort of weight to the subject matter of art is dangerous; something similar actually happened in Soviet Russia but with a different ideological justification.

Geoffrey Jellicoe's humanist ideals are, of course, very far removed from Tolstoy's fundamentalist dogmatism, but the form of his mistake is the same. Jung's theory of the collective unconscious may be a rich and illuminating idea, but for Jellicoe to make it the sole yardstick against which landscape architecture is judged as art is surely wrong; there will be some landscape design which we want to call art but which has nothing whatsoever to do with Jung, the unconscious, archetypes or whatever.

The similarity between Langer's theory and Jellicoe's lies in the fact that both require the work of art (whether it be painting, musical passage or landscape) to perform a symbolic function, but Langer's view is more sophisticated than a naive communications approach. For Langer the primary purpose of a symbol is not to communicate but to give form; the ability to create symbols is a vital part of apperception.

Jellicoe may not be wrong to believe in the subconscious, nor even to adhere to the Jungian version. Nor is he to be faulted for making this a cornerstone of his personal vision; it led, after all, to the production of some memorable work. However, he is mistaken in his attempt to make it into the rigid foundation of a theory of art, which in turn must support a theory of landscape architecture.

Family resemblances

The entire search for a *single* criterion by which we can divide works of art from other things may be a mistaken enterprise. Wittgenstein disagreed fundamentally with all attempts at essentialist definitions (Wittgenstein, 1953) Taking the concept of a tool, he asked what quality all tools had that everything that was not a tool did not have? Was it the ability to cut? What about a hammer? Perhaps it was the ability to alter materials? What about a ruler? And so on. He concluded that in the place of a single quality there was a criss-crossing network of similarities which he called 'family resemblances'. This has proved a very powerful analytical notion which can be applied in all sorts of areas. It can certainly be applied to the concept of art.

There is likely to be a whole family of similarities between those things we choose to call works of art. Some will stir feelings, some will not. Some we may call beautiful or sublime, others not. Some may be non-discursive symbols of feeling, but perhaps not all. Some may reach into the many layers of our unconscious minds – but some will not. There may be many ways in which an object can come to be considered a work of art. Some will have stronger claims than others. In terms of landscape, we may feel that Stourhead, which involves the creation of an idealised landscape and includes an allegory drawn from Virgil, has a very strong claim, that the careful arrangement of landform and planting around a reservoir has a weaker claim, and that a screen of cotoneasters around a car park has little to recommend it as art at all.

To argue against essentialist definitions of art is not to say that just anything can be art. Even the Institutional Theory did not make this claim. An object which might be considered a work of art in one period of history, would not count as such in another. Stephanie Ross (1998) seems to be in general agreement with Arthur Danto, who propounded a contextualist theory of aesthetics (Danto, 1981) in which he argued that artworks must *say* something about the world. A blue necktie which Picasso has mottled green may be a work of art, whereas a blue tie daubed by a finger-painting 3-year-old would not be. Ross says that the same sorts of things can be said about landscapes: a wildflower garden carefully constructed by an ecologist in a sunny woodland clearing would be a work of art, whereas a similar, but entirely natural, array of plants in a similar location would not be.

This raises interesting possibilities. On this view, where a landscape designer has intervened in nature with the primary intention of creating aesthetic effects, we might be inclined to say that he or she has produced a work of art. Significantly, the green political theorist Robert Goodin (1992) takes a very different view of this matter. For Goodin the ultimate source of value is 'naturalness' – the manipulated landscape is never going to have as much value as the pristine landscape. This even applies to those cases where a very skilful ecologically attuned designer has simulated natural habitats and plant associations. In the interviews reported in Chapter 5 attitudes from both sides of this argument were expressed.

We will never find a single criterion against which to judge those things which aspire to be works of art, and we are mistaken to look for one, but it will probably benefit landscape architecture if at least some of its products are considered to merit the appellation 'work of art'. To this extent its status is more than an academic question. There is not, I am certain, one right or guaranteed way of producing such work. Some will see that as a problem, others as a liberation. Which schemes are works of art, which are not, and which lie on the borderline, will always be matters of judgement and debate. Perhaps, as Steven Bourassa has suggested, we need professional landscape critics, just as we need professional art or theatre critics (Bourassa, 1991). In making our judgements, one of the things we will have to take into account is the intention of the landscape architect. Practitioners are often called upon by clients or employers to tidy up or 'make seemly' a visually displeasing piece of land. Many landscape architects do this kind of work for their entire careers, without once attempting to make design into art.

Art and nature: nature and art

The second general question we set ourselves at the outset of this chapter concerned the relationship between art and the aesthetics of nature. Within philosophical aesthetics we find two quite contradictory accounts of this relationship.

The first is the view that the aesthetic experience of nature is conditioned by art. The critic Apollinaire writes for example that 'without poets, without artists . . . the order that we find in nature, and which is only an effect of art, would at once vanish' (Apollinaire, [1913] 1949: 14). Similarly, Shepard considers that 'the history of scenery is the history of painting and tourism' (Shepard, 1967: 119).

The dramatic change in Western perceptions of mountain scenery is often quoted in support of this view. As Simon Schama relates in *Landscape and Memory* (Schama, 1995: 430) in medieval times mountain ranges like the Alps were considered to be infested with demons and dragons, which were responsible for the stormy weather found in such regions. A particularly unpleasant creature was thought to inhabit the summit of Mons Pilatus near Lucerne, but in 1555 the naturalist Conrad Gesner decided to scale the peak and lay the legendary serpent to rest. In his account of his climb he notes the fragrance of the wild flowers, the purity of the air, and the verdancy of the pastures. During the eighteenth century similarly positive opinions came to be expressed by painters and poets who had visited the Alps, and, as travel through the mountains became easier and less perilous, so this more appreciative attitude became dominant on the part of the general public. A similar thing happened in the nineteenth century in England as, under the influence of Wordsworth and his contemporaries, the Lake District became an object of cultural tourism.

Although there can be no doubt about the reality of such cultural shifts, it would surely be wrong to say that the activities of the writers and painters *created* the qualities they described, for surely the verdure of the grass or the perfume of the flowers were always there, waiting for Gesner to notice them – and no doubt they *had* been noticed by generations of anonymous shepherds before the naturalist described his expedition in print.

On the view we are considering, however, our notions of scenery and our aesthetic reactions to landscape are entirely culturally conditioned. The central idea is that artists teach us how to see, and presumably until we have been taught we are only partially sighted. Such a belief sits squarely with Jellicoe's high opinion of painters as the scouts or pathfinders of the visual arts. 'Only the infinite patience of generations of painters,' he writes, 'each advancing the relationship of objects in space, could force attention on such a grand conception of natural environment' (Jellicoe, 1970: 2).

Such a stance is, however, at odds with the biologically based theories explored in Chapter 2. The opposing view is that the appreciation of art is conditioned by appreciation of nature.

'Go out to nature', writes Humphrey, 'and learn from experience what natural structures men find beautiful, because it is among such structures that men's aesthetic sensitivity evolved' (Humphrey, 1980: 73). This is similar to the line taken by the American philosopher, John Dewey, in his *Experience and Nature* (1929). Art, for Dewey, is 'a continuation, by means of intelligent selection and arrangement, of natural tendencies of natural events' (Dewey, 1929: 389).

Bourassa concludes that both the biological and cultural camps are offering partial truths, and that any successful paradigm for landscape aesthetics must take account of both. His suggestion, worked out in considerable detail in *The Aesthetics of Landscape,* is a tripartite system in which biological drives are modulated by cultural conditioning, but creative individuals may break free from both to create personal perceptual or design strategies. Through their expression in the arts, these personal strategies may in time come to be part of the cultural fabric. He writes:

> If human nature generally has both biological and cultural components, and if one subscribes to Dewey's argument that aesthetic experience is a heightened, more intense form of everyday experience, it is logical to conclude along with Dewey that aesthetic activity has both biological

(or instinctual) and cultural (or learned) components just like the rest of human nature.
>
> (Bourassa, 1991: 49)

The complexity of the interaction between nature and culture is illustrated by the Picturesque tradition. Adherents to Picturesque theory can be placed in the Dewey camp, for nature was their ultimate model. However, as Sutherland Lyall puts it, 'nature was not always perfect in its designing'. The landscape designer's task according to this theory, says Lyall, 'was to re-compose nature with a better design than nature was sometimes able to create' (Lyall, 1991: 16). The desired end result was to create a landscape which, though composed with a painter's eye, appeared to have been the work of nature's unguided hand. 'Here', says Lyall, 'was art imitating nature imitating art' (ibid.: 17). We could also see it as an example of what Dewey would describe as 'intensifying, purifying, prolonging and deepening' the satisfactions which unaltered nature already affords.

Landscape architecture and the other arts

During the ascendancy of the Picturesque theory the relationship between painting and landscape design was explicit. Turning their backs on the geometric order of Italian and French formal gardening, the landscape gardeners of the English Landscape School took the paintings of Claude Lorrain, Poussin, Salvator Rosa and Hobbema as their models. Jellicoe goes so far as to say that there would have been no English Landscape School had it not been for 'the infinite patience of generations of painters, each advancing the study of the relationship of objects in space' (Jellicoe, 1960: 2).

Landscape architecture is never, according to this view, going to keep abreast of painting. What it must do, however, is to make sure that it stays firmly attached to the towrope, for Jellicoe believes that when landscape loses its connection with painting, as it did in the nineteenth century, it loses its way.

Writing in 1966, Jellicoe's prescription for landscape architecture was Modernist, but despite his advocacy a Modern school of landscape design hardly appeared in Britain. Lyall suggests that for Modern Movement architects landscape was something which could not easily be reconciled with their dominant preoccupations with function, order, progress and the advent of the machine age. He notes that there was no landscape design course at the Bauhaus and that the landscape elements of Modernist architectural drawings were generalised indications of naturalistic planting. Only in the Americas, during the post-war period, did enough influential Modernist landscape designers emerge for it to be possible to talk about a movement. The eminences of the period were figures like Thomas Church, Lawrence Halprin, Garrett Eckbo, Isamu Noguchi, Luis Barragan, Dan Kiley and Roberto Burle Marx. Many of their landscapes – Halprin's urban waterfalls, for example, or Church's kidney-shaped swimming pools – have achieved iconic status within the landscape architectural profession, but their impact outside the profession has been less marked.

Significantly the title of a recent book about American Modernists is *Invisible Gardens,* and its authors note that the work of American landscape architects between 1945 and the late 1970s has 'slipped beyond even the peripheral vision of art historians' (Walker and Simo, 1994: 3). They suggest that something about the professionalism of landscape architecture, which could be taken for commercialism or materialism, was antipathetic to

the artworld of the 1950s and 1960s.

Ross (1998) offers a different explanation based upon the interpretation of modernism offered by Clement Greenberg in his essay, 'Avant-Garde and Kitsch' (1961). Greenberg offers the insight that abstract art develops when 'turning his attention away from subject matter of common experience, the poet or artist turns it upon the medium of his own craft' (Ross, 1998: 88). This introspection has been the engine of the avant-garde, resulting in an escalating minimalism in the works themselves, while theoretical exposition of the works has spiralled out of control, a process ridiculed in Tom Wolfe's *The Painted Word* (1989) Although it proved possible to create gardens or landscapes with a sparse Bauhaus aesthetic, Ross does not think that garden or landscape designers took up the challenge of 'art about art'. She tries to imagine what such a garden might be like:

> [it] might emphasise the process and materials of gardening, or deny such traditional garden values as beauty, variety and originality. Imagine a garden that displays hoses, tools and fertiliser as prominently as flowers, or one with nothing but marigolds covering varied settings and terrain that might otherwise lead us to expect roses, lilacs, lupins, hollyhocks, daffodils and more.
>
> (Ross, 1998: 89)

In fact at least one such garden exists – Martha Schwartz's Stella Garden[4] (inspired by Frank Stella's 1970s relief paintings) consists of brightly coloured shards of Plexiglas in a bed of gravel.

Ross's contention is that while garden and landscape design, whether from timidity, pragmatism, or commercial hard-headedness, did not join the Modernist project, and therefore failed to develop an avant-garde, this vacuum was filled by land artists like Robert Smithson or Walter De Maria who eschewed both the gallery and the corporate plaza to make works in deserts and wildernesses. Smithson, for example, created his *Spiral Jetty* (1970) by piling a 1,500-foot-long spiral mound of earth into Utah's Great Salt Lake. De Maria created *Lightning Field* (1977) by erecting 640 lightning conductors on a one-mile-square grid in the middle of a desert. Environmental artists, Ross argues, are the true descendants of the eighteenth-century's landscape gardeners:

Figure 4.4 Thomas Church's kidney-shaped swimming pools have iconic status within the profession. This plan for a Californian garden is from 1948.

My claim comes to this: these twentieth-century works are works of art, like gardens; they address the relation of work to site, like gardens; they can be ideological, like gardens; they can be beautiful, or sublime, like gardens. Overall they force us to think deeply about nature itself, about our relation to nature, and about nature's relation to art.

(Ross, 1998: 94)

Put in these terms it seems that environmental artists have stolen the artistic limelight from landscape architects. In one sense this vindicates Jellicoe, because it is surely another case of landscape architects not keeping up with developments in the other visual arts. A more positive way of regarding this is to say that landscape architects, with social and environmental values to weigh against purely artistic ones, eschewed an unhealthy avant-garde introspection that would ultimately be self-consuming. But if we assent to this, we cannot also maintain that it is always a good thing for landscape architecture to tag along in the train of other arts.

It emerged during the course of the interviews that many British landscape architects respect the American land artists and also the work of Andy Goldsworthy and Richard Long, but the exigencies of practice seem to deter them from turning admiration into emulation. The situation appears to be different in America, where designers like Peter Walker and Martha Schwartz work in a minimalist idiom which has clearly been influenced by developments elsewhere in the artworld.

There is also a new breed of artists whose work in public places overlaps significantly with that of professionally qualified designers. Tess Jaray, for example, was employed under a Percent for Art budget to prepare paving designs for Centenary Square in

Figure 4.5 Sheepfold sculpture by Andy Goldsworthy, Raisbeck, Cumbria, 1996.

Figure 4.6 Drove Stone, Casterton, Cumbria, Andy Goldsworthy.

4.7

4.8

Birmingham (1991). The sculptor John Maine was employed on a similar basis to work alongside planners, engineers and landscape architects on a new road system for the London Borough of Lewisham (completed 1994), and Susan Tebby constructed two courtyard landscapes at the Department of Health's new headquarters at Quarry House in Leeds (1993) (perhaps the most comprehensive piece of landscape design to have been undertaken by an artist). If artists undertaking landscape-style commissions produce works of art, then it surely follows that landscape architects could do the same, but so far the trade has been mostly in one direction. Kathryn Moore is right to say that more landscape architects lack the confidence to see themselves as artists. During my interviews with practitioners I found ample evidence of a great willingness to collaborate with artists, but a corresponding reluctance to assume the mantle of artist.

4.9

Figure 4.7, Figure 4.8 and Figure 4.9 Newcastle Draw Dock, Isle of Dogs, London. This collaboration between landscape architects Tate I Hopkins and Turner Prize winning sculptor Grenville Davey also involved open evening/drop-in sessions for local residents. It is a good example of the way in which respected artists are becoming involved in collaborative design processes in the public realm. **Top**: perspective drawing showing the view towards Davey's *One* and *Four Thirds* and the bosque of cherry trees. **Middle**: the view of the Thames from Newcastle Draw Dock. **Bottom**: Two of Davey's *Four Thirds*, gently kissing seats. Notice also the listed cannon bollard, an original feature of the site. (Photo © Martin Jones.)

Case study 4.1: Uppermill Cemetery, Saddleworth, Greater Manchester; Camlin Lonsdale

Though some landscape architects yearn to make bold statements in their designs, Robert Camlin's thoughtfully conceived design for a small cemetery on the edge of the Pennine moors eloquently demonstrates that it is possible to combine powerful ideas with vernacular traditions. This design whispers its grand statements about life and death and is all the more affecting precisely because it does not shout.

The design not only respects the particularities of the site, but draws much of its inspiration from them. The strongest elements in the design are

4.10

4.11

4.12

Figure 4.10, Figure 4.11 and Figure 4.12 Robert Camlin: Uppermill Cemetery. (Courtesy of Camlin Lonsdale.)

belts of indigenous woodland and drystone walls built from the gritstone which is characteristic to the area. But in the skilful hands of this designer, these everyday materials become infused with the deepest of meanings.

While the belts of planting reflect the informality of the surrounding landscape, the dignity and seriousness of the burial rites are expressed in the formality of an Infinite Axis which leads to views of the distant countryside. The sense of physical procession along this axis, and metaphorically of our inexorable progression through time, is reinforced by the inclusion of drystone niches, each containing a single yew tree. In Britain the yew tree is traditionally associated with churchyards, at least 500 of which contain yews which are at least as old as the churches themselves, if not a good deal older. Doubtless the longevity of this species has suggested its use in places dedicated to the contemplation of human mortality. At Saddleworth the eternal and the transitory are brought into conjunction. Crossing the Infinite Axis there lies a Finite Axis bounded by wooden obelisks and bollards and boundary markers in the same gritstone as the drystone walls.

The resulting landscape is both intimate, familiar and comforting, yet deeply symbolic of the mysteries of life and death. This is a functional design for a working cemetery and also a careful exercise in harmonious aesthetics; but it is far more than this. Whether or not the designer set out to make a work of art, there can be little doubt that in this instance he has created one.

The discussion so far has suggested that although it is possible to produce works of landscape architecture that may be considered as works of art (in the classificatory sense), aesthetics can provide no certain formula for creating them. Attempts to provide some sure criterion, and the most notable of these in the landscape architectural literature has been that of Geoffrey Jellicoe, have thus far failed, and it seems likely that the whole project is misguided. Nevertheless, we have seen that not just anything counts as art – the context in which the work is made and experienced is always relevant, as are the intentions of the artist. Art, in general, is *about something*, and as such is often an attempt to express or communicate emotions or meaning through some form of symbolism, whether overt or subtle.

We have noted that there will be paradigmatic cases of landscapes which are loaded with symbolism and meaning – Stourhead we identified as one;

another would be the Elysian Fields at Stowe, which according to John Dixon Hunt (1986: 83) embodies an anti-Stuart, anti-Catholic, pro-British message; and another, in a very different way and a very different age, is Bernard Tschumi's Parc de la Villette, which, for all its vaunted deconstruction of conventional meanings, has become emblematic of a postmodern world-view. The cemetery design by Robert Camlin described in Case Study 4.1 is surely a work of art; it even meets Jellicoe's rather stringent conditions.

The cotoneasters around the car park, or the screen planting around the open-cast mine, lie at the other extreme. They say *something* about our values, what we approve of and what we would like to hide, but generally it cannot be said that they carry a sufficient load of symbolic meaning, and we would not usually consider them to be art. To use Jellicoe's term, they are about making things 'seemly'.

In between lies the majority of landscape work, where seemliness and aspirations towards art are mixed. Moreover, landscape architects, like architects, do not have the freedom of painters or sculptors to pursue self-imposed agendas. They work in response to briefs, budgets and the requirements of clients and users.

On top of all this, as we shall see in a later chapter, they must address another layer of values derived from the ethics of environmental concern. The question of whether something is or is not a work of art is completely independent of questions about its ethical value. To say otherwise is to fall into the same error as Tolstoy or the Soviet government. Unecological art is as possible as ecological art.

Figure 4.13 In his design for the plaza of the China Trust and Investment Headquarters, Hong Kong, John Hopkins used a cascade which apparently flows from a pool on the square into the basement to symbolise money pouring into the bank!

Figure 4.14 Bernard Tschumi's Parc de la Villette is becoming emblematic of a postmodern world-view.

Should landscape architects seek to be artists?

In this chapter we have devoted much space to examining the views of Geoffrey Jellicoe, who, perhaps more than anyone else this century, has tried to re-establish landscape design as a fine art. But it is interesting to note that even Jellicoe makes reference to higher values than the value of 'art for art's sake'. He tells that 'the effect upon human beings is the ultimate objective of all landscape design' (Jellicoe, 1966: 7), and that it should thera-peutically reconcile the unchanging tempo of our bodies to the increasing tempo of modern life. Jellicoe therefore puts a humanistic value at the apex of his system. The aspiration towards art is made subservient to a higher purpose.

The alternative would be to put the aspiration towards art at the top of the pyramid, but if this chapter has shown anything it is that the whole question of art is problematic. It cannot be defined and we cannot be certain how to make it. It would seem unwise for any profession to make such a difficult concept into the keystone of its system of values. As we shall see in the following chapter, very few practising landscape architects are driven by an urge to make art, and few would regard it as a necessary, or even sensible, starting point for design. One can address matters of aesthetics without trying to be an artist.

We have nevertheless seen that it makes sense to talk about landscape design achieving the status of art, and also, on Langer's view, that it is possible to make art, as it were, by accident, as in the case of everyday objects which 'function as non-discursive symbols of the inner life'. A healthy way for the profession to think of art, therefore, is as a possi-bility, rather than an imperative. In Chapter 10 I will be arguing that the richest work in landscape architecture embraces social, ecological and aes-thetic agendas. The artistic imperative can be regarded as one way to pursue the aesthetic part of this mission.

Some possibilities

The list that follows suggests some ways in which landscape designs might be considered as works of art. The categories below are not necessarily exclus-ive – a grand gesture, for example, might also have symbolic significance. In some cases these possibi-lities link closely with the aesthetic strategies suggested at the end of the previous chapter.

1 Art as the grand gesture   The self-conscious striving after artistic merit is likely to produce work which embodies the grand gesture. One thinks immediately of Le Nôtre's grand axes, which have been evoked in the contemporary work of Dani Karavan at Cergy-Pontoise and Peter Walker at Solana. Formal qualities such as symmetry, order, balance and proportion play an important role. This approach elevates culture above nature. Grand gestures certainly found their place within the Classical tradition, but it is also possible to think of Modernist gestures or Postmodern gestures.

2 Art as the avant-garde   Although there has not been a significant history of avant-garde landscape design, it is possible to conceive of work which presses against the limits of what landscape archi-tecture might be. Such work would be radical, challenging and provocative. It may take the form of a grand gesture.

3 Art as consummate skill   In popular discussions of art it is very often the skill of the artist that is admired. This accounts for the enthusiasm that people often show for paintings which they consider to be 'realistic'. An opposing view would regard skill alone as indicative of craftsmanship rather than truly artistic achievement. A wildflower garden carefully constructed by an ecologist in a sunny woodland clearing could be a work of art. What seems to be admirable here is the artifice and the skill employed to achieve a natural effect. There is a strong connec-tion between this possibility and the varieties of biologically based aesthetic satisfactions explored in the previous chapter. Many would feel, however, that without greater symbolic content this achieve-ment remains technical rather than artistic.

4 Art as picture making   This applies both to the Neoplatonic approach recommended by Hogarth and Burke, and described at the end of the last chapter as 'Beautiful Improvement', and to the Picturesque tradition that followed. In both cases the art seems to consist in making painterly rearrange-ments of nature. Here again, formal qualities such as balance and harmony play an important role in creating compositions.

Figure 4.15 Studley Royal in North Yorkshire. Nature recomposed with a better design than nature could create?

5 Art as symbol making On this view, neither skill nor painterly composition alone is enough. The finished work must be *meaningful*. Jellicoe places the locus of meaning in subconscious processes, but there is no reason to exclude more conscious or overt symbol making. Langer's theory can also be invoked to explain why even everyday objects like dry stone walls or hedgerows might act as symbols of the inner life.

Notes

1   This classification is taken from his essay 'The Problem of Definition', which forms an opening chapter in O. Hanfling, ed., *Philosophical Aesthetics: An Introduction* (1992, Open University/Blackwell, Oxford).
2   William Charlton likens this to the formal apparatus of algebra: 'the same piece of music can be used by different hearers on different occasions as a vehicle for the conception or intuition of different emotions; in this way the elements in a piece of music are rather like algebraic symbols or functions in the mathematical sense than like numerals: a piece of music might be compared with $2(\ )^3 + (\ )$ which we can fill with our own arguments' (Charlton, 1970: 26).
3   Reproduced in G.A. Jellicoe, *Studies in Landscape Design*, Volume II (1966).
4   However, as Ross notes, Schwartz's Stella Garden is a private garden, created in her mother's backyard. Ross contends that this isolates it from the mainstream of the artworld.

Bibliography

Apollinaire, G. ([1913] 1949) *The Cubist Painters: Aesthetic Meditations*, trans. L. Abel, George Wittenborn, New York.
Bell, C. ([1915] 1958), *Art*, Capricorn Books, New York.
Bourassa, S.C. (1991) *The Aesthetics of Landscape*, Belhaven Press, London and New York.
Burke, E. ([1759] 1968) *A Philosophical Enquiry into the Origin of Our Ideas of the Sublime and the Beautiful*, edited by J.T. Boulton, University of Notre Dame Press, Notre Dame, Ind.
Charlton, W. (1970) *Aesthetics*, Hutchinson and Co., London.
Colvin, B. (1948) *Land and Landscape* (2nd edition), J. Murray, London.
Danto, A. (1981) *The Transfiguration of the Commonplace*, Harvard University Press, Cambridge, Mass.
Dewey, J. (1929) *Experience and Nature*, Minton, Balch, New York.
Dickie, G. (1974) *Art and the Aesthetic*, Cornell University Press, Ithaca, N.Y.
Goodin, R.E. (1992) *Green Political Theory*, Polity Press, Cambridge, England.
Greenberg, C. (1961) 'Avant-Garde and Kitsch', in *Art and Culture*, Beacon Press, Boston.
Humphrey, N.K. (1980) 'Natural Aesthetics', in B. Mikellides (ed.) *Architecture for People*, Cassell, London, and Holt, Rinehart, Winston, New York.
Hunt, J.D. (1986) *Gardens and the Picturesque, Studies in the History of Landscape Architecture*, The MIT Press, Cambridge, Mass.
Jellicoe, G.A. (1960, 1966, 1970) *Studies in Landscape Design* (3 vols), Oxford University Press, Oxford.
Jellicoe, G.A. (1983) *Guelph Lectures on Landscape Design*, University of Guelph.
Jung, C.G. (1978) *Man and his Symbols*, Pan Books Ltd, London.
Kant, I. ([1790] 1952) *The Critique of Judgement*, trans. by James Creed Meredith, Oxford University Press, Oxford.
Langer, S. (1953) *Feeling and Form*, Routledge and Kegan Paul, London.
Langer, S. ([1942] 1957) *Philosophy in a New Key*, Harvard University Press, Cambridge, Mass.
Langer, S. (1957) *Problems of Art*, Routledge and Kegan Paul, London.
Lyall, S. (1991) *Designing the New Landscape*, Thames and Hudson, London.
Mikellides, B. (ed.) (1980) *Architecture for People: Explorations in a New Humane Environment*, Cassell, London, and Holt, Rinehart, Winston, New York.
Moore, K. (1993) 'The Art of Design', *Landscape Design*, No. 217 (February): 28–31.
Moore, R. (1993) 'The Senses Engaged', *The Royal Academy Magazine*, No. 38 (Spring): 46–48.
Newton, N.T. (1971) *Design on the Land*, Belknap Press, Harvard, Cambridge, Mass.
Repton, H. ([1806] 1969) *Inquiry into the Changes of Taste in Landscape Gardening*, Gregg, Farnsborough.
Ross, S. (1998) 'Gardens and the Death of Art', *Landscape Architecture*, 88(7): 64–96.
Schama, S. (1995) *Landscape and Memory*, HarperCollins, London.
Shepard, P. (1967) *Man in the Landscape: a Historic View of the Aesthetics of Nature*, Knopf, New York.
Tolstoy, L. ([1930] 1994) *What is Art?*, trans. A. Maude, Bristol Classical Press, London.
Walker, P. and Simo, M. (1994) *Invisible Gardens: The Search for Modernism in the American Landscape*, MIT Press, Cambridge, Mass.
Wittgenstein, L. (1953) *Philosophical Investigations*, Blackwell, Oxford.
Wolfe, T. (1989) *The Painted Word*, Black Swan, London.

5 In practice: but is it art?

Can a designed landscape be a work of art?

One of the questions I asked each of my interviewees was whether they believed that a designed landscape could be a work of art. If they thought that this was a possibility, I also asked them whether they thought, as the late Sir Geoffrey Jellicoe apparently did, that landscape architects should be striving to create such works. Most replied that in certain beneficial circumstances, which generally included a wealthy and sympathetic client or patron, there was no reason why a landscape could not achieve the status of art, but hardly anyone believed that the desire to create art was a necessary or realistic starting point for most landscape design.

Let us begin with the people who were most sympathetic towards Jellicoe's philosophy. Interestingly, one of these was Rebecca Hughes, whose background is in the sciences and whose career has taken her into landscape planning. Nevertheless she told me:

> Given my time again, I could easily see myself going to art college and not being an ecologist at all, because I have a great interest in sculpture and land art generally that is totally different from my biological interest. I used to do a lot of sculpture before I went to university and it's something that is definitely there. It doesn't go away. I'm fascinated by it, and Jellicoe really epitomised that in landscape design for me.

Hughes also spoke enthusiastically about the work of artists such as Richard Long and Andy Goldsworthy:

> They are more important to me in the way that I think about landscape than the sorts of jobbing landscape architects who do schemes round the latest office block or conference centre . . .
>
> Somehow what they do seems to get at the essence of what a place is all about . . . It adds further meaning to a location . . . and the fact that Goldsworthy's work is so unegotistical, but it shows something to do with the beauty of nature and place that, to me, is just perfect art in terms of landscape, but is not covered or done in any other way.

I asked Hughes what significance she thought these artists had for the profession of landscape architecture:

> For the landscape profession, it's take-it-or-leave-it. There are some of us who really relate to that sort of thing and the meaning it can infer to place – 'Yes, that's it! That's absolutely perfect for that location.' It's an emulation [sic] of place that you can't often get through landscape design.
>
> Possibly the value of their work, though Richard Long may be a bit too abstract for some people, is getting across to the ordinary person the meaning or nature of a location which otherwise may be invisible or missed entirely. We can't do that in our profession. We're locked in by conventional and client needs, if you like, whereas they can be much more freely creative . . . well that's an artist's prerogative of course!

Perhaps one of the reasons that landscape architects admire land artists is because they share an approach which respects the inherent qualities of places. The land artist who works *in situ* is responding to the *genius loci* in a way that is similar to the landscape architect, although the latter may systematise his approach in terms of site survey and analysis. As we saw in Chapter 3 a respect for place is one of the values which all landscape architects seem to hold dear.

Hughes's assessment of the prowess of landscape architects in communicating the qualities of a place is perhaps an unduly negative one, but she believes that Jellicoe was more successful than most in communicating meaning through landscape design:

> I think Jellicoe might have been one of the original Andy Goldsworthys of this world. You know, that sort of land art on a grand, grand scale. I admire the way he brought meaning into his designs. There was quite often a very deep and integrated approach to the whole design and I found that really stimulating.

Another enthusiast for Jellicoe was Tom Robinson of Newcastle-based Robinson Penn:

> Jellicoe believed that the work was design and that at its best it could have sufficient content to rank with other significant branches of culture, certainly architecture, but I suspect he also thought it could be as good as painting. He took design seriously. He took the idea of design seriously, and what's more he believed in ideas in design, and that's as rare as a ten-bob note.

John Vaughan, a landscape architect who is now the Director of the Great North Forest,[1] is also enthusiastic about Jellicoe's contribution. I asked him whether his ideas played any part in his current thinking:

> Yes. Not his Jungian ideas *per se*, but his basic belief that there is more in design and more in landscape than the physical product that meets the eye. I think that it's immensely important and I think one of the things that has been lost in terms of design is the idea of underlying layers of meaning in things. I wouldn't go with Jellicoe in the sense that I think there is a definitive set of symbols and there's a definitive approach, in the same way that I think it would be very difficult, if

you step back, to say that everyone has to believe in Jungian philosophy. There are lots of different philosophies, but what I think was important about his work was that there was more to it than the functional use of the environment, the functional use of land . . .

> . . . so while I wouldn't go with his stereotyped symbolism, I think the great thing that Jellicoe brought was a belief that there should be layers of meaning, in the broadest sense of the word, underneath things, to which people respond emotionally or subconsciously or in some cases intellectually. It's enriching people's relationship with the environment . . .

Vaughan believes that landscapes are complex and multi-layered. Like Hughes, he believes that the accomplished designer can reveal hidden aspects of a landscape and prompt people into asking questions about their relationship to it:

Figure 5.1 *Stone Cone* by Colin Rose who was sculptor in residence in the Great North Forest 1994–5. (Courtesy of the Great North Forest Project.)

Figure 5.2 This seat, by Richard Caink, was one of four created by the artist alongside members of Kibblesworth Youth Club for the Marking the Ways Project promoted by the Great North Forest and Gateshead Council. Kibblesworth is a former mining village. The pine cone and the acorn are intended to symbolise regeneration, the emergence of new life and hope for an area which has experienced tumultuous change.

That's relatively easy to do in Northumberland because it's big, it's fairly hard, it's a strong environment. It's very much more difficult at the smaller scale. There I think you have to do what Jellicoe did. You have to make conscious decisions and to build these layers in and ask 'well what will this evoke in people?' and 'can I put hooks in here that people will respond to?' 'Or clues that people will respond to?' Shapes, textures, spaces, voids, all the colours and all the smells, all those sorts of things which will bring to people's minds not 'what am I looking at?' but 'what does this all mean?'

For these reasons, Vaughan is an enthusiast for placing art into natural settings such as the Great North Forest. Its purpose is not so much to provoke as to prompt people to ask questions such as 'how did this thing get here?' or 'why was this site chosen?' This, he believes, will stimulate them into thinking about their lives, the environment and their place in it.

John Hopkins[2] took a very similar view:

Art is how we relate to the environment. It's how we abstract ourselves. It's how we express ourselves in the environment. It's how we understand ourselves in the environment. So art is absolutely critical. The only way you can get art into the environment, into landscape, is through design, so design is critical. It's not just a question of finding out what animal species, plant species or ecosystems there are. We have to work out new ways of tying ourselves into that ecosystem, into an expression of ourselves and our values in that environment.

Hopkins was sympathetic to the idea that the landscape itself could be the artform, but struggled with the specifically Jungian content of Jellicoe's theories:

I think where I disagreed with Jellicoe was with his notion of this Jungian idea, notions of the subconscious. I find the whole idea of the subconscious difficult to deal with. Yes, there is a spiritual dimension to our lives. I'd rather call it

Figure 5.3 Waymarker at Newbottle by Felicity Watts for the Marking the Ways Project promoted by the Great North Forest and Gateshead Council.

noumenal than spiritual, which has kind of religious overtones.

I suggested that Jellicoe had been wrong to make access to the collective subconscious a necessary condition for creating art. Initially I was surprised by Hopkins's reply, because it seemed at odds with his previous scepticism about the unconscious. In fact he seeks to reinterpret this idea in terms more consonant with science:

> Well no, I think I agree with Jellicoe's views. They relate to Lévi-Strauss[3] and anthropological ideas, and Chomsky's research into language[4] that showed language is innate. In the same way I think our ways of understanding our environment are innate. I think that's why there are universal designs. That's why Africans, Chinese, whatever ethnic background, can appreciate certain universal designs. I think Jung would define that as the collective unconscious. I would think it was biological and genetic and be more Darwinian

Figure 5.4 The posts of this stile in Kibblesworth village have been carved in the form of a cockerel crowing at the rising sun, part of the Marking the Ways Project promoted by the Great North Forest and Gateshead Council. The sculptor was Chris Sell.

about it, but it's part of our make-up as humans.

There were some out-and-out disbelievers however. Peter Fischer believes that Jellicoe was a good intuitive designer but has little time for his psychological and philosophical speculations:

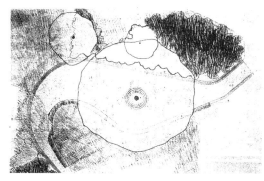

5.5

Figure 5.5, Figure 5.6 and Figure 5.7 (opposite) The landscape itself can be the work of art, as shown by these images of One Tree Hill, designed by Hopkins I Tate for Greenwich Royal Park. This subtle, low-key, fitting and functional scheme provides a romantic contrast to the seventeenth-century classical layout of the park. a) plan of One Tree Hill. This subdued and restful look-out area is very much part of the hill top landscape; b) the refurbishment of One Tree Hill provides new seating taking advantage of views to the River Thames and the City of London; c) the inscription on the curvilinear seats is taken from a poem published in the *London News* c.1770.

5.6

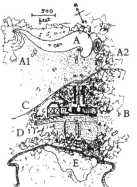

A   Lake and site for more sculptures
A1 The man hill
A2 The woman hill
B   Paradise and Secret Garden
C   Kitchen Garden
D   Ben Nicholson Sculptured Wall
E   Grotto and cascade

Figure 5.8 Geoffrey Jellicoe's sketch for the symbolic landscape of Sutton Place.

I'm going to be heretical here … I remember going around Sutton Place[5] when there was a guided tour. The South East Chapter[6] arranged it and Jellicoe was there and he gave this talk, and having walked around the scheme, the one he was particularly talking about was the walled courtyard, and when he talked about it, it was, to me, post-rationalisation, totally and utterly. He'd had an idea, quite a nice idea, quite interesting, but then he tried to impose on that all these classical allusions which I don't think were sustainable and that devalued his approach in my eyes. I felt if he does it here, he must do it all the time …

I may be wrong, but having heard him speak twice, talking about his work, I got the impression that he was an intuitive designer. He could come up with something that looked good and you could say it was a work of art, but I wasn't convinced that the symbolism wasn't imposed on it afterwards. He came from a classical training perhaps, so maybe I'm doing him a disservice. It's impossible to know. I think people react to the

5.7

sense of place, the site, and try to build on that, and at the same time to be thinking of how to impose symbolism is almost a preconception, and I believe what I was taught at university, that you shouldn't have preconceptions about your site before you deal with it. So to try and build up this thing about symbolism, to me is a post-rationalisation of what one has designed, and something which is probably going to be lost on the majority of us. I'm not a Jellicoe enthusiast, but that's not to knock his designs. It's not to say I don't like them or don't think that in parts they are attractive and enjoyable. I think the symbolism, for me, was overdone.

Attitudes towards symbolism

Opinions on the place of symbolism in landscape design ranged from those who fully endorsed it to those who thought it had little place. Pauline Randall thought that it might be appropriate in certain sorts of private commission, such as a garden for an individual or a religious community, but had great reservations when it came to public urban spaces:

> There are some public spaces which have symbolic artwork in them which are fantastic. They work extremely well and they tell you a lot about the politics of the era when they were created. Symbolism has its place, but I don't think it's a starting point.
>
> There's always an element of taste in art. I think the best landscapes are those that actually get the structure right for the users, but also are shaped in such a way that they are a work of art in themselves. I think when designers make the creation of art the starting point of landscape design, the users' needs and everything else seem to leave the designer's brain. The landscape becomes a work of art and all works of art are essentially egotistical. That's what fine art is about. These landscapes don't necessarily work well or survive in the public realm.

Randall seemed to be saying that the wish to create a work of art was a bad starting point for design. I put this to her:

> It's only a bad starting point if it's the only starting

point. I think it's okay to include it as one of the starting points. I don't think there's ever a single starting point for a landscape. It's much more complex than that, isn't it, because it's an interaction of so many different things.

There is a sense in which any design which responds harmoniously to its site can be said to symbolise aspects of that site. Rebecca Hughes made an interesting distinction between using symbolism in a focal sense, perhaps concentrated upon a single object in the design which attempts to capture particular qualities of the place, and a more diffuse form in which the whole designed landscape in some way is a symbol. James Hope, who has a practice near Edinburgh and also teaches at Heriot-Watt University, made a similar distinction. In his view the broader form of symbolism is far more profound. When discussing the landscape design for office buildings, he made the following observation:

> A lot of landscape art is symbolic. It's concerned not with this-object-symbolises-that. That's naive. It's that this place in some way symbolises the attitude of the management to the people who work here. That's a much more profound and satisfying form of symbolism, although students are always saying 'we've got this pillar here . . . it symbolises aspirations and infinity and man's relationship to space . . . you see how it looks like a rocket!' That's okay for a student, but the symbolic element is much deeper, I think, than that.

For Ivor Cunningham symbolism could provide the key to unlock a troublesome brief. He entertained me with an anecdote, supported by copious sketch-pad doodles, about a private garden commission he had undertaken:

> I did a design of a small garden . . . chap rang me up, went round to see him. I said 'Yes, I can design your garden.' When I got back I thought, how the bloody hell do you design a garden? The house was there and the road was there and the railway embankment was there . . . and so I started doodling and got nowhere. What do I know about these people? And I wasn't asking myself that question as a sociologist; I just wanted to find some way of turning the key in the lock. There is a key somewhere – you turn it and it

opens. So what do I know about this fellow? Well, he's quite keen on sailing; he's not really into gardening, and his partner's an American woman. And in their front room there's a grand piano . . . that's it! So I designed a garden for a pianist and a pirate! There's the boat, there's the water, there's the piano terrace and on here there would be a contrast of black and white. Ground cover is acting as water. Larger plants were boulders . . . these were islands. The spiky plants were sea-serpents, or as far as the pianist was concerned they were critics! And the pergola . . . I even put fish faces on the front. I didn't want to do something literally, but I needed something to just make a statement.

Intellectual content

A few of my interviewees had gained their greatest satisfaction from having produced designs which were symbolically based upon complex intellectual ideas. It mattered little to them whether this work was classified as art or as design. One such

was James Hope, who described a scheme that he designed for the Cummins Diesel factory at Shotts.[7]

> It was a very bold concept. It was to build geometric pyramids to complement a highly faceted building. And not only that, it was to symbolise two or three things which in some way related to the company. The precision of the mounds related to the diamonds that cut the tools that made the precision motors that Cummins built. There was the interlocking of the mounds. It was an interesting device – I used to have a model of it – where we actually melded mounds into each other in a very interesting way, and that was seen as the co-operation of management, workers, unions and bosses. That was the story we sold . . .
>
> . . . Not only that. Partly for my own satisfaction, and there's an element of deviousness in this, there is a hidden geometry in it all. The orientation of the bings, the facets of the bings, relate to the confines of the site, to the building . . . and so there's an esoteric element here of hidden geometry. Now that's very satisfying to someone with a mind like mine, because it has associations with numerology, with cabbalism, all those things . . . I'm really getting to the mysteries of the universe now! (Laughter.)

There was a mischievous glint in Hope's eyes as he told me this. His delight in the ingenuity of his design was palpable. Later in the interview he admitted:

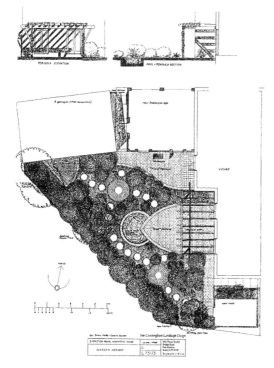

Figure 5.9 Symbolism unlocks a difficult brief. Ivor Cunningham's garden design for a pianist and a pirate.

Figure 5.10 Pyramidal landscape, Cummins Factory, Shotts. (Courtesy of James Hope.)

I'm much more concerned with . . . being clever, I think. That's a real admission of human frailty . . . being clever! There's nothing so satisfying as being clever is there? It's intellectual, aesthetic arrogance of the nth degree, and I now realise it, I realise it!

Relatively few design commissions offer the scope for such aspirational work. The only other person to describe a project of similar content was Tom Robinson who worked on a Belgian project called the European Recreation Centre while employed at RPS Clouston in Durham. The project, which was not

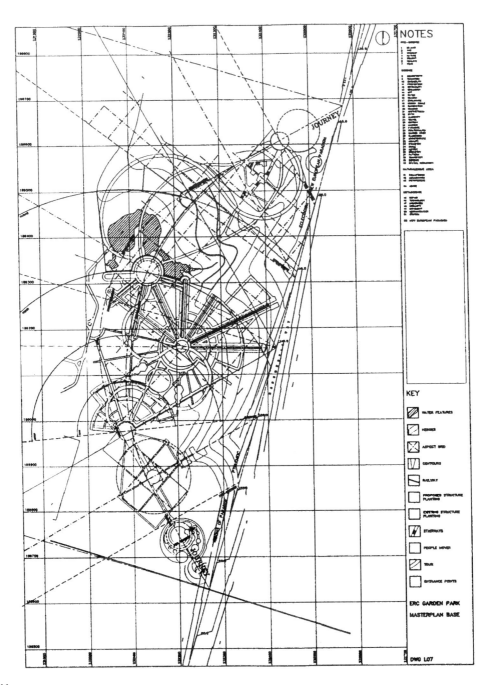

5.11

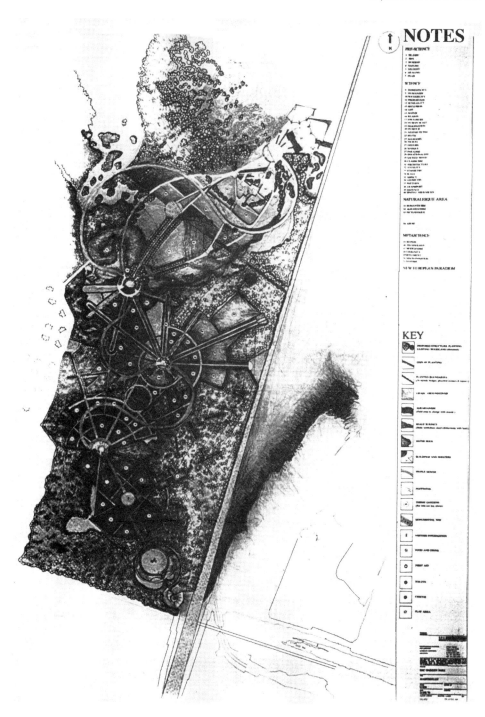

5.12

Figure 5.11 and Figure 5.12 Tom Robinson described this (sadly unrealised) scheme for the European Recreation Centre in Belgium as the 'most interesting, challenging design' he had ever been involved in. The main path through the site represents a journey through history. Philosophical standpoints associated with particular periods are related to the spatial organisation of the garden park. (Courtesy of RPS Clouston.)

realised, was to have been a theme park on the site of a former colliery. A garden park of some 35 hectares was required by the brief, and this was to have reflected European values. In some ways the project is reminiscent of Jellicoe's proposals for the Moody Gardens in Galveston, Texas. Robinson says of this commission:

> I spent about five months working on it, and it was then – and still is – the most interesting, challenging design I've ever been involved in. I think the reason that I say that is that the site was complex. It had complex technical problems. Part of it included a spoil heap . . . there were complex level changes, there were water lagoons, there was a wood. And we had this sophisticated design idea of trying to create a narrative of different landscapes in Europe over two thousand years, but doing it in such a way that we built the essences of these landscapes rather than a series of theme gardens.
>
> It was intellectually very very rich, far richer than anything I've worked on since . . . This was, if you like, an aesthetic design problem, because we had to find a way of creating spaces that were recognisably of their period, yet stripped down so they could all fuse into a sequence of spaces, in distinct areas, that could, for instance, all sit together as the Renaissance period, the Pre-industrial period, the Classical world, and it forced us to find out what the essences were of, for instance, Italian Renaissance gardens . . . and how could we represent that in such a way that you can create a convincing link to later Baroque Italian gardens.

I asked Robinson whether he thought this thematic complexity raised the project to the status of art:

> I would be nervous about that. I really would. I'd certainly call it design with a capital D. I'd be reluctant to use the word 'art'. Proudly, it wasn't art, it was good design.

The place of emotion

Several of my subjects suggested that the artistic aspects of their work were concerned with the expression or the communication of emotion. Nevil Farr told me:

> I think art has a soul to it. I can't define it for you, but I like to think it's the result of the release of some emotion . . . and I think you can recognise the difference, which means that an awful lot of the schemes we've got are not art. I can think of some that probably are. There are certain schemes that you put an awful lot of yourself into, sometimes just for the sake of the job, sometimes it's for a good cause, or sometimes just for the heck of it, and I would go along with that being the response of an artist. And long may it be so. If it ever became just the Lego-brick syndrome, we'd be losing out badly.

My discussion with Farr took place in a white-walled exhibition space which was part of the business centre in which the Donaldson Edwards Partnership's Liverpool office is situated. As we talked about art we were surrounded by contemporary examples. Farr found much in common between art and design:

> Let's look at some of the paintings and sculpture in here. I would like to think that they were all done for the artist himself. They look a bit odd some of them. However, I would like to think that they have a discipline, they have an intent, that every mark made on that painting is there for a reason. Every line we draw on our drawing boards is there for a reason and you need to be able to justify it. That sounds very precise and analytical, but I do actually think that art is intended and it has a rationale behind it.

Another designer who told me that he put a lot of personal emotion and energy into his work was James Hope:

> For people like me, who lead a fairly rich emotional life, landscape provides that medium, because I can sit at my drawing board and I can put some Mendelssohn or Bach on, and I can reach an incredible high, an emotional high, and you enter another realm . . . like Robert Burns or MacDiarmid drinking whiskey! They got maudlin as well as emotional. I don't become like that, but I can become very emotional and that's a device. It's a way of releasing a certain energy. And you end up with a product. Whether it's a poem or a landscape doesn't matter.

It was clear, listening to Hope and to Farr, that landscape design could for them be a deeply involving process, and in this they might be every bit as absorbed as an artist. Peter McGuckin, on the other hand, made a very cool separation between the functional, problem-solving aspects of a design and its emotional content. He described his own approach to design in the following terms:

> You do a survey, and it's important that that is mechanical, to be accurate, it's systematic, and then you do the analysis and you begin to bring in a bit of interpretation. It's a filter, the beginnings of it becoming less mechanical. The design is emotional, so you're moving through a range there, from the mechanical to the emotional, and it's that last bit, putting the spin on it that makes it, to my mind . . . well it would be wrong to say either good design or bad design because that's like saying that there's something that's right and there's something that's wrong . . .
>
> If I think it's a good design, I don't shove it down people's throats at presentations. I just seek to explain, first of all the functionalism, the mechanical part, how it actually came through that design process, and then I explain some of the emotional aspects of how I arrived at that design and they can either agree or disagree with the latter. It's hard to disagree with the former.

As we will see, McGuckin is not alone in laying great emphasis upon the functional aspects of a design, nor in wishing to keep the consciously artistic elements firmly in their place, but it is also worth noting that he believes that without an emotional 'spin' a design can be dead.

Frustrated artists?

It does not seem that the majority of landscape architects are frustrated artists, although one or two gave this impression. Cheryl Tolladay, Principal Landscape Architect for Groundwork East Durham, described an exhibition she had recently seen about land art:

> There was a really interesting panel about the circle and its potency as a symbol and as I was reading it I felt like someone who had been in the desert and been given a drink. I was reading it and thinking

'this is wonderful'. How often does a landscape architect think 'What am I going to do on this? I think I'll read a tome on ancient myths and legends to inspire me.' They just think 'I'll use Marshall's Tegula'[8] on this.'

James Hope is another who wears his frustrations on his sleeve:

> So what some of us are doing is we're uniting the philosophical, the scientific, the emotional and artistic, and so on, in whatever we do. And in a way one of the frustrations of landscape is that it appears to be such a very poor vehicle or medium in which to indulge such heroic ideas. I mean, had we been Brown or Kent or Le Nôtre or Shenstone, or any of these people, we might have been able to achieve it. But now we bugger around with bloody paving and pedestrian precincts and put a few tubs here and there, and you think 'bloody pathetic!' We're unable to create great art. We may be incapable of producing great art. That's more likely to be true! We're just not the stuff that great artists are made of.

One senses that the real source of Hope's ire is a conviction that landscape architecture has the potential to achieve very great things indeed; it is just that it is circumscribed by all manner of practical, pragmatic and financial constraints which prevent these possibilities from being realised. For many people in practice this is simply a fact and it does not trouble them unduly. When I asked Phil Moss whether he used symbolism in his designs he told me:

> No, hand on heart, I don't think . . . well you might do it subconsciously. I don't know. Certainly in my design, no. I've never got to that level of philosophical depth. Ain't got enough time. I've got too many things to do, when I've got a client on the end of the phone . . .

Art and elitism

One of the concerns that some landscape architects expressed was that the kind of artistic aspirations which Jellicoe urges upon the profession are elitist. Peter McGuckin suggested that the use of symbolism in design presented particular difficulties:

You know, if something's going to be symbolic it has to be reasonably obvious to the majority of people, and to some people's taste, those who have a more subtle sense of design values, that will be too overt. It'll be over the top . . . If you were doing something for a school playground, you wouldn't want it to be so obscure that it would take a kid that's qualified to go to Cambridge to figure it out, and there are a lot of abstruse examples of landscape design, where the landscape architect says this, this and this about the design and you think 'Gerroff! That's not there!'

While Nigel Marshall was not completely dismissive of the contribution that artists could make to landscape, he thought it was of limited importance and he was suspicious of landscape architects who put artistic aspirations at the centre of their work:

I'm not one who says that landscape architects should be out for an ego trip – to create something just for the sake of it.

Marshall took his landscape qualifications while working for the Greater London Council Parks Department, and this experience was formative. He recalls that the values taught on his college course were different from those he was forming in practice:

One thing I did find that I had to do was to adopt a slightly different mode of mind when I was doing the college stuff to what I was doing at work, but for me as someone who is not – this might sound rather critical of some landscape architects – but not an airy-fairy artist landscape architect, being at the earthy end of it, that was right, actually . . . being able to see from day one the practical implications of what I was doing at college was right for me.

Of all my subjects, Pauline Randall was the one who was consistently the least enamoured with art. Talking about her time studying landscape architecture at Sheffield she commended the course because:

There was a minimum of what I would call artistic language that I think confuses the issue of landscape.

When asked what kind of landscape work she most admired, she replied:

I admire quite a lot of land reclamation work that goes on, a lot of that is sound, but I don't think it is often improved by attempts at land art.

Landscape architects like McGuckin, Marshall and Randall take a certain pride in being no-nonsense or down-to-earth designers. Art, for them, is not quite an irrelevance but something which needs to be seen objectively and not allowed to obscure other values.

Not art but 'good design'

Having completed my series of interviews, one firm conclusion I was able to reach was that Jellicoe's grand objective of producing not just good landscape designs but works of art was not a vision shared by many practising British landscape architects. While landscape design as art was a logical possibility for most, it did not assume a primary position in their value systems. What was far more common was to hear practitioners talk about 'good design', and it became clear to me that there was a cluster of values associated with this concept which were different to the values that grouped around the notion of art. Peter Fischer put this distinction very succinctly:

If a landscape design doesn't achieve the correct functional use that I think it ought to be achieving, for people to use, then you might call it a work of art but it's not a successful landscape. Okay, you might be able to create a work of art that isn't successful in other ways. At the same time, if one creates something that is successful in terms of the way that people use it, they enjoy it, it works well on a number of different levels, its maintainability, its support of wildlife, then that for me is what it should be doing. If at the same time some people see it as a work of art, then that's fine.

Here then are some of the attributes which my interviewees thought good design should possess:

Function

The idea that a good design is one that functions well was widely held. Peter McGuckin, for example, told me:

I think I'm very much a firm foundations individual and so fundamentally the scheme has to function correctly. I don't just mean that prosaically – that a wall has to have a well-detailed foundation – I mean that everything that is relevant is called to mind and influences the design. That's from a functional standpoint, and once I've convinced myself that I've satisfied those requirements, I almost put them to one side. After that it becomes purely a question of making it look good . . .

Injecting some spirit, some emotion into the design comes within my value system. It's just not top of the pecking order. I feel that if the design, first and foremost, doesn't work, for whatever reason, then much of the spirit of that design will be unpicked through time. It will be abused . . .

. . . I feel so strongly that you have a once and only chance to get a design right and that is why I apply, at the top of my value system, this systematic approach to design. The feeling, the spirit, the emotion come second on the list of priorities for that reason.

For Tom Robinson, good design is confident design, and this in part is concerned with function:

Well, I do think I can recognise when a design has worked and when it hasn't and one of the things that you recognise is that good design seems to have a confidence about it. It's not fussy or . . . where it's intricate one would never describe the intricacy as fussy because it's appropriate to it, and confidence is something I think you recognise in all good designs.

You have some things you need to resolve and part of the confidence would be the success with which you resolve these design problems, so if it's to screen some things off, and to accentuate others and to make the public spaces leading from A to B pleasant, that's more than just aesthetic. There's a function to be carried out there and you can instinctively feel whether it has been carried off well, carried off half-heartedly or not carried off at all.

However, the belief that a design must function does not commit one to a belief in *functionalism*. Solving functional problems does not necessarily address aesthetic ones. Robinson puts it thus:

I don't actually believe that in landscape design form necessarily follows function. I think it's a good generalisation, but if you try to apply it, you very quickly end up with squares and right angles and diagonals and all the grace and the pixie-dust have gone. But having said that, the thing that landscape architecture, like architecture, has to do is to work.

Space and scale

When I asked my interviewees what they thought constituted good design they often mentioned an awareness of the qualities of places, which is something we have already explored in Chapter 3. Closely related to this was the widely held belief that landscape architects have a particular expertise in understanding and manipulating spatial characteristics. For Dougal Thornton this is the most interesting aspect of the job:

The main thing that attracted me to landscape architecture was . . . it's a visual experience primarily, but it's more than a visual experience . . . I think the core of what we do is space. It's handling space, and the hardest thing is scale. People can get all the components right and get the scale wrong. I think the movement through space is the most fascinating thing we deal with, and how people interact with that space and how they respond to it.

Pauline Randall also believes that handling space is an essential skill and one which it takes years to develop:

To create a space that's comfortable to be in and that really works you've got to understand the dimensions of spaces and you've got to have experience of it. It's something that develops over time.

Peter Fischer told me that he admired the urban landscape work done in Glasgow by Ian White Associates (of Stirling) because it combined simple elegant detailing with an understanding of scale and function. On the other hand, he believes that much contemporary urban work has lost its way:

To me scale of space is fundamental. A hobbyhorse of mine is that a lot of urban design work of late is pattern for its own sake – circles and squares and diamonds and whatever. To my mind it's not what design of an urban space is about. It should be how it functions. It should be very simply paved and very carefully detailed and Ian White can do that – and has done it two or three times in Glasgow. I think he's always had an attention to detail and he understands that scale and function are the essence of a landscape, rather than what I call patterns.

Similarly Pauline Randall was very unhappy about the revamping of St Anne's Square in Manchester, which she described as a complete waste of public money. The original scheme had been done by her partner, Edward Thorp, in the days of Greater Manchester Council:

> It worked very well except that the paving, inevitably over a ten-year period, needed redoing. It had a good structure of trees. I can remember him doing the design. The Royal Fine Arts Commission were involved in the design because St Anne's church is a historic church and the Royal Exchange Building, another historic building, is on the square. It was an understated paving design, a good structure of trees, seats and a relocated statue. It worked extremely well, people loved it, buskers were down there all the time. The city council decided to revamp it two years ago, and rather than just redoing the paving which was what it needed, they spent, I'm not sure whether it was £250,000 or £500,000 or more, on redoing the entire thing . . . ripped out all the trees which had been growing for ten years, replaced them with these round concrete 'Barcelona balls' that are kicked about and graffitied, 'very stylish' seats that look as though they'll snap if you jumped up and down on them, and they've put the direst fountain in the middle.

The love of details

In talking to landscape architects about good design, I was struck by the frequency with which they referred to the quality of detailing as a kind of touchstone. As we observed in Chapter 3, they seldom refer to Neoplatonic theories when dealing with the broad scale, yet when it comes to the details, a species of formal purity seems to become important. Most of the people I talked to seemed to agree with Mies van der Rohe's dictum that 'God is

in the detail'.[9] Simon Rendel expressed it quite poetically:

> I have a lot of appreciation of detail. When I see a landscape architect who's got a hold on detail, I realise that that is the summit of design . . . perhaps because I'm not very good at being able to predict the outcome at that level. If I tried to do that I could produce a sensible solution, but not something that really sings in some particular way. And I can see it when someone's done it. I can appreciate that it does sing.
>
> . . . You see a piece of design and you say 'Yes, this guy really has his sense of proportion right . . . the way he's bolted it together', which really does show up best in the details.

Elizabeth Banks describes herself as a perfectionist and she is intolerant of badly executed work.

Figure 5.13 God is in the details? This crisply detailed handrail from Insite's Newcastle East Quayside scheme subtly refers to the site's history while providing a tactile cue (rope texture) for the visually impaired. (Courtesy Insite.)

She thinks that it is the details which get noticed:

> I was very insistent that the quality of the work should be of the highest quality from design down to the implementation and when it got slipshod or showed a lack of care, then I got very upset.
>
> . . . it is that constant desire to have the detail right, when you get down to doing the grand design, and it's the detail, to my mind, that actually will in the end be the visual manifestation.

The same sentiments were expressed by Phil Moss of BDP in Manchester, for whom the importance of detailing came as a revelatory experience on a field trip to Switzerland as a student:

> I saw the quality of external design in Zurich and Geneva and I thought 'what we are doing is absolutely appalling, especially in the case of hard landscape'. I really did think it compromised the nature of the British people and therefore British designers had a lot to answer for. And you saw this quality and thought that they really thought through their detailing. I've always had a bee in my bonnet. I think 'I'm going to be very critical of myself and my own designs, and certainly any designs within BDP' . . . It's the quality and attention to every detail, and I still think that . . . we've improved, but by God we needed to, and we've still got a long way to go.

What they don't like: meretricious stylism

Appropriateness to place, a sense of space and scale, sound functioning and well-conceived and constructed details are the features which constitute good design for landscape architects. The characteristics which they least admire can also be concisely stated: landscape architects do not like flashy, trashy, gimmicky or meretricious design and they are often very hard on the designers they perceive to be guilty of the crime of stylism.

Nevil Farr believes that good design is robust and that designers must not become precious about their work:

> So much of so-called good design is a bit precious and 'Oh, you mustn't change that. If you change it, it has spoiled the whole concept!' . . . actually

things used by people have to change . . . It's just like the Albert Dock. Those buildings are so big that actually if people want to have hanging baskets on the side of them, that's fine. It doesn't mean anything. It'll accommodate them and you haven't lost anything.

As we have already noted, many designers, despite recent criticism of the Survey–Analysis–Design methodology, continue to believe in a systematic approach to design and are suspicious of more intuitive methods. Peter McGuckin told me:

> I'm frustrated at people who seem to arrive at designs which . . . I look at those designs and come to the conclusion that they aren't sustainable, that they aren't well thought through, and often the people who have this more haphazard approach to design . . . it's almost like a freestyle . . . speak so passionately about it.'

Simon Rendel thought that too much emphasis could be placed upon design. If it is reified into an end for itself, one can lose sight of the landscape itself, which is the important thing:

> I think that when you think about a landscape at the broad level, the design should be at the back of your mind, must be at the back of your mind. It shouldn't intrude. It should somehow . . . it's this iterative process I was talking about just now in terms of my own garden. If you try and impose things too much it loses some of the magic it might otherwise have had. You know, when I see pictures of Derek Jarman's garden,[10] I realise he was after something which I find really interesting.

Perhaps because Heather Lloyd started to train originally as a fashion designer, she had very little time for style without substance:

> I was doing fashion actually, fashion and textiles, but it didn't seem very meaningful. It seemed ever so shallow and you had to get all psyched up to design stuff and then it didn't make any difference to how the world was going to change, or be, or anything else, and so I suppose landscape architecture had that side to it, and also it was big scale . . .
>
> I haven't got any time of day for all these prima donnas of designers who go round with some

concept in their head and they chuck it out and then it doesn't make any sense. It's got no relation to what is really required, and I think if you can't speak to users who are going to end up using it, and ask them what they want, and it's not just what they want, but also what they really need, because sometimes people have different ideas about what they want and what they actually need, and I think as a designer it is up to you to find that out.

The practitioner who expressed the strongest dislike for stylistic approaches was John Hopkins. He recalled an interview for a commission with the architect, Terry Farrell:

> I mean every new job that you work on, you're always trying to create something that's new, that's different, and that is growing from that particular place and those particular community values, ecological values – whatever is there –trying to draw off that. I remember in an interview with Terry Farrell he said 'Well, what's your style?' and we said 'We're landscape architects. We don't do style. We do design, which comes from wherever that particular place is.'

Hopkins did not get the job, and is inclined to regard Farrell as a stylist who selects a particular aesthetic for a job and then designs to it. He also thinks that many of the European influences in landscape architecture are stylistically driven and he is very sceptical about them:

> I think British landscape architects have been enamoured with stylistically projected landscape architecture from Europe. I don't see many landscape architects in Europe who are doing very good thinking and designing.

I wondered whether he was including the resurgence of open space design in Barcelona, which has certainly had a great impact upon landscape education. What was his opinion about that?

> It looks very nice, but I don't think it will stand the test of time. I think it's just stylism. It's okay for the 90s, but in 2000–2010 they'll be doing a different style. But think the idea of what they're doing, refurbishing their open spaces, is very good.

The project that brought out the strongest reaction was Bernard Tschumi's Parc de la Villette:

> Oh that's just crap. That's a load of bullshit. It's about Tschumi and Derrida[11] and stylism . . . any time anybody says 'This is the new wave, this is the way we must do things . . .'
>
> . . . I think Derrida is unintelligible. How does he help me? It's like Heidegger. Okay, I get the sense, the intuition, that there's something to Heidegger, but with Derrida I don't . . . so, you know, I'm a busy practitioner. I want people to make things clear to me and when I look at a lot of architectural landscape it's just crap because it's just unintelligible.

The designers whom Hopkins admired were mostly Americans, not just the older generation of Modernists like Kiley, Eckbo and Halprin, but contemporary figures like Michael Van Valkenburgh, George Hargreaves, and Peter Walker. He sees these people as serious thinkers and designers, not merely stylists:

> I'm very much influenced by the development of landscape architecture in the States because I went there to study. I think that Garrett Eckbo is probably the greatest American philosopher in landscape design. He came up very early on with the ecology, community and art, the triadic relationship. He identified that as the most basic principal from which we now need to build the future of landscape architecture on . . .
>
> I admire George Hargreaves because he is very much reintroducing art back into landscape design, and tying it in with the ecology and the community. Van Valkenberg because I think he's doing the same although he's much more at the higher end of design.

Commodity, firmness and delight

On my visit to the Manchester area, a number of interviewees mentioned the same phrase, 'commodity, firmness and delight', in response to my questions about good design. This turned out to be more than just coincidence. For those who do not recognise the reference, it comes from a treatise called *The Elements of Architecture*, written by Henry Wotton and published in London in 1624:

'The end is to build well.
Well building hath three conditions, Commoditie, Firmenes, and Delight.'

Several of my interviewees had worked together in the former Greater Manchester Council, where, it seems, this expression was in currency. Pauline Randall explained what it meant to her:

By which one means that it's fit for its purpose, i.e. the users – commodity, consideration of the users; firmness, being that it's well built, which means that it would be enduring – sustainable; and delight, of course, meaning that it has to please the eye, inspire, whatever, be artistic. If you can get the balance between those three then you often get a good sustainable design.

This, it seemed to me then, was a useful addition to the conceptual armoury of any designer, and the title chosen for this book pays homage to Wotton. In particular I have made use of his word 'delight', which seems so much fresher than 'aesthetic appeal' or any other synonym I might have found. I have used this word in my title because it seems to encapsulate all of the aesthetic concerns explored in Chapters 2–4. It includes not only the delight that we all feel when walking in unspoilt countryside, but the satisfactions we may get from walking in spaces that are well proportioned and harmonious, from noticing 'details that sing' or from contemplating a symbolically rich and evocative piece of landscape art.

Some conclusions

The main conclusion to be drawn from this chapter is that most landscape architects do not see themselves as aspiring artists, which is not to deny that some landscape design can attain the status given to art. Rather than striving to be artists, most practitioners endeavour to be good designers, and there is a large degree of consensus about what constitutes good design. Sensitivity to the qualities of place must come high on the list, as must an understanding of spatial scale and skill in detailing. Landscape architects are impressed by designs that function well – that meet the social needs they

address, and also by designs which, through firmness of construction and a basis in sound ecology, are enduring or sustainable.

Notes

1 The Great North Forest is one of twelve Community Forests being developed on the outskirts of English towns and cities by the Countryside Commission in partnership with the Forestry Commission. The aim of this project is to increase tree cover in England from 7.5 per cent to 15 per cent by the year 2050. The Great North Forest covers 160 square miles and overlaps the boundaries of five local authorities.

2 At the time of the interview John Hopkins was an associate of the London office of EDAW Ltd.

3 Claude Lévi-Strauss (1908–), the anthropologist and ethnographer, is a leading exponent of structuralism. He believes that beneath the apparently diverse forms of myth, ritual and symbolic representation there lies a deep grammar of mythical thought which unites this multiplicity of meanings and forms.

4 Noam Chomsky (1928–), the American linguist and philosopher, believes that the reason children from a huge range of social and cultural backgrounds, and with varying degrees of intelligence, all learn to speak their native languages at about the same age is that they share an innate faculty for language characterised by a universal grammar. This is part of their biological endowment as human beings.

5 In 1980 Geoffrey Jellicoe was commissioned by Stanley Seeger, a millionaire, to prepare designs for his house, Sutton Place in Surrey. Tom Turner has described this as 'the magnum opus of modern English garden design' and as 'the most significant private garden to have been made in England since the war' (*English Garden Design*, 1986, p. 218).

6 South East Chapter of the Landscape Institute.

7 Shotts is a town to the east of Glasgow.

8 The name of a style of concrete block paving much used (overused?) by British landscape architects.

9 Personal motto of Ludwig Mies van der Rohe. See 'Mies van der Rohe' in *Macmillan Encyclopaedia of Architects*, Vol. 3, edited by Adolph K. Placzek, New York, Free Press, Macmillan, 1982.

10 Shortly before he died the late Derek Jarman created a garden at Prospect Cottage, his house on the beach at Dungeness, which has been widely admired. Jarman utilised maritime species and materials discovered during beachcombing expeditions to create a sensuous and inventive garden which is in close harmony with its setting.

11 Tschumi has said that he was influenced by the writings of the French Deconstructivist philosopher Jaques Derrida.

PART II
COMMUNITY

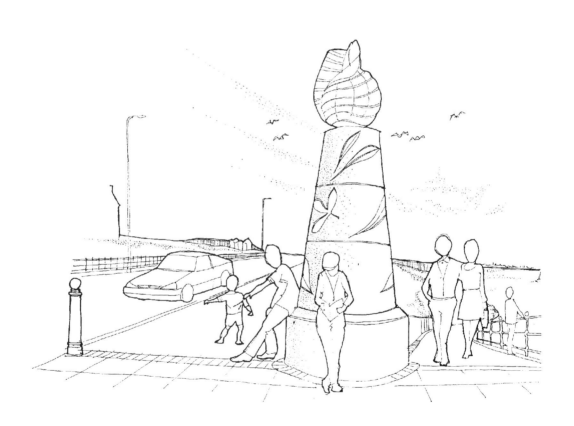

Sketch by John Elm showing proposals for Seaham Promenade, County Durham (overleaf). (Courtesy of Groundwork, East Durham.)

6 The social value of landscape architecture

Landscapes of the powerful

This chapter will discuss the social mission of landscape architecture, but let us be clear that it has not always had one. Every student of landscape history must have felt a buzz of *schadenfreude* when told the story of Nicolas Fouquet, Louis XIV's corrupt finance minister, who employed André Le Nôtre to create his magnificent formal garden at Vaux-le-Vicomte. To create these gardens three villages had to be moved out of the way (I seriously doubt whether anyone asked the villagers what they thought about this idea). So pleased was he with his grand estate that Fouquet invited the king and his court to an elaborate reception. A big mistake. Louis was consumed with anger and envy and it was not long before Fouquet was imprisoned, while his chief gardener was commandeered to work on the king's even grander garden at Versailles.

The point of this homily is to demonstrate the historical links between landscape architecture, ostentation and power. The classical traditions in design described in Chapter 2 are particularly open to this kind of conscription. It is extremely ironic that Versailles should have appealed so strongly to Thomas Jefferson when he was casting about for a prototype for the capital of America's fledgling democracy. L'Enfant's masterplan for Washington is based upon Le Nôtre's plan for Versailles, the perfect embodiment of absolutist royal power.

In the early years of the twentieth century, and despite the arrival of Modernism, this tradition kicked again. The City Beautiful Movement, headed by the Chicago-based architect, Daniel Hudson Burnham (1845–1912), took its inspiration from Versailles and from Haussmann's reconstruction of Paris.[1] Burnham's monumental visions were easy to sell to the burghers of the emerging commercial cities of the American Midwest, but City Beautiful thinking also appeared in the Lutyens–Baker plan for New Delhi (1913) and in the plans for other colonial capitals like Lusaka and Nairobi. This monumental language of civic prestige and ostensible power later appeared in Mussolini's compromised plans for Rome and in Speer's grandiose but unbuilt vision for Berlin. What all of these visions had in common was 'a total concentration on the monumental and on the superficial, on architecture as symbol of power; and correspondingly, an almost complete lack of interest in the wider social purposes of planning' (Hall, 1988: 202). Behind the façades of Haussmann's Paris, Burnham's Chicago or Stalin's Moscow lay chaotic slums and poverty.

Functionalism and the rise of Modernism

If the classical style has often served those in positions of power, Modernism, with its emphasis on function, its abhorrence of ornament and its rejection of ordering devices like symmetry and the axis, might have been expected to have produced a more socially concerned and democratic form of architecture. Sadly it became every bit as theory-driven and rule-governed as the styles it replaced, lending itself to yet more 'top-down' design in which the needs of users were often ignored.

Functionalism has a distinguished pedigree and, at first glance, it seems like an entirely commendable

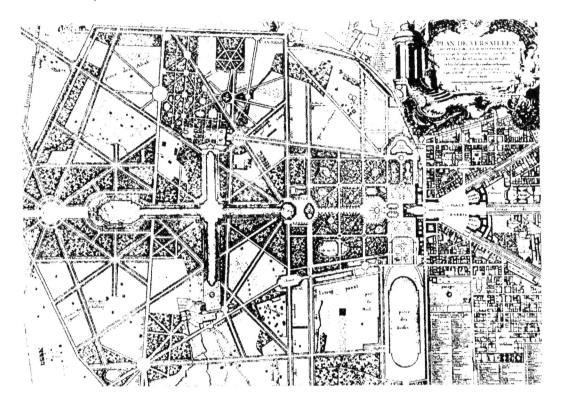

Figure 6.1 Plan of Versailles made by Abbé Delagrive showing the gardens as completed by Le Nôtre by 1700.

idea. It is the belief that an object which is most suited to fulfil its function will be both a good object, in an evaluative or moral sense, and a beautiful or aesthetically pleasing object. Plato, as we noted in Chapter 2, considered that the Form of an object was identical with its essential nature or function. Thus the good knife is the knife that cuts well – it will also be a beautiful knife. The same idea is found in the first chapter of Hogarth's *Analysis of Beauty* entitled 'Of Fitness'. Here we find the proponent of the line of beauty arguing that the fitness of parts contributes to the beauty of the whole, and praising ship-builders for the functionality of their designs; 'When a sailing vessel sails well, the sailors call her a beauty; the two ideas have such a connection' (Hogarth, [1753] 1971: 32–33).

Functionalism was entirely consistent with the rationalistic and mechanistic world-view which rose to become the dominant European ideology in the seventeenth century. Believing, as they did, that the cosmos was a complicated clockwork, Descartes, Newton, Bacon and their ilk maintained that it could be analysed, reduced, investigated and ultimately controlled. If the universe is a machine, it is easy to

assert, as did Le Corbusier, that a house ought to be one.[2] It was this connection with science which ultimately distanced the functional approach from ordinary people and delivered it into the hands of technocrats. This did not begin to happen until the emergence of the social sciences in the nineteenth century, when functionalism became linked with ideals of social progress and revolutionary political developments.

Nikolaus Pevsner has given a very full account of the emergence of the Modern Movement.[3] He suggests that three main tributaries converged to form the mainstream of Modernism. The first was Art Nouveau, which, in its youthfulness, freedom and inventiveness, represented an attack on historical precedents, even though its curving, bulging forms were anathema to the Modernists. The second was Morris's Arts and Crafts Movement, which emphasised the social duty of art to produce useful objects, although it looked backwards towards medieval craftsmanship and shunned machine production. The third was the stream of nineteenth-century technological and engineering innovations, which included the structural use of iron in the

A Potomac River
B Eastern branch
C Tiber River
D Approximate escarpment
E Georgetown (existing)
F President's house
G Capitol
H Public landscape
I Expanding city
J View to hills
K Canal
L Statue of Washington

Figure 6.2 L'Enfant's plan for Washington (1791) based firmly on French formal principles.

erection of bridges, conservatories and railway stations, and the development of reinforced concrete for use in industrial buildings. Modernism's emphasis on functional requirements, upon rational problem solving and scientific rigour, was principally derived from this third source.

That functionalism was fundamental to Modernism is evident in Louis Sullivan's often quoted (and usually misquoted) aphorism 'form ever follows function'.[4] As we have seen, this, in itself, was not a new thought, but the Modernists took the insight a stage further by condemning all decoration that had no functional justification. The corollary of the Modernists' preoccupation with function was their opposition to all that was simulated or sham, and this took on the force of a moral crusade. Thus the French architect, Tony Garnier, who designed the rigorously functional Cité Industrielle at the turn of the century, could condemn most of the work of earlier architects as dishonest: 'Like all architecture based on false principles, ancient architecture is an error. Truth alone is beautiful. In architecture, truth is the result of calculations made to satisfy known

necessities with known materials.'[5]

It was perhaps inevitable that a movement which had dedicated itself so energetically to the eradication of slavish adherence to styles should finally produce a style of its own and promote it as the *only* style appropriate to the spirit of the age. In 1931 Henry-Russell Hitchcock and Philip Johnson prepared an exhibition on Modern Architecture for the Museum of Modern Art in New York. The catalogue, published the following year, was entitled *The International Style* and asserted that the 'contemporary style, which exists throughout the world, is unified and inclusive, not fragmentary and contradictory like so much of the production of the first generation of modern architects'.

The International Style made a virtue out of disregard for climate, culture and site. The only criteria that were important were that architecture should be seen as enclosed space (as opposed to load-bearing mass) allowing flexibility of plan, that there should be an attempt to introduce modular regularity (premised on the industrial prefabrication of standardised components and replacing axial symmetry as an organising principle) and that there should be no superimposed decoration. The new style was taken to heart by corporate bureaucracies around the world, and is embodied in thousands of anonymous glass boxes. It is the antithesis of design which responds to the 'Spirit of the Place'.

Many of the early Modernists were social revolutionaries of one stamp or another. The desire to create a new architecture accorded with the aspiration to forge a new social order. It was easy to characterise the old styles and applied ornament as decadent and bourgeois, while the new architecture, rationalised and standardised, would lend itself to the redress of social ills. In practice, however, Modernism could be as ruthlessly insensitive to individual human aspirations as Stalinism. As Le Corbusier's Modulor[6] notoriously demonstrates, some Modernists believed that they should design for standardised human beings. Nevertheless, this socially conscious strand in Modernism is of significance to the present study because it was a cause taken up strongly by many landscape architects, particularly in the United States.

The impact of Modernism on landscape architecture

As we have seen, a major factor in the rise of Modern architecture was the discovery of new materials and the advent of industrial production. Landscape designers who admired the developments in architecture were presented with a problem, because the main components of landscape design – earth, water and plants – had not altered. They could, however, identify with the Modernists' attack on symmetry, historical styles and superficial ornamentation. The most positive contribution that Modernism had to make for landscape architecture, however, was the notion that function should be the starting point for design, rather than any preconceived idea of what is beautiful or picturesque, a shift from aesthetics towards the notion of usefulness.

Tunnard, Eckbo and Rose

Modernist landscape architecture found it hard to make headway in Britain, where naturalistic yearnings and horticultural traditions were strong, yet its first manifesto, *Gardens in the Modern Landscape,* was written in England in 1938 by Christopher Tunnard (who was, however, born in Canada). Tunnard's doctrines have three roots: the first is a functionalism taken directly from the Modern Movement in architecture; the second is his admiration for Japanese traditions in architecture and garden design; the third is the conception that a garden should be, in its entirety, a work of art.

Tunnard cites Adolph Loos and Le Corbusier in his initial attack on the academic styles, and promotes 'fitness for purpose' as the touchstone for a new kind of landscape architecture:

> It will be apparent . . . that the modern garden should be the logical outcome of the principle of economy in statement and the sociological necessities which have influenced modern architecture.
>
> (Tunnard, 1948: 75–76)

Tunnard argues for a stripped-down functional style which takes the needs of users as its departure point. Indeed he finds it necessary to chide Le Corbusier for a passage in *Precisions* in which the great rationalist betrays what Tunnard regards as a dangerously romantic form of nature worship. Le Corbusier's new town is set in a meadow where twenty blocks of housing tower above grazing cattle:

> Grass will border the roads; nothing will be disturbed – neither the trees, the flowers, nor the flocks and herds. The dwellers in these houses, drawn hence through love of the life of the countryside will be able to see it maintained intact from their hanging gardens or from their ample windows. Their domestic lives will be set within a Virgilian dream.
>
> (Tunnard, 1948: 78 [quoting Le Corbusier])

Tunnard however would prefer to see the meadows levelled and turned into recreation grounds. The landscape must be planned in accordance with human needs (Tunnard, 1948: 78). But notice that he does not suggest that the people should be consulted about their requirements.

Japanese design appealed to Modernists in its simplicity and functionalism. Tunnard notes that 'the Japanese come at the beautiful by the way of the necessary' (1948: 87). He finds that they are able to imbue even the most ordinary everyday objects with a spiritual quality. He finds in Japanese design an alternative to classical symmetry in the principle of 'occult balance' in which dissimilar objects can be counter-balanced in an asymmetrical design, and he maintains that the same principle is at work in modern architecture. Moreover, in oriental religions such as Shinto and Buddhism there is a sense of personal identification with Nature. He calls this the 'empathetic attitude' and finds it reflected in a unity of design between house and garden which also has parallels in Modern design. This attitude can also be seen to be compatible with the more humanistic theories within environmental ethics (to be discussed in Chapter 8), in that Tunnard is suggesting that the antagonistic, masterful attitude towards nature should be abandoned.

Tunnard's thinking is more convoluted when he comes to consider his third influence, modern abstract art. In places his opinions seem very close to those of Geoffrey Jellicoe (explored in Chapter 2) in that he would like to re-establish gardening as an art form. He suggests that most garden ornament, whether it be in the form of Italian stone benches or florid wrought iron gates, is anachronistic and should be removed. However, he does not seem able to embrace a rigorously functional aesthetic which might have no place for works of modern art as embellishment.

Tunnard attempted to apply his design philosophy to the design of gardens for a number of medium-sized country houses in England during the 1930s, including Serge Chermyeff's Bentley Wood in Sussex and his own home at St Ann's Hill, Chertsey (architect: Raymond McGrath), but he did not find Britain sympathetic towards Modernist experimentation. In 1939 he emigrated to the United States to teach initially at the Harvard Graduate School of Design, where Gropius was already teaching, and later as an associate professor of city planning at Yale. Lance Necker observes that many of the young American landscape designers who were to become influential after the Second World War – in particular the classmates, Garrett Eckbo, Dan Kiley and James Rose – gained their introduction to Modernist thought through contact with Tunnard in the design studio (Necker, 1993).

Eckbo's career as a designer began during the closing years of the Depression, when he worked for the Farm Security Administration from 1939–42, and was involved in the site planning for new settlements for farm workers. Influenced by Gropius and Tunnard at Harvard, he became an advocate of the need to address social issues through landscape design. His most important contribution to the theoretical literature is *Landscape for Living* (1950) which develops some of the themes explored in an earlier series of articles written by Rose for the magazine *Pencil Points* (predecessor of today's *Progressive Architecture*) in the late 1930s.

Rose's overriding concern was with the utility of spaces. Design, he argued, should not be about creating patterns in plan or contriving picturesque sequences. 'We cannot live in pictures, and therefore a landscape designed as a series of pictures robs us of an opportunity to use that area for animated living' (*Pencil Points*, November 1938). This emphasis on gardens as places in which to live, also led him to attack axial geometries: 'By selecting one or two axes, and developing a picture from a given station

Figure 6.3 Parks are for people: schoolchildren learning to be trees in New York's Central Park.

Figure 6.4 Parks are for people – and dogs too: canine toilet in a New York park, a great meeting place for pets and also for their owners.

point, we are losing an infinity of opportunities' (*Pencil Points*, October 1938).

Rose echoed Sullivan in arguing that form is something which develops out of consideration of the function to occur. There may be functional designs which are also symmetrical – such as a cinema auditorium – but we must never begin to design with any preconceived notions of form. Instead it is often wise to look to circulation – 'not an opportunity for persons to find their way around within an imposed pattern, but circulation as a structural part of design' – as the first guide to the creation of the more skilful arrangements 'for greater utility and for the expression of contemporary living' (*Pencil Points*, February 1939). This is the keystone of a functionalist value system, and once it is in place the values which have to be relegated are precisely those aesthetic ones which we examined at length in Chapter 2.

Rose was caustic about the role of plants as embellishments:

Ornamentation with plants in landscape design to create 'pictures' or picturesque effect means what ornamentation has always meant: the fate call of an outworn system of aesthetics. It has always been the closing chapter of an art with nothing more to say.

(*Pencil Points*, November 1938)

For Rose, plants must be considered as materials, the soft equivalents of bricks, steel or concrete; but just as these latter materials have their own characteristics, which should be expressed rather than disguised in the process of building, so too must the inherent characteristics of plant species be allowed to express themselves in a landscape design. Plants are not to be bullied, pruned or clipped to fit preconceived patterns – instead their natural habits must be a factor in the equation, alongside use and circulation, which ultimately determines the overall design.

The view of planting put forward by the Modernists is directly opposed to classical traditions, and opposed to romantic traditions to the extent that these are based upon pictorial composition, yet the scope for conflict is less with the latter since naturalistic design is sympathetic to the innate habits of plant species. For the same reasons, a reconciliation between the Modernist and ecological schools is possible, although Modernists were inclined to use plants in isolation or in single species groups, rather than assembled into ecological associations and communities.

Treib's six axioms of Modernist landscape architecture

Compared with the polemical outpourings of the architects, Modernism in landscape architecture was an altogether more tentative affair. Nevertheless, Marc Treib (1993), who has conducted an extensive investigation of the movement in America, is prepared to identify an 'imperfect, ill-formed and implicit manifesto'. This manifesto has six axioms which can be summarised as follows:

1 A denial of historical styles. Instead landscape expression derives from a rational approach to the conditions created by industrial society, the site and the programme.
2 A concern for space rather than pattern, deriving a model from contemporary architecture.
3 Landscapes are for people. Although addressed to a variety of purposes, landscape design ultimately concerns making outdoor places for human use.
4 The destruction of the axis. The modern landscape, perhaps influenced by cubist space, is multifaceted and omnidirectional.
5 Plants are used for their individual qualities as botanical entities and sculpture.
6 Integration of house and garden, not 'house-and-then-a-garden.'

It is doubtful if any of these is truly an axiom, in the strict sense of a statement which is accepted as self-evidently true. Numbers 1 and 3 are the strongest contenders, and they express an essentially functionalist credo. Axiom 3 embodies the essentially homocentric thrust of Modernism. Ultimately it is the usefulness of outdoor spaces for human beings that is to be the landscape architect's overriding concern. The first axiom states that this ultimate goal is to be achieved through rational means, implying a methodology which will have the objectivity of science.

Survey–analysis–design: a rational approach to landscape design

Ever since the first academic course in landscape architecture was established in Britain some fifty years ago, the orthodox approach to education has been based upon Survey–Analysis–Design, the so-called SAD methodology. Quite where this terminology entered into professional discourse is difficult to determine. Turner (*Landscape Design*, October 1991) suggests that SAD had its origins in the eighteenth century, but he does not elaborate. Lancelot Brown earned his nickname of 'Capability' by analysing sites for their 'capabilities' (Brown's synonym for potentialities), while Repton is famous for his Red Books in which he presented before-and-after drawings of his clients' estates. Both approaches could be said to follow a pattern of Survey–Analysis–Design.

Patrick Geddes, however, is the more direct progenitor of the SAD approach. The 'father of town and country planning' was also the first person in Britain to adopt the professional title of 'landscape architect'. At the turn of the century he advocated an approach which was encapsulated in the aphorism 'survey before plan'. How this metamorphosed into SAD does not seem to be recorded, but the approach became enshrined in the Landscape Institute's own examination system. Even today the SAD orthodoxy is the basis of much of British landscape education, although its adequacy has been questioned by many, and it has been completely rejected by some.

SAD seems to be least problematic where large-scale landscape planning projects are concerned. Ian McHarg's influential *Design with Nature* (1969) essentially refines SAD and introduces the powerful tool of suitability analysis (a form of overlay sieving), which has, in turn, influenced much contemporary work in GIS applications. However, the inadequacies of SAD become more apparent when the work in hand is towards the more creative, intuitive end of the design-planning continuum. We must examine some of the objections to it, but this is better done within the context of an overall critique of functionalism, and to this we turn next.

What is wrong with functionalism?

David Pye, formerly the Professor of Furniture Design at the Royal College of Art, argues that the whole edifice of functionalist aesthetics is based upon a fiction (Pye, 1978). Function implies purpose, but objects only have the purposes that people assign to them. Plato was wrong to say that the essential

function of a knife is to cut; the same object might be used to whittle tent pegs, peel an apple or spread jam. Pye agrees that for an object to attain a given end, there will be some basic arrangement of parts and some essential geometric relationships must obtain, the materials used must be strong enough, and it must be possible to access the object for use (these four requirements he calls the *requirements of use*), but beyond this the designer has enormous freedom to determine form.

The purpose behind Pye's assault on functionalism is to re-establish the importance of the requirement of appearance, and to reinstate workmanship to a place of honour and importance. He provocatively refers to workmanship as 'useless work', but denies that useless means ineffectual:

> 'Design', to many who practise it, must mean, simply and solely, useless work. Nothing they do is concerned with the requirements of use, economy, and access. Such are graphic designers, designers of printed textiles, of decoration on pottery, wallpapers and similar things. To engineers, designers for industries, architects, and naval architects, 'design' means something quite different; yet in all the things they design useless work is invariably done and sometimes a great deal of it.
>
> (Pye, 1978: 77)

Landscape architects do not feature in Pye's list, but clearly they would be included in his argument. They would lie somewhere in the middle of his design continuum; like architects and engineers they have a responsibility towards clients and users to make their landscapes functional and safe, but, like graphic and textile designers, they pay great attention to the aesthetics of their designs. Pye's conclusion is that both function and aesthetics are essential to design, but that one cannot be reduced to the other.

While Pye's defence of aesthetic requirements reads like a rearguard action against the aesthetics of functionalism, more recent critics have suggested not only that Modernism is misguided, but that the whole rationalistic edifice that has dominated Western thinking since the Renaissance is also flawed.

The reductionist, materialist and mechanical model of science has come under attack from philosophers of science and scientists themselves. Relativity and quantum mechanics overturned the

Newtonian model of matter in space behaving like billiard balls on a table. They also undermined the idea of the totally objective observer independent of the events observed. Meanwhile, Popper convinced many scientists that they could never conclusively prove anything; instead science advances by devising the best hypotheses to fit the observed facts, then attempting to *disprove* them. Kuhn similarly showed that science advances by replacing one model of reality with another that has more explanatory force. These developments have left the door open to the argument that science is a social construction; what is to count as a 'fact' depends upon the collective decisions of a community of scientists. This is to overstate the case, but nevertheless science is a lot less certain than it used to be.[7] As a result the Modernist ideal of basing design decisions upon hard scientific evidence also looks shaky.

The death of Modernism

In his 'Modern Movements in Architecture', Charles Jencks (1995) dates the death of Modernism to the dynamiting of the Pruitt–Igoe flats in St Louis in 1972, a Modern housing scheme based upon the theories of Le Corbusier and the Congrès Internationaux d'Architecture Moderne (CIAM) which had proved to be a social catastrophe. The collapse of the Ronan Point block had a similar impact upon the British psyche. But if Modernism was dead, what was to replace it? To revert overnight to an interest in historical styles and ornamentation would have caused architects too much psychological discomfort. They had to find a way of reassuming former ways without ignoring or belittling the corpus of Modernist work and theory. The way out of this bind was Post-Modernism, an architectural style which took on the historical styles, but in an ironic, knowing manner. Jencks identified the Post-Modern building as one which possessed a 'double-coding'; on one level it was Modern, yet it was also something else: vernacular, revivalist, contextual or metaphorical. Eclectic architecture was back in fashion.

We must be careful with the term 'Post-Modern' however. Capitalised in this manner it refers to an architectural style, but spelt 'post-Modern' we are talking about an epoch, not a style, and spelt 'postmodern' it can refer to a social condition, a broadly based cultural movement or even a world-view. Post-Modernism in architecture was just a particularly visible manifestation of postmodernism as a cultural phenomenon, one which also made itself felt in areas as diverse as fiction, literary criticism, product design, geography and town planning. Postmodernism rejects the idea of a totalising world-view and seeks to embrace pluralism. Uncertainty is certainly part of the postmodern condition, and at worst this can degenerate into relativism or nihilism. More positively, in design it can result in playful experimentation.

To complicate matters, the movement known as Deconstructivism or Deconstruction followed swiftly upon Post-Modernism. This was a more aggressive creature, determined to tear down structures in an attempt to understand them, a mission which soon became an assault on all symbolic meanings and conventions. Deconstruction is a postmodern movement, but it is possible, in architecture, to distinguish it from the style known as Post-Modernism. In landscape architecture there are too few postmodern practitioners of any note to make such discriminations worth while.

However, there is at least one paradigmatic piece of postmodern landscape design and this is Bernard Tschumi's design for the Parc de la Villette in Paris. According to Tschumi, his design for La Villette superimposes (randomly, if he is to be believed) three ordering systems: a point grid of 'folies', a path system which consists both of axes and a meandering circuit called the *Promenade Cinématique*, and a spatial system based upon the formal geometries of the square, circle and triangle used in an unconventional way. Tschumi has claimed that he actively pursued fragmentation and 'madness' (Tschumi, 1987). In fact La Villette functions rather well; dead-straight covered walkways give easy and direct access and one of them links the two main buildings, the 'folies' distribute facilities evenly throughout the park, while the lazy promenade allows visitors to explore in a leisurely way.

Many of the things of which postmodernists and deconstructivists seem to approve would seem to be the mere opposites of Modernist values. Thus artificiality replaces honesty in materials, playfulness replaces seriousness of purpose, complexity replaces simplicity, and so on. In the same vein, one might expect design self-indulgence to have usurped social responsibility, and critics of postmodernism would say that this has indeed happened. Modernism

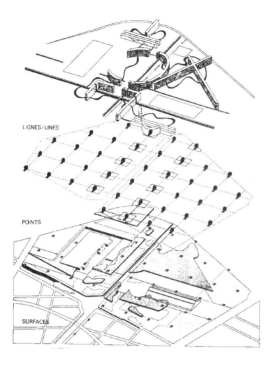

Figure 6.5 La Villette: superimposition of points/lines/surfaces, 1982.

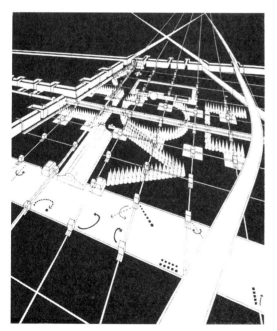

Figure 6.6 La Villette: computer perspective (1983): 'madness serves as a constant point of reference throughout the urban park of la Villette because it appears to illustrate a characteristic state at the end of the twentieth century – that of disjunctions and dissociation between use, form and social values', Bernard Tschumi, *Cinegram Folie,* 1987.

adopted a technically elitist view – plans drawn from God's-Eye viewpoints were supposed to be objective prescriptions for rationally perfectible worlds. Postmodernists may have rejected the viewpoint, but they seem to have replaced it with the elitism of a knowing *cognoscenti.*

However, to see the change from Modernism to postmodernism as the substitution of one set of values for another is to miss an important implication of the shift towards pluralism. Unlike Modernists, postmodernists *cannot* claim to have discovered a set of universal values, since they are committed to the idea that there are diverse sources of value. Postmodern social science recognises the existence of a plurality of different groups, each with different 'lifeworlds' or views of reality and different sets of values. Some groups are powerful, others are marginalised or excluded. In complex societies there need to be ways in which values and objectives can be negotiated, and the concerns of the less powerful given voice. As we shall see, where these issues concern the environment, landscape architects and planners may find themselves holding the ring.

Our principal interest in the rest of this chapter will be in just those social purposes which Modernism and City Beautiful design pushed out of view, but we must undertake some reconnaissance in the fields of social and political theory before we can take this investigation much further.

Ethics and political theory

Political theories rest upon conceptions of what is moral behaviour, of how we should behave towards one another. The two great traditions which underlie much political thought and public policy, particularly in the West, are utilitarianism, classically expounded in the nineteenth century by Jeremy Bentham and John Stuart Mill, and the deontological approach (from the Greek word for 'duty') which was forcefully argued by Immanuel Kant.

Utilitarianism is a consequentialist ethics. The rightness or wrongness of an action does not depend upon the nature of the act itself but upon its outcome. For Bentham and Mill the outcome which was universally desirable was the greatest happiness of the greatest number. A more sophisticated version of the theory requires people to choose between their preferences and to put them in order of rank. It can readily be seen that utilitarianism has much in common with market economics, where people must make choices between various goods with the aim of maximising their satisfactions.

Huge swathes of public policy are also determined along utilitarian lines. When government has to decide whether to build a new road or protect a beautiful landscape, a utilitarian calculus comes into play. Which will bring the greatest increase in total happiness: the road or the landscape? Several of my interviewees echoed a claim often made by landscape architects that it is their purpose to harmonise development with the landscape or with the environment. Behind this lies the utilitarian assumption that the greatest overall benefit lies in allowing the development to proceed, but only with 'amelioration' measures which will minimise the loss of other sources of happiness, such as pleasant views. Of course the difficulty lies in assessing such different sources of happiness. Because happiness is notoriously difficult to measure, attempts are made to translate all goods into the same form so that comparisons can be made. The surrogate usually chosen is money, hence it can be seen that utilitarian thinking lies behind all the recent efforts of environmental economists to weigh aesthetic or environmental benefits in monetary terms.

Utilitarianism appeals to policy-makers because it seems to offer a decision procedure, and because it seems inherently democratic. Since, in the utilitarian calculus each individual counts equally, the rightness and wrongness of actions is determined by the manner in which they affect the majority. The Modern Movement was essentially utilitarian as the language used by the founders of the CIAM in 1928 clearly demonstrates. They demanded the 'reduction of certain individual needs' in order to 'foster the maximum satisfaction of the needs of the greatest number'.

However, critics of utilitarianism point out that there are some acts which seem wrong, regardless of their outcomes in terms of overall happiness.[8] An example can be given from environmental ethics:

In recent years, many environmentalists have fought to prevent logging in the old-growth forests of the Pacific Northwest. Logging activities were threatening to destroy the habitat of the spotted owl, an endangered species. The spotted owl was threatened with extinction if logging continued. On the other hand, signifi-

cant social benefits would follow from a growth in the logging industry. Because the owl has no known use and because it does not contribute to society in any obvious way, a utilitarian calculation might suggest that the logging be allowed. However, environmentalists charged that causing the extinction of a species is wrong in principle, even if doing so would result in a net increase in beneficial social consequences.

(Des Jardins, 1997: 26–27)

The alternative mainstream tradition in ethics, deontology, is based upon notions of rights and duties. In this tradition, individuals are held responsible for their acts in themselves, not for the consequences that may follow from them. This seems reasonable, for surely we can only be brought to book for things we can control? The consequences of our actions may be impossible to predict. Kant believed that we had a fundamental ethical duty to treat people as *ends* rather than as *means*. This duty falls upon all human beings, which means that each one of us has the right to be treated by others as an *end*, not a *means*. The whole language of human rights and civil liberties was generated by this insight. Kantian ethics serve as a check upon the tyranny of the majority, which might prevail under a purely utilitarian system of governance.

However, the view of society inherent in a rights-based ethics is an atomistic one of autonomous individuals contracting together, but only if they choose to and only in their own interests. One of the problems with this is that some individuals, such as slaves, children, the mentally ill, or women, have historically been excluded from the contract. These injustices may have been remedied to a large extent, but some environmentalists argue that plants, animals, ecosystems and even natural features like islands or lakes should now be given moral standing. As things stand it is doubtful whether the spotted owls mentioned above have rights. This is a matter to which we will return in Chapter 8. Neo-liberals tend to believe in this atomistic view of human life (Margaret Thatcher famously said that there was no such thing as society), but for the philosopher, Mary Midgley, biological science provides better metaphors for human society than outmoded notions of physics:

Leaves relate not only to other leaves, but to fruit, twigs, branches and the whole tree. People appear not only as individuals but as members of their groups, families, tribes, species, eco-systems, and biosphere, and have moral relations to these wholes.

(Midgley 1995: 92)

The sociological perspective

Both of the main traditions considered thus far have taken free and equal, autonomous individuals as their starting point, but it is clear that individuals are not equal in the talents they are born with nor in the opportunities offered to them by their station at birth. Neo-liberals shrug and say that is the way the world will always be. Competition between individuals is part of the natural order, they say, but fortunately this competition serves society well overall (a utilitarian argument, of course). It was this belief in the efficacy of markets and competition which generated the largely discredited 'trickle-down' theory of the 1980s. Opponents of this view argue that the disadvantages which people suffer in life are not unavoidable facts of nature at all. They are produced by social forces.

Max Weber, writing at the turn of the century, saw society divided into social classes and noted that these discriminations were not the result of personal striving but were largely accidents of birth (Healey, 1997). Social life is not just a competition between individuals, or even between groups. It is a game played on an uneven field, in which those with higher social positions are able to maintain control of the best situations. It has been suggested that the whole of the British planning system has a class bias, in that it is largely a mechanism for the protection of the countryside and with it the privileged lifestyle of a landed elite (Williams, 1975; Marsden *et al.*, 1993). If this is a fair criticism of planning, it may also apply to the activities of landscape architects, many of whom have been involved in the designation of protected landscapes, but I doubt whether anyone who was interviewed for this book would be willing to accept the reproach. Most saw their main task to be the improvement of conditions within towns and cities, some were involved in increasing access to the countryside for city dwellers, while those who set great store by the protection of countryside believed that they were doing it as much for those who might visit from towns as for the people who lived there.

Marxism suggested that the inequalities and injustices of the class system were produced by the relationship of the various classes to the ownership of the means of production. Conflict within the system was inevitable because workers had different interests to capitalists. Marx predicted that the supposed contradictions within capitalism would inevitably lead to its collapse. Marxism becomes an ethical theory when this hypothesis is turned into an injunction to hasten the process through revolution. Once capitalism is overthrown it will be replaced by a true socialism in which the power of the state will wither.

For Marxists, tinkering around with the built form of cities, as might planners, urban designers or landscape architects, is about as significant as the proverbial rearrangement of deck chairs on the *Titanic*. It does nothing to bring the downfall of capitalism closer. Indeed, if it is seen as offering the working class palliatives in the form of better housing or more parks it can even be characterised as an impediment to the formation of the class consciousness necessary for a revolution. For environmental design professionals such an analysis is disabling. It can offer a theory which explains the inequalities and injustices of society, but cannot offer a prescription for them, or at least not one which would fall within a professional ambit rather than appear on a revolutionary manifesto.

In the present era such ideas have an anachronistic ring. The division of society into just two blocks, workers and the bourgeoisie, is seen to overlook the myriad differences in interests that characterise our pluralistic society, while the demise of capitalism seems more remote than it has been for decades. Polarisation, however, is still in full swing, as evidenced by the rise in homelessness and social exclusion. Meanwhile, in those countries which had communist revolutions, the predicted withering away of the state did not happen. Instead the cadres which led the revolutions metamorphosed into elite governing classes who lost touch with the people they had once championed. As for the role of planning and design it is clear that this is every bit as necessary in a post-revolutionary socialist state as it is in a pre-revolutionary capitalist one. Good environmental design has relevance to people's everyday lives under whatever political and economic system they may live.

Landscape architects, as we shall see in the next chapter, believe that by changing people's environments they can improve their lives. This is almost a necessary article of faith. However, the relationship between environment and behaviour is a very complex one, and professionals need to maintain a critical stance towards their own interventions. To illustrate this we can consider the vexed issue of 'designing out crime'.

Crime, safety and environmental determinism

During the 1980s the British geographer Alice Coleman suggested that it was possible to reduce crime by altering the layout and design of housing areas[9] (Coleman, 1985). Her work amounted to an indictment of many 'Modern' forms of architecture, such as deck-access flats, and approbation for the conventional suburban street with gardens to the front and rear of the dwellings. While she regarded both fully public and fully private space as naturally self-policing, she was very critical of some forms of semi-public space, particularly that which she labelled 'confused', which was shared by too many people to permit self-policing. Outsiders could not be distinguished from residents. Her ideas were welcomed by a right-wing government which did not wish to look for wider social causes for worsening crime figures, but critics accused Coleman of a simplistic environmental determinism. Nevertheless the idea that good design can reduce crime has persisted, and was mentioned by several of my interviewees, particularly those who had worked in inner-city housing areas. There is, doubtless, some truth in it. Research has linked opportunities for criminal behaviour to Prospect and Refuge Theory (see Chapter 2). People feel threatened where they cannot see an obvious escape route, while would-be assailants take comfort in the sort of concealment afforded by dense shrub planting or poor lighting (Fischer and Clarke, 1992).

Meanwhile Jacquie Burgess and her collaborators have used focus groups to discover attitudes to both urban greenspace of various kinds (Burgess *et al.*, 1988; Burgess, 1994a) and to urban fringe woodlands (Burgess, 1994b). In the urban situation they found that while people have an intense desire for contact with nature, and that oak woodlands were preferred to semi-wild scrubland, managed parkland, or (least favoured of all) closely mown common, the landscapes people said they liked were, paradoxically, those that could also be most threatening. This was borne out by the woodland study which discovered some important gender differences. While men were generally not afraid of being mugged, most women said that they would be afraid to go in the woods alone. For most white women, one companion would be enough to allay these fears, but the women from ethnic groups said that they would need to be in larger groups in order to feel secure.

Such findings make the landscape architect's axiomatic belief in the efficacy of planting to improve life in urban situations somewhat problematic. There is sufficient evidence to prove that people link dense planting to possible danger. It hardly matters that this fear may be unfounded, for fear of crime can be as socially disabling as crime itself. The onus is upon the landscape architect to take notice of these concerns. Consultation is essential in these circumstances. The landscape architect has to respond to genuine concerns, but, equally, must fairly represent other values in the situation. Is the knee-jerk removal of soft landscape the best policy, or will it contribute to a general appearance of decline which will, in the longer term, make the social situation even worse? Good design requires dialogue. This is our next concern.

Collaborative planning and design

Many urban commentators now regard the Marxian analysis given above as too simple. In characterising the social order in terms of homogenised classes and 'us-and-them' relations, it has missed the complexity of social existence. Rather than all power arising from the spheres of political and economic organisation, there are other sources of power 'characterised not by the language of material inequality but by concern with domination, with oppression and limitation and with obvious and subtle forms of discrimination and exclusion' (Healey, 1997: 117). Much of the transformation in the debate can be attributed to powerful feminist critiques, but there have been other articulate and effective pressure groups, in particular those representing people from minority ethnic groups and people with disabilities.

In the 1960s an American planner, Paul Davidoff, suggested that the planning system should be radically changed and democratised (Davidoff, 1965). Rather than allowing a centralised bureaucracy staffed by technically trained planners to impose their unitary plans upon the citizenry, various groups with an interest in the outcome should be encouraged to produce their own plans, and assisted in doing so by professional planners – so there might be a plan for the shopkeepers, a plan for single mothers, a plan for the elderly, and so on. Planners would act as 'advocates' for these different visions which would be resolved in a quasi-legal process. While Davidoff's ideas had a limited impact upon planning systems, they were influential in changing planning education and in recasting the way in which planners thought of themselves.

In Britain the Royal Town Planning Institute instigated Planning Aid, whereby community groups could receive advice from professional planners on how best to make their voices heard when engaging with the planning process. In a parallel development, architects inspired by Rod Hackney's entrepreneurial approach to community architecture[10] formed a Community Architecture Group within the Royal Institute of British Architects (RIBA), and the cause was taken up by Prince Charles in the mid-1980s. Community Technical Aid Centres (CTACs) emerged as an alternative to private practices involved in community architecture. Usually formed as limited companies with charitable status, CTACs provide their communities with the services of architects, planners, landscape architects and graphic designers. They cater for groups which traditionally have been denied access to technical and professional expertise (Rook, 1989).

Landscape architects have also emerged as key professionals in the locally based Groundwork Trusts, the first of which was formed in 1981 in St Helens and Knowsley under the auspices of the Countryside Commission. There are now forty-two Trusts affiliated to the Birmingham-based Groundwork Foundation. The Groundwork philosophy promotes partnerships between the community, the private sector, the voluntary sector and local and national authorities. Freed to some extent from the rigours of local authority financial systems (which often demand that designers must spend their budgets before the end of the financial year or lose them altogether), Groundwork Trusts have often been able to engage in close, long-term community collaborations, though it must also be said that many Groundwork schemes have been quite small in scale.

Meanwhile, planning theorists like John Forester (1980) and Patsy Healey (1997) have sought to find a new theoretical rationale for mainstream planning practice, basing their ideas on the work of the German philosopher and social theorist Jürgen Habermas. Forester's suggestions for a new approach to planning practice could also be applied to landscape architectural practice. Landscape architects reading this could try substituting 'landscape architecture' for 'planning' in the following passage:

> By recognising planning practice as normatively role-structured communicative action which distorts, covers up, or reveals to the public the prospects and possibilities they face, a critical theory of planning aids us practically and ethically as well. This is the contribution of critical theory to planning: pragmatics with vision – to reveal true alternatives, to correct false expectations, to counter cynicism, to foster inquiry, to spread political responsibility, engagement and action. Critical planning practice, technically skilled and politically sensitive, is an organizing and democratizing practice.
>
> (Forester, 1980: 277)

Peter Hall, commenting on this, thinks that if 'collaborative planning' and 'communicative action' are stripped of their Germanic philosophical justifications they come out as old-fashioned democratic common sense. The prescription is to

> cultivate community networks, listen carefully to people, involve the less organised groups, educate the citizens on how to join in, supply information and make sure people know how to get it, develop skills in working with groups in conflict situations, emphasise the need to participate, compensate for external pressures.
>
> (Hall, 1988: 339–340)

Participatory design

There is an extensive literature on participation in planning and design, much of it dating from the 1970s when the political concerns of the late 1960s began to influence professional practice. Those who studied this development soon realised that public participation could be a very uneven process, rather like a layer cake in which the thinnest layer is made up of the most active participants. It was noted that low-income citizens were less likely to participate than those from higher socio-economic categories. Attention shifted to those groups who were not given, or could not find, a voice in participatory activities. Leonie Sandercock and Ann Forsyth (1992), writing from a feminist perspective, note that we cannot assume that all groups are able to articulate their interests in equal manner: 'Given the current socialisation of women, particularly women who suffer multiple disadvantages because of class, race, education, health and self-esteem, this simply may not be the case' (Sandercock and Forsyth, 1992: 51).

They cite the experience of one feminist planner who had great difficulty in encouraging women to speak at neighbourhood meetings. She responded to this problem by asking people to sit in small groups and tell a story about their neighbourhood. In this setting people had no difficulty in speaking out about their lives and community and previously silent or hesitant participants joined in.

Conducting participatory exercises is clearly a highly skilled business. It is perhaps not surprising that some designers see the public as 'a professional hazard'. This jibe is taken from an article by Judy Rosener in which she observes that for many public officials 'the involvement of citizens is viewed as being time-consuming, inefficient, irrational and not very productive' (Langton, 1978: 113). Although these remarks were written twenty years ago, these attitudes are still common. Some of the designers whose views are described in Chapter 7 thought that public participation was largely a waste of their time. Some thought it was extremely hard work, though important in many projects and essential in some. What then are the purposes and benefits of public participation?

For Henry Sanoff (Neary *et al*. 1995: 110–111) there are two main purposes. The first is to involve citizens in design and planning, thus increasing their trust and confidence and making it more likely that they will accept whatever designs, plans or decisions that are forthcoming. There is some degree of social control involved, in the sense that those in authority would prefer the public to work within the system to find solutions. The second is to provide citizens with a voice in design and planning in order to improve the eventual quality of the designs and plans that are produced.

There are benefits in this process for all concerned. From the social perspective, the consultative process should increase the probability of the users' needs being met and thus reduce the likelihood of

resources being squandered on inappropriate work. The individuals involved in the process will also benefit in less tangible ways, including a sense of empowerment and greater understanding of the way in which decisions about their local environment are made.

For the designer, public participation can be seen as a means of obtaining the best possible brief from the eventual users of the landscape and accessing information about the site and the community which could easily be overlooked in any conventional sort of site survey. Participation should also provide a very rich source of design inspiration. Perhaps the most satisfactory aspect, from the designer's point of view, is the knowledge that a scheme produced in a collaborative manner is going to have a far greater chance of long-term success than one which has simply been imposed.

Figure 6.7 Schoolchildren help to plan the future of the Ridgway Canal with Groundwork Black Country (see also Chapter 7). (Courtesy of Groundwork Black Country.)

Figure 6.8 Public exhibition, Bold Moss, organised by Groundwork St Helens, Sefton and Knowsley (see also Chapter 7). (Courtesy Groundwork St Helens, Sefton and Knowsley.)

A cynic might say that the benefits of public participation exercises accrue to the authorities that initiate them, by providing them with an instrument to achieve their own goals without transferring any real power. Sherry Arnstein, writing the year after the revolutionary student protests in France, suggested a ladder of participatory processes which had palliatives at the bottom and citizen control in the highest position (Arnstein, 1969).

Without going into a rung-by-rung critique of this model, I would suggest that for most designers public participation is best regarded as a partnership whereby the professional and the client-users collaborate to produce the best possible solution for the design problems set by the brief. My interviewees were somewhat divided on the question of who should have the final say. Some thought this should be the designer – this was their responsibility, what they got paid for. Others were clear that the users should have the final word. It was a nonsense to consult, if one was not prepared to follow the wishes of the public as revealed in the consultation. The truth probably lies somewhere between these positions. A certain decisiveness is required of the designer. Some conflicts between participants may be impossible to resolve. In such cases designers must take their lead from the wishes of the majority and seek to bring the process to a conclusion. On the other hand, the exercise will clearly have been futile if the designer imposes a solution which is not supported by the consensus.

If we accept that public participation is a desirable goal, the question of the most appropriate form of participation next arises. Writing at the end of the 1970s, perhaps the heyday of participatory theory, Rosener lists an alarming thirty-nine different ways of conducting the exercise. Time has whittled her list down somewhat, and the jargon has also shifted. We can reject some on the grounds that they are not genuinely empowering. From the remainder we can identify those which seem most appropriate to the role of the landscape architect. Another source has been *The Guide to Effective Participation* (Wilcox, 1994), which has an excellent A–Z compendium of topics and methods for participation. I would propose the following list, which I have sought to authenticate by cross-checking with the techniques mentioned by professionals during the course of my interviews.

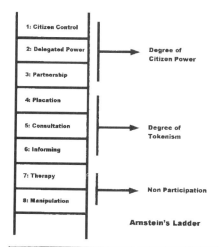

Wilcox (1994) offers the following explanations.

8 Manipulation and 7 Therapy. Both are non participative. The aim is to cure or educate the participants. The proposed plan is best and the job of participation is to achieve public support by public relations.

6 Informing. A most important first step to legitimate participation. But too frequently the emphasis is on a one way flow of information. No channel for feedback.

5 Consultation. Again a legitimate step - attitude surveys, neighbourhood meetings and public enquiries. But Arnstein feels this is just window dressing ritual.

4 Placation. For example, co-option of hard-picked "worthies" onto committees. It allows citizens to advise or plan ad infinitum but retains power holders the right to judge the legitimacy or feasibility of the advice.

3 Partnership. Power is in fact redistributed through negotiation between citizens and power holders. Planning decision-making responsibilities are shared e.g. through joint committees.

2 Delegated Power. Citizens holding a clear majority of seats on committees with delegated powers to make decisions. Public now has the power to assure accountability of the programme to them.

1 Citizen Control. Have-nots handle the entire job of planning policy making and managing a programme e.g. neighbourhood corporation with no intermediaries between it and the source of funds.

Figure 6.9 Arnstein's Ladder; this version is taken from Wilcox (1994).

Methods of public participation

Charrette

The word '*charrette*' is French for 'pushcart'. In design circles it has come to refer to a type of time-limited brainstorming exercise (Condon, 1996: 11). The word was coined by members of the School of Architecture at the École des Beaux-Arts in Paris at the end of the nineteenth century. At the end of a difficult design exercise a *charrette* would be trundled past the drawing boards. Finished or not, the students' projects had to be thrown into the cart. To miss it was to fail.

The word is now used of various kinds of idea-generating activity in which designers take the leading part, though other interest groups (which might include governmental organisations, community groups and business representatives) may participate. The parties convene for intense, interactive meetings, which in some cases may last for several days or even weeks.

One form of *charrette* is the RUDAT (Regional/Urban Design Action Team),[11] an idea pioneered by the American Institute of Architects in the late 1960s and still widely used. These involve bringing in a team of outside experts to a town or city for a lengthy brainstorming exercise (see, for example, Peter Fischer's involvement at Blackburn in Chapter 7). However, these exercises often involve professionals to a greater extent than local people and therefore cannot always be regarded as fully participatory.

Workshops

These are similar to *charrettes* in that they bring together professionals and other stakeholders, particularly users, to discuss a technical or design issue thoroughly, though they are generally more focused and more time-limited. They can, of course, be linked in series to form a more continuous participatory process.

Planning-for-Real

This is a powerful technique promoted by the Telford-based Neighbourhood Initiatives Foundation. The method is really a development of the design workshop approach in which individuals and groups are brought together to make decisions about their neighbourhood or a particular site by building a three-dimensional model which is then exhibited locally and forms the basis for further participatory group design work. This method, or variations upon it, has found great favour with landscape architects, particularly those working in the public and voluntary sectors.

Design game

Developed by Community Land and Workshop Services, this is similar to Planning-for-Real in that a scale plan of the site is used, together with pieces, drawn to scale, representing, for instance, play or sports facilities, which are moved around by the participants. A fairly large number of people can thus be involved in a complex design process.

Public meetings

These are an efficient way to inform communities about initiatives in their area and to obtain some general feedback. They are, however, subject to all kinds of difficulties. They can easily be dominated by articulate minorities while less confident participants are cowed into silence. While it may be important to hold public meetings, particularly when one is seeking general approval for a stage of design and a brief to proceed with the next, much of the fine-grain discussion, explanation, negotiation and consensus-building involved in participatory design may be easier to accomplish with smaller groups.

Steering group

Here the designer, or design team, is answerable to a committee made up of representatives of the users. Regular meetings are held throughout the design and implementation stages of the process. At its best, this method of working can be genuinely empowering in that the eventual users of the scheme effectively become the client.

Focus group(s)

Quantitative methods of measuring public opinion, such as the questionnaire survey, can be criticised on two main grounds. First, by restricting the range of questions and therefore the possible answers, issues are likely to be skewed towards those which are of most concern to the questionnaire designer. Issues that are important to the people being surveyed may be totally overlooked. Second, the nature of the process restricts interaction between the design professional and those for whom he or she is designing. An alternative is a qualitative approach based on small discussion groups, where people can voice their aspirations and concerns in their own terms, while the informal nature of such meetings should encourage the development of understanding and trust. The composition of the groups can be devised to explore issues of concern to particular groups, e.g. young single mothers, the elderly, people with disabilities, etc.

Community forum

This is a regular meeting of community activists (including interest groups such as local businesses, religious groups, etc.). A forum is a good means of highlighting issues and generating discussion, but without some other, more ends-directed, organisation, it may not be able to turn discussion into action.

The legacy of Functionalism

Cultural movements swing wildly from excess to extreme and babies are forever being dispatched with bathwater. In particular the reappraisal of Functional*ism* as an ideology and an aesthetic does not mean that we have to jettison functionality as a positive value. Indeed, as the interviews with practitioners discussed in the following chapter reveal, the idea that a design should function well is still central to most designers' concepts of good design, and it is hard to imagine many clients paying-out fees or designs that do not work, that create problems rather than solve them. The emphasis upon madness and folly in some deconstructivist writing takes matters too far, and will, I believe, be a transient phenomenon. The more valuable aspect of the postmodern turn is the rejection of universalising ideology in favour of a value-pluralism which recognises the differences amongst people. What seems to be required is a more subtle and responsive kind of utilitarianism, tempered by considerations of individual rights, which takes the variety of human needs and aspirations into account, and does not close down opportunities for imagination and creative expression.

Negotiating values

It is a premise of this book that all landscape architects hold a varied set of values drawn from the aesthetic, the social and the ecological spheres. While these values may be mutually supportive, situations may arise when they are in conflict. If an individual designer believes that the social aspects of his job are very significant and that consultation is important, then that designer's situation becomes correspondingly more complicated, for now he must not only reconcile his own conflicting values but must give particular weight to the values of others. It is this which turns consultation into a dialogue and a negotiation, a two-way flow of ideas and information. In the following chapter we will learn how the practitioners themselves view this complex activity.

Notes

1 George-Eugène Haussmann's reconstruction of Paris under Napoleon III was undertaken for military as much as for aesthetic ends. He was assisted by an engineer and landscape designer named Adolph Alphand.

2 In *The Death of Nature*, Carolyn Merchant has demonstrated how mechanistic metaphors have dominated the Western worldview for the last 300 years (San Francisco, Harper and Row, 1980).

3 See N. Pevsner (1936) *Pioneers of the Modern Movement*, reissued in 1949 with amendments as *Pioneers of Modern Design*. Also his *Sources of Modern Architecture and Design*, Thames and Hudson, London, 1968.

4 See 'The Tall Office Building Artistically Considered' by Louis Henri Sullivan, *Lippincott's Magazine*, March 1896.

5 Tony Garnier in *The Builder*, lxxx, 1901: 98.

6 Le Corbusier developed his proportioning system during the 1940s. It was published as *The Modulor: A Harmonious Measure to the Human Scale Universally Applied to Architecture and Mechanics* in 1948. A second volume, *Modulor II*, appeared in 1954. It was a system based in part upon the mathematics of the Golden Section and Fibonacci Series and in part upon a standard or ideal notion of the human figure.

7 Undoubtedly the attack on scientific rationality, championed by many postmodern French philosophers and cultural theorists, has been carried much too far. Alan Sokal and Jean Bricmont have led a devastating (and enormously entertaining) counter-attack on behalf of the scientists. Read their *Intellectual Impostures*, Profile Books, London, 1998.

8 An example I was given as a philosophy student concerned a sheriff in a town in the American South who had arrested a black man on suspicion of raping a white woman. Outside the jail was an angry lynch mob demanding that he should hand over the accused for summary execution. If he did not, they assured him that they would burn down the black quarter of the town, possibly killing many innocent people. The sheriff, no racist, but a good student of J.S. Mill, duly handed over the suspect. This strikes most people as wrong!

9 Coleman's work closely resembles the earlier investigations carried out in America by Oscar Newman, and reported in his 1972 book *Defensible Space: Crime Prevention and Urban Design*, Macmillan, New York.

10 Hackney's involvement in community architecture began in Macclesfield in 1971 when he organised his neighbours to fight the proposed demolition of their terraced houses. By 1987 he was heading a £4 million a year business with twenty regional offices, and had successfully defeated the official candidate to become President of the RIBA.

11 There are also UDATs (Urban Design Action Teams).

Bibliography

Arnstein, S. (1969) 'The Ladder of Citizen Participation', *Journal of the Institute of American Planners*, 35(4): 216–224.

Burgess, J. (1994a) *The Politics of Trust: Reducing Fear in Urban*

Parks, Working Paper No. 8, Comedia/Demos Study, 'The Future of Parks and Open Spaces'.

Burgess, J. (1994b) *Growing in Confidence: Research into Understanding People's Perceptions of the Urban Fringe*, Technical Document, Countryside Commision, Cheltenham.

Burgess, J., Harrison, C.M. *et al.* (1988) 'People, Parks and the Urban Green: A Study of Popular Meanings and Values for Open Spaces in the City', *Urban Studies*, 25: 455–473.

Coleman, A. (1985) *Utopia on Trial*, H. Shipman, London.

Condon, P. (1996) *Sustainable Urban Landscapes: the Surrey Design Charrette*, University of British Columbia, Vancouver.

Davidoff, P. (1965) 'Advocacy and Pluralism in Planning', *Journal of the American Institute of Planners*, XXI(4), November: 331–338.

Des Jardins, J.R. (1997) *Environmental Ethics: An Introduction to Environmental Philosophy* (2nd edn), Wadsworth Publishing Company, Belmont, California.

Fischer, B.S. and Clarke, R.V. (1992) 'Fear of Crime in Relation to Three Exterior Sites: Prospect Refuge and Escape', *Environment and Behaviour*, 24(1): 35–65.

Forester, J. (1980) 'Critical Theory and Planning Practice', *Journal of the American Planning Association*, 46: 275–286.

Hall, P. (1988) *Cities of Tomorrow*, Blackwell, Oxford.

Healey, P. (1997) *Collaborative Planning: Shaping Places in Fragmented Societies*, Macmillan, Houndsmills, England.

Hogarth, W. ([1753] 1971) *The Analysis of Beauty, Written with a View of Fixing the Fluctuating Ideas of Taste*, Scolar Press, Menston, England.

Jencks, C. (1995) *The Architecture of the Jumping Universe*, Academy Editions, London.

Langton, S. (1978) *Citizen Participation in America: Essays on the State of the Art*, Lexington Books, Lexington, Mass.

McHarg, I. (1969) *Design with Nature*, The Natural History Press, Garden City, New York.

Marsden, T. *et al.* (1993) *Constructing the Countryside*, UCL Press, London.

Midgley, M. (1995) 'Duties Concerning Islands', in R. Elliot, ed., *Environmental Ethics*, Oxford Readings in Philosophy, Oxford University Press, Oxford.

Neary, S.J., Symes, M.S. and Brown, F.E., eds (1995) *Urban Experience*, Routledge, London.

Necker, L. (1993) 'Christopher Tunnard: The Garden in the Modern Landscape' in M. Treib, ed., *Modern Landscape Architecture*, MIT Press, Cambridge, Mass.

Pye, D. (1978) *The Nature and Aesthetics of Design*, The Herbert Press, London (first published as *The Nature of Design* in 1964 by Studio Vista, London).

Rook, A. (1989) 'Landscape Aid', *Landscape Design*, No. 180: 10–13.

Rose, J. (1938/9) *Pencil Points*.

Sandercock, L. and Forsyth, A. (1992) 'A Gender Agenda: New Directions for Planning Theory', *Journal of the American Planning Association*, 58(1) Winter.

Treib, M. (1993) 'Axioms for a Modern Landscape Architecture', pp. 33–67 in M. Treib, ed., *Modern Landscape Architecture: A Critical Review*, MIT Press, Cambridge, Mass.

Tschumi, B. (1987) *Cinegramme Folie*, Princeton Architectural Press.

Tunnard, C. (1948) *Gardens in the Modern Landscape* (revised 2nd edn), Architectural Press, London, and Scribner, New York.

Wilcox, D. (1994) *The Guide to Effective Participation*, Partnership Books, Brighton.

Williams, R. (1975) *The Country and the City*, Penguin, Harmondsworth.

7 In practice: social workers in green wellies?

Designers with a social conscience

Landscape architects, my interviews would indicate, are people with well-developed social consciences. Three of my interviewees expressly stated that they placed the welfare of people at the summit of their personal value systems, and many more justified their aesthetic or ecological endeavours by saying that, in some way, they were undertaken for people. Matters like natural beauty or ecological balance may also be important, but there is generally a social dimension to such concerns.

Dougal Thornton was one of those who plainly put social matters first, and he explained how this priority had shaped his career:

> I probably went into local government on the basis that maybe there was a better opportunity working there. Your hands were less tied as to whom your clients were, and you could actually get involved in trying to redress the imbalances in society in some way.

In Stirling Council many of his colleagues were concerned about the protection of areas of high-quality landscape, of which the authority has several, but Thornton was more interested in those areas which are disadvantaged. He told me that he took part in many policy discussions at the time that this new local authority was formed:[1]

> My mission statement was 'first the worst'. We do have areas of crap environment. They're not vast, but we do have areas of poor housing and we should actually be concentrating on the worst bits first. The good bits . . . we do need to pay attention to them as well, to make sure we're not losing them, but my philosophy is to try and focus on the areas of deprivation.

Another local authority landscape architect, Fiona Sim, expressed very similar sentiments:

> I work for a local authority because I'm not interested in designing gardens for rich people. Not only can I not do it very well, but it doesn't seem to serve a great purpose. I enjoy being in this environment, where you see things develop over a period of years and where you build up links with the community, and because people are very cynical about changes and about spending money on the environment when they've got roofs that are leaking . . . when you can demonstrate that you are improving their quality of life . . . I enjoy that because we can prove people wrong.

John Vaughan, presently the Director of the Great North Forest, looked back on a career spent entirely within the public sector and felt able to say:

> The one great thing I've always held is that . . . it's the one thing I polish my halo for . . . is that I can feel that in my entire working career, that all of it has been devoted to trying to make life better in one way or another. All of my work has been directed towards a sense of the public good and I get a lot of satisfaction from that, from the way in which I have not had to compromise my principles in terms of balancing issues in terms of the public good. It's a very smug position and it's very convenient to be in. It enables me to take the moral high ground.

However, like Thornton and Sim, he has had to face the reality that landscape is often nowhere near the top of a community's most pressing problems, and his social concern is tempered by a longer-term view of environmental issues:

> I've always been privileged to be in a position where I can say that what I'm doing is geared towards improving people's lives, to a small degree or a great degree, but I've also had to balance that with the fact that the work I do doesn't tackle a lot of the more immediate problems in people's lives . . . why can't I fix their roof and their windows and why can't I get them a job? In a way, I lift myself above that and say that the concerns I'm dealing with are very much longer term. In some ways that's very arrogant because it does include having to say that there are some things which are more important than people's short-term interests.

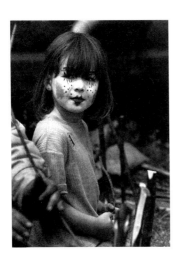

Figure 7.1, Figure 7.2 and Figure 7.3 Community craft workshop at the Great North Forest 'Success Festival' Newbottle, 1997.

Figure 7.4 Great North Forest Penshaw Festival, 1996.

Improving the quality of life

A central idea is that by improving people's surroundings one can make their lives better. This is sometimes expressed in terms of improving their 'quality of life', a phrase which landscape architects use as freely as they once used the expression 'amenity' – which now seems to be less in fashion. Public sector landscape architects do not have a monopoly on these finer feelings. Phil Moss of the Liverpool office of BDP used both terms in a single sentence. He was describing his time at Warrington New Town:

> If you remember what was there before, certainly in Birchwood, which was a horrible, derelict piece of land, a massive amount of land, and also look at what sort of housing was generally being created as environments in those days, I still think the quality of the external environment and the impact it has hopefully on the quality of a person's life living there, and the amenity that we tried to get into it, then I think the New Towns on the whole don't stand out too badly.

This belief in the efficacy of environmental improvements to better people's lives is tantamount to an article of faith for many practitioners. One of the more forceful statements of this creed came from Tom Robinson, of Newcastle's Robinson Penn Partnership:

> Despite all I was telling you today about how tedious it can get, I do believe that landscape design and/or environmental design, formal or informal, green or hard, with or without architecture . . . the design of external environment can just so improve the quality of life, directly and indirectly, there should be a government department for it!

A corollary of this belief in the possibility of improving the quality of people's lives is the view that landscape architects should be more concerned with urban environments than with rural ones, because it is within towns and cities that most people live. Three of my interviewees took exactly this position. One of these was Rodney Beaumont of Gillespies, who, as we saw in Chapter 3, believes that as cities are where the population is concentrated they should be exciting places with exciting

public spaces. Another was Dougal Thornton who told me:

> By and large, the bulk of the time, I'm much happier working in an urban environment than I am in the rural environment. I feel that's where people live, where people work and that's where we should concentrate our resources.

The third was Peter Fischer. During our discussion I asked him whether he found rural work or urban work more satisfying. He hardly hesitated:

> Very difficult . . . the urban work. I live in the city. I always have done and I believe in the social structure of the city. I'm most interested, I suppose, in the design of enclosed open spaces for people to use, whether it's the urban town centre or the parks.

Social values in the city

How then do landscape architects believe that they can make life better for those who live in cities? In general they believe that they can influence both their physical and, perhaps more significantly, their mental well-being. Landscape architecture, conceived thus, is a therapeutic enterprise. James Hope, for example, believes that while landscape architecture may aspire to the status of art, the art is only a stepping-stone to its true purpose which is to affect minds:

> I think that if you see art as a way of affecting people's minds, then yes, that's what we are trying to do. We're trying to introduce beneficial effects into people's lives . . . These are, as in the case of all art, psychological. These effects have the ability to affect people's minds in particular ways. Now whether they do that through symbolism or signification or through simple things like pattern, colour, texture and so on doesn't really matter as long as one is aware of the rules that govern these things.

Hope went on to catalogue some of the particular benefits that landscape architecture can provide:

> Well-being is something to do with it, I think. Relief, I suppose, is another aspect of it. Identity is another important element . . . that one is able to create in a place an identity for that place which is

unique to it, and that that identity in some way relates to who and what these people are and to what happens here, because identity is important to everybody.

Relief

Let us consider Hope's idea of 'relief'. It is almost axiomatic for landscape architects that the provision of green spaces and vegetation in urban areas affords city dwellers some form of psychological respite from the harshness of built forms and the dominance of hard materials like brick, stone, concrete and glass. Pauline Randall told me that growing up in Ealing, London, she had realised at an early age how important parks and trees were in people's lives. The borough had had some of the finest parks in the capital apart from the Royal Parks and at some point Randall had realised that somebody had to be responsible for providing and maintaining these amenities. The purpose of landscape architecture, Randall believes, is to provide places which give pleasure, and consequently she is sceptical about some recent continental projects which seem more concerned with the aesthetics of high design. She told me about her reaction to an issue of *Landscape Design* magazine which had been devoted to contemporary park design:

> There was one in Germany,[2] where the space was designed to be a blank space to show off the city and I looked at it and I thought that it looked like a very blank and boring space that would be very windswept, very uncomfortable in a lot of different conditions and although some people might find it attractive in a photograph, or maybe in real life . . . in terms of understanding human needs for shelter, greenery, things that lift the spirit, the majority of people wouldn't like it. If you look in people's homes, they don't live in cold bare homes with no ornaments. They live in warm humanised places and that is what we like.

John Vaughan has spent much of his professional life, both on Tyneside and in the London Borough of Lambeth, seeking to provide or enhance open spaces within the inner city and is a firm believer in the benefits that such areas can bring, but his current role as Director of the Great North Forest is rather different. The Forest is essentially an urban-fringe concept and part of its *raison d'être* is that it can provide opportunities for countryside recreation to city inhabitants. Vaughan's philosophy is that access to the Forest area should be greatly improved, and this means both physical access, in terms of 'gateway sites', car parks, better public transport, footpaths, signposting and so on, and also psychological access in terms of countryside interpretation, which involves far more than just providing leaflets and nature trails. The policy of encouraging artists to work in the Forest is a way of stimulating an emotional reaction to the landscape. Vaughan's team also organise events, exhibitions and minibus trips to the Forest for urban groups. Like Randall he is very aware of the therapeutic possibilities of landscape:

> We're doing a lot of work here trying to unpack how people respond to landscapes and what role landscapes play in people's lives, either a conscious role or an unconscious role, and I'm not sure you can produce a simple package . . .
>
> We spend a lot of time taking people out from Gateshead, Sunderland and South Tyneside who have had no contact with the countryside, no contact with the natural environment, whose environment is essentially both a hard urban one and also socially a fairly stressed one. Their responses to the environment are very simplistic, very simple, in terms of the way they get pleasure from it and the way in which it impinges upon them as something which is attractive . . .
>
> We've taken groups from South Tyneside to Penshaw Monument[3] and we've got a whole list of quotations about what a wonderful time they've had, and, more particularly, that they'd never realised that places like that existed, how great it was to get away from town for a while, just to be out amongst grass and trees and greenery and some space, how wonderful it was to have some space for the kids to hare around without constantly getting under their feet, how nice it was to have no shops so they weren't constantly being nagged by their kids 'can I have this?', 'can I buy an ice-cream?' – and the sense of relaxation they get from it. So in that way, it's a very simple sort of escape. It's something simple. It's something pleasurable.

Identity, morale and economic reconstruction

James Hope, as we have seen, believes that a sense of community identity is one of the specific social benefits that landscape architecture is able to deliver. This idea is closely related to aesthetic notions about the particularity of places and the importance of local distinctiveness. John Vaughan is also concerned about these matters:

> I think regionalism is important. I think people do need to recognise that they are individuals, they are different. That's quite straightforward in the home. You create your own space around you. You create a space that to some degree reflects your personality, your interests, your values. And that when people are clustered together in some way, that cluster of people has values of its own which are derived from the interactions of all those individual values, plus the sort of weight of culture and history that comes with it. People do

> need some way to express that within the environment. If that ceases to be, then you find a mismatch between people and the environment. You find people's perceptions operate on one scale and the environmental design process operates on another scale. People will become disorientated to the extent that if you step out of an aircraft anywhere it will be like stepping out of an aircraft in London. You get the same shops as you get in Paris, so what's special about Paris?
> . . .
> You do need in some way to allow the design process to be influenced by regional characteristics and of those regional characteristics, some will be physical. They may be types of material, they may be peculiarities of design which are related to local climate, local topography or whatever, or they may be related to the way people feel about the place.
> We could put concrete block paving on the

Figure 7.5 Bustling crowds during the annual International Seafood Festival at West India Quay, Isle of Dogs, London. Close to Canary Wharf, this site for urban festivals was designed by EDAW. It involved the renewal of the coping stones on the dock walls, new paving, railings and furniture and the refurbishment of the dock cranes, and includes a steel water sculpture 'Archimedes' by Bill Pye and a new bridge by Future Systems. (Photograph © Martin Jones.)

moon if we wanted to, if we threw enough money and technology at it. At some point people may begin to realise that that's engendered an arrogance, that that's engendered a carelessness with the detail in life. The detail in life is what's important . . . to people. It's important to people feeling secure in where they belong, and if they feel secure in where they belong, they'll feel secure in dealing with other people.

. . . so I suppose I'm a fan of individual expression, and expression at the community level of what their values are, and that's design values as much as anything else. This is what we like. This is what we're comfortable with. This is what means something to us, but to express that is very difficult because so much of the design process is undertaken in rarefied atmospheres of international finance and big business decisions and the rest of it. People quite often don't have a chance to, not so much to influence individual designs, but to say 'Well hang on, we think there are some things which are of value here'. So you end up with the imposition of bland overriding sort of designs. At the other end you get 'Well let's go back to chair-bodging and be self-sufficient and grow lots of hazel coppice'. Somewhere in the middle you've lost this idea of 'Do we have a regional identity? Do we have a community?'

In the case of the New Towns and the new city of Milton Keynes, designers were attempting to create feelings of identity, local character and belonging from scratch. One of the criticisms most often voiced about them is that, designed as they were on Modernist principles of zoning, and planned with motor transport much in mind, many failed to engender this sense of a distinctive local identity. However, some of my interviewees thought that there had been some notable successes, Warrington and Milton Keynes being the two that were most frequently mentioned. In both cases the designed landscape played a large part in creating this local character. For Neil Mattinson, Milton Keynes has been an inspiration throughout his career. He had become aware of the New Town movement before he decided to study landscape architecture; now his firm occasionally wins commissions in Milton Keynes; he

has been able to follow the city's development closely:

> That's been another thing . . . to watch it grow from something that was fairly stark . . . but you know, it's taken them what? . . . twenty-eight years now, plus, to achieve what they've got, and, for me, to see that landscape maturing into something that is actually contributing to the environment . . . I mean, it was just millions of sticks for many, many years, but if you drive through Milton Keynes now, the reaction you get from people who live there – it's tremendously positive for the majority of people. I mean they live for that structure of footpaths and highways. The Redway system is fantastic; you can cycle from one end of Milton Keynes to the other without crossing any major roads. And that was all part and parcel of this pure, structured approach in which landscape architects were absolutely fundamental.

Another significant project for Mattinson was the redesign of Newcastle's Walker Park, which he had undertaken while working for the Durham office of SGS Environment. Here, he believes, the refurbished park was able to act as a focus for community identity and to restore feelings of self-respect within the neighbourhood:

> For me, the pride that came back into that park from the people who lived around it was immense. I mean, we suffered tremendous vandalism in the first two years. Everything we put in was snapped or broken, but then slowly we built up this real spirit in the area of Walker and that park became part of the community again.

Another interviewee who thought that landscape architectural interventions could restore community pride and self-confidence was Cheryl Tolladay of Groundwork East Durham. Interestingly Tolladay was somewhat sceptical about the Groundwork organisation's emphasis on community consultation and participation, feeling that it was very labour-intensive in terms of the landscape architect's input, but that the results were often small scale. She contrasted this with the dramatic changes that could be brought about by a large-scale intervention, describing a large project in the former pit town of Seaham on the Durham coast:

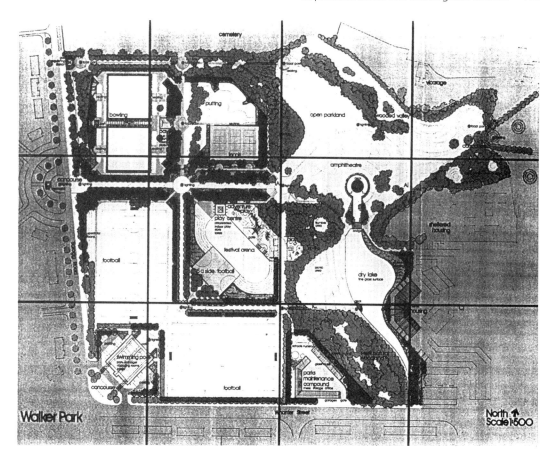

Figure 7.6 Walker Park, Newcastle: redesigned by SGS Environment (formerly Woolerton Truscott).

We're doing this big scheme at Seaham. It was even on the TV last week. We've just done a display at the council offices. It was in a window and apparently the pavement was deep with people looking at the exhibition because they were so interested. We did a quarter of a million pounds worth of schemes in Seaham last year – very high profile schemes on junctions and such like. And they were extremely high-quality items – hard landscape, the new frontage to the park, all these railings with gold tops . . .

. . . that's not so much to do with public participation as with us delivering the goods and not doing just a quiet little scheme . . . It's 'Well, you can have Hyde Park in Seaham if you want! Anything as good as Buckingham Palace railings, if you want.' And I think that can be just as powerful a tool as public participation. It doesn't empower people . . . but it still gives them a huge boost.

Several of the people I interviewed told me that they saw their role as contributing to the pride and self-esteem of disadvantaged communities, and indeed to assisting with the task of economic regeneration. John Hopkins directly related these two aspects of his work:

A sense of community comes from its economic vibrancy, how it sees itself, how it relates . . . how individual members relate to each other, and how they see themselves as a vibrant, living organism almost.

Talking to practitioners in cities like Liverpool, Manchester and Newcastle, which have all suffered the throes of industrial decline and economic restructuring during the 1980s and 1990s, these themes emerged frequently. Perhaps they were stated in the most forthright manner by Tom Robinson:

Figure 7.7 Proposals for Seaham Promenade, County Durham, showing the landmark Portland stone sculptures by Paul Mason. Sketch by John Elm, courtesy of Groundwork East Durham.

Look at the recent architectural congress at Barcelona. Barcelona has had a policy for about fifteen years now of major investment in the spaces between its buildings to make it . . . to win back the idea of fine living in a city. And on the back of that they got the Olympics as well and it's a surging region in Spain economically and actually it is reckoned to become one of the economic hot-spots of Europe, because it's also an attractive place to live . . . very inventive people down there, an attractive lifestyle, an attractive city.

If you see it in the wider context, what they're doing is investing in these squares . . . you can't put a value on the one square but you can put a value on a series over a time. It must affect major economic decisions. The quality of space and the quality of life is going to become . . . is already . . . an economic locator. You don't need to locate next to the coal and water any more. Well that gives us, as landscape architects, tremendous power and

that's one of the reasons why I said at the very beginning of this that I was a firm believer in economic reconstruction. That's why I like to work up here, because I believe that we're doing our little bit to rebuild the economic base of the North-East.

Raising public morale and providing a focus for identity is seen as part of the landscape architect's role, but there seems to be a recognition that this alone is not enough. Above all communities need jobs, and many practitioners believe that there is a link between the image of an area, which is something that they can use their skills to improve, and the possibility of attracting inward investment, with all the social and economic benefits which that can bring. Working in the private sector, Peter McGuckin tries to persuade his clients that spending money on good landscape design will add value to their developments:

Yes. I say financial value, but say it was aesthetic value instead. The client says 'Well that has no value on my balance sheet', but I could advance an argument that good design adds value, that if you want to get a prestige company, a blue-chip company, to relocate from the South East to the North East they're used to looking at M4 corridor standards of business park design. How actually are you going to do that unless you invest in good-quality design? An awful lot of the people you're going to ask to relocate are going to say 'Oh the North East, pit heaps and chemical industries . . . I don't want to do that.' If however they are given a paragon of excellence, of good design, that could convince them, and that's worth an awful lot to a developer, but to pay for it, to recognise that! He thinks he can procure that for bottom dollar. That's sad.

While there may be strong philosophical arguments against attempting to translate the kinds of values examined in this book – ecological, social and aesthetic values – into monetary values, many landscape architects in private practice would be delighted to be given a formula which allowed them to calculate the financial value that any particular amount of spending on landscape works could add to a development. They feel intuitively that some sort of relationship exists, and it would be so much easier to attract clients if this were transparently obvious. But while it is possible to point to developments throughout history, including Beverly Hills and the apartments that face New York's Central Park, to demonstrate that landscape design can be phenomenally successful in this regard, any kind of general law seems an impossibly remote prospect. In its absence landscape architects will continue to argue and cajole clients into believing that good design is much more important, and potentially more lucrative, than mere prettification.

Designing out crime

Crime and the fear of crime are particularly prevalent and insidiously corrosive aspects of contemporary urban life. As we saw in Chapter 6, all the environmental design professions are regularly exhorted to 'design out crime'. I was interested to see whether my interviewees had included this on their social

agendas, and whether or not they believed it could be done.

Many of the landscape designers interviewed seemed to give credence to the theories of 'defensible space' put forward originally by Oscar Newman and updated in the 1980s by Alice Coleman. Dougal Thornton, for instance, described some work he had undertaken on a Stirling housing estate. In Scotland it is common to find four flats under a single roof (the buildings superficially look like semi-detached houses until one counts the numbers of doors), but the land around these blocks is not divided up into private gardens:

> We've got small pockets of pretty down market housing with big social problems. You know, you read the press page every week and you can tell where most of the crime is going on, and going into these places we had consultations about open spaces . . . These houses, they're 'four-in-a-block' mainly, so there were problems of who has the ground outside, you know, because it's not like semi-detached housing where you've got a front door and you've got a back door and you've got a wee patch and you can say to the tenant 'that's your bit'.
>
> Now what had happened over the years was that these back gardens – which were huge back gardens – had got into a terrible state, so the council just wiped the slate. So all you had were tarmac drying areas and grass and the odd bit of metal play equipment. There was no private space at all. And I tried . . . we'd loads of meeting with tenants . . . we tried to convince them they should have wee back gardens. It was a major task. You know what we should have done? We should have given them a shed. We never gave them a shed. We spent about £30,000 refurbishing their houses and the environmental improvements came on the back of that package and we gave them the fencing, we gave them a wee gate to go in and out of the common area which still existed, and we gave them nice landscaping which got torn apart fairly quickly, which again was me thinking . . . My aspirations didn't meet their social objectives, or the social problems that they have.

Working in such areas landscape architects cannot avoid questions of crime. Not only will such issues be at the top of the residents' lists of priorities, but if they get the design wrong, or if they mishandle their dealings with the community, the landscape works themselves can easily become the target of vandalism. Of course, this can still happen if they get the design right and handle the community consultation as well as possible. Defensible space theories have an intuitive appeal, but the complexity of social issues means that deterministic design solutions alone are rarely going to be successful. As Thornton indicates, the obstacles can be formidable:

> But I think initially I did have real problems of trying to superimpose my design objectives on them and we compromised. We did make half-hearted attempts to try to take them to other areas, in a sense, because they said 'We don't want trees. We don't want this and that because they'll just get vandalised.' Trying to break out of that spiral of designing down to a Colditz kind of environment, where it's all metal, all metal fences. 'We don't want wooden fences because they just get cut up and sawn up.' When the miners were on strike, you know, we arrived on site and all the wooden fences had disappeared onto the coal fires. It's very hard to come up with something that takes people forward in a way that they're happy with and is meaningful.

Often 'designing out crime' leads not to defensible space but to defensive design. In some areas, every design decision, from the thickness of the fence-posts, to the height of the lighting columns and the choice of shrub species, is mentally checked against a crime prevention criterion – is this going to make a crime easier to commit and therefore more likely? Indeed, the defensiveness goes a stage deeper because the actual probability of a crime occurring is often not the issue. The issue is whether people in the area perceive a place to be unsafe. Fear of crime can be as disabling as crime itself.

One of the most unfortunate results of this widespread apprehensiveness is that vegetation has come to be regarded with mistrust by many urban residents. It is seen as providing hiding places for potential assailants. Landscape architects have had to take account of this fear. Some local authorities have actually been taking shrubberies out of parks and residential areas, and when considering new plantings designers are urged to use low-growing shrubs and to keep shrub beds back from the edges of paths. This defensive approach is in many ways the antithesis of the ecological ideals which were being imported from Holland in the 1970s. These called for mass plantings, more relaxed plantings and an altogether shaggier, more naturalistic style of landscape design. I asked Perry Twigg, a senior landscape architect for Salford City Council, what he thought the public's attitude to ecological planting might now be:

> Maybe they think it just looks overgrown and it looks a bit of a mess. I think a lot of it does boil down to personal security and if they do feel threatened in these areas. It was a common fault that kept coming up, and I think a lot of these areas have now actually gone, or we've replaced the planting in the urban situations. It's just a sign of the times really. Something we've had to do. I think most people, when they actually design, do think of lower-growing shrubs in these areas.

While landscape architects like Twigg may feel regret about the defensive approach, and perhaps would, under different circumstances, like to see more native vegetation within the urban area, ultimately they put the community's wishes first. Some designers however think that this defensiveness has already gone too far, that it is a reaction to media-generated hysteria, and that it ought to be resisted. Peter Fischer holds this view:

> I think one of the problems that we have suffered from is the risk of litigation . . . and the concerns about sex attackers and so on – the shrubbery that people can hide behind, the attitude that you can't have children going off and playing in undergrowth and all this kind of thing. Maybe sociologists can prove me wrong, but surely there have always been those sorts of risks. They are maybe made more of in the media today than they were before the war, for example, but you know, if one goes on the laws of averages about things like that, there have always been dangers. There always will be a certain percentage, but should we find ourselves designing out enjoyable landscapes, particularly for children, just because of safety in its broadest sense? I think it's gone too far, personally
> . . .

All this fencing things off. And then people go to, say, Barcelona, and there's that recent development for the Olympics where you walk across this bridge onto this island off the main quayside and it's just this timber boarding. There's not even a handrail and, okay, people could fall in, but it's like the quayside on a fishing port. You don't start putting fences up to stop people falling over. Yet, when I worked for Milton Keynes Development Corporation, there was a tragedy where a child fell into the canal and drowned. They were building housing near the canal, so there was this manic pressure for the whole of the canal towpath to have a fence along it, and that's not the way to approach the problem I think. I know I could be vilified but I think we have to live with a bit of danger rather than trying to design it out all the time. It doesn't work. It reduces the quality of the landscape in its widest sense.

The relationship between social, ecological and aesthetic values

If it is true, as much of this chapter has suggested, that landscape architects generally place social objectives towards the top of their value systems, how then do they resolve conflicts with other sorts of values? Many do it by giving precedence to the social values. David Appleton, for example, believes that one must be very careful about trying to impose a new landscape aesthetic based on ecological thinking upon people who do not value it:

> I think we have to be very conscious of the society in which we live and work. Whether we like it or not, we are a nation of gardeners and there are a lot of people for whom ecological landscapes are the equivalent to a lack of social care. Now it is easy for us to say we can just re-educate people. That in itself can be very dangerous, and if we have got something in our national psyche which is that, as a society, we associate certain things with being good and other things as being bad, that in itself is not necessarily wrong.

Heather Lloyd, who now works for Westminster City Council, would agree with this. She described a project she had undertaken in a previous job with a London borough. As a landscape architect

schooled in ecological concepts she often seeks opportunities to introduce planting into her schemes, but she recognises that the people she is designing for must have the ultimate say:

> There was one project I was involved with where I wanted to plant more trees. There were a few trees, but they were quite mature and coming to the end of their lives, and I said let's put some more trees in, and I go through all the reasons why we should put more trees in from an ecological as well as an aesthetic point of view. They just weren't interested, and I could have spent £5,000 on tree planting and they'd all be ripped out. So you can just try your hardest to educate people, but there is no point doing something just because you fancy it or you think it's right.

Dougal Thornton, as we have already seen, places community aspirations at the apex of his value system. He told me about the consultations he undertook in preparation for the design of a country park. Rather than emphasising nature conservation or ecology, which was a possible approach, Thornton chose to give the community the power to say what kind of park they preferred:

> We've wheeled these people around other country parks and said 'What are your aspirations? Is this the model? Is it this recreation model?' Or, 'Here's a wildlife model? What do you think of that?' . . .
>
> And out of that came high aspirations for jobs because of the unemployment. The level in the village is quite high. Moderate aspirations for wildlife. Some of the folk were quite keen on wildlife. They were keen on having something that was vibrant, and with lots of people working on it, rather than something that was giving a lot to nature and had a warden and nobody else.

These examples show that, whether from pragmatism or from a principled belief in the supremacy of people's wishes, ecological ideals often take second place to social objectives. There are also cases where aesthetic objectives are similarly relegated. If it came to a choice between artistic goals and functional objectives, for example, landscape architects tend to regard the latter as more important. Earlier in this chapter I quoted

Pauline Randall's criticisms of the kind of art-house urban design which does not meet people's needs. Perry Twigg is more enthusiastic about placing art in the environment but he finds it more convincing if people can relate to it or find it useful:

> You can introduce artwork into a scheme, whether it's through signage or seating or everyday elements that people use, and I think that way is like making an art statement, but at the same time people can relate to what's been done, because it's something that they use, whereas if you stick a pile of bricks at the end of a pedestrian street, people might think 'Well, what's that all about? What a waste of money!'

Where there is a conflict between a designer's aesthetic sensibilities or ecological ideals and the community's aspirations it may be possible for the designer to persuade people to accept their point of view. This can be an important part of the consultation dialogue which is discussed more fully below. However, if persuasion fails the designer has to decide whether to go with the community's wishes. It would be wrong to suggest, in a simplistic way, that wherever there is a difficult choice between a social objective and an aesthetic or ecological one, landscape architects invariably opt for the social goal. Life is not as straightforward as that, and every dilemma must be addressed on its own terms.

I am inclined to believe, on the basis of this series of interviews, that landscape architects are more likely to resist community pressure in matters of design aesthetics than they are in matters of ecology. Perry Twigg, for example, told me about a project to improve the image of Eccles[4] town centre by co-ordinating the street furniture and reducing visual clutter. Having achieved these aesthetic objectives he was frustrated to learn that others within the council were about to introduce CCTV cameras on tall columns in response to a request from local businesses concerned about security. Similarly Fiona Sim, who at the time of our interview worked for the London Borough of Newham, got annoyed about the introduction of bobbly pink paving for the visually disabled into one of her completed pedestrianisation projects.

Part of their annoyance, of course, was that they, as designers, were not consulted before these intrusive alterations were made. In each of these cases there might have been a design solution which addressed the respective social needs without compromising the appearance of the schemes. But there might not have been such a solution. During the writing of this book I have come to the view that the various values which landscape architects espouse can, and on some occasions do, turn out to be incommensurable. There is nothing for it, at such times, but to make a difficult choice.

Public consultation

Landscape architects are divided on the question of public participation. Some are great enthusiasts, some think it is largely a waste of time, or at best a necessary chore they must do to keep the clients happy. The majority of those interviewed took a middle path, believing that for works within residential areas, particularly socially disadvantaged ones, consultation is absolutely fundamental to success, whereas for many other kinds of work, such as commercial work on business parks, it is largely an irrelevance.

We will consider the doubters later. For the moment let us hear from two of the believers. One of them is Perry Twigg, perhaps because he works mainly in existing urban communities:

> The rewarding thing is that when you actually carry out community consultation, whatever form it's in, you actually get people coming along who are genuinely interested in improving an area and genuinely want to take part in improving the area that they live in. But that doesn't stop the minority who live in that area from having no interest in it and destroying what's been carried out. Having said that, I think the schemes that do involve public participation have a much better success rate. We carry out a number of art work schemes throughout Salford whereby we've involved art groups working together with landscape architects, working together with local community, whether it's school children or youth groups, to actually come up with the designs themselves and they are incorporated as part of the scheme and in those instances those schemes will remain virtually intact, no vandalism at all, because it creates a sense of ownership and responsibility, so that side of things is quite rewarding.

The second is Tim Gale, but he puts the horses-for-courses view:

At the moment we do a lot of housing renewal work and public consultation is absolutely an essential ingredient. You have to start there, otherwise it's a waste of time and effort. On the other hand I personally believe that it's not always going to give you particularly helpful answers on some other schemes, commercial schemes for example.

Gale believes strongly that if one does decide that consultation is the appropriate thing to do, then one must accept the results of that consultation:

Ultimately you've got to go with the wishes of the community, but as I say the word *ultimately* is the significant one. If you believe something strongly you have to put forward strong cogent arguments in support of it. If you're not successful in being persuasive then you have to follow the will of your client or not do the job. That's really what it boils down to, ultimately. I think its obviously completely ridiculous to consult with people and they tell you really clearly what they want and then you do something else. That's just self-indulgence.

Gathering information

Of the interviewees who were well-disposed towards public consultation, most believed that its purpose was to access information which might otherwise be unavailable, in order to refine the brief or to supplement survey information gathered in other ways. Peter Fischer, for example, told me:

I do think it's essential to have people on the ground involved, whether it's council officers or the public, explaining how they use the place, because whether you work for a local authority or whether you're a consultant coming in from outside, you can't be there for a long enough period of time to know really how the place works and you have to listen to what people say.

Similarly, David Appleton said:

You can use consultation as a design tool, in as much as there will always be people that know more about their locality and their needs than anybody else, and I think it's an important ingredient to allow you to do the job properly, and particularly if you're doing urban renewal schemes

or housing refurbishments, you've got to listen to them.

However, while some people I spoke to thought that the public could become more involved through community-arts projects, no one believed that they should actually become the designers. Indeed some thought that this would seriously compromise the landscape architect's position and expertise. Pauline Randall, for example, said:

I certainly don't think the public should play a part in the spatial arrangements because I think that's a highly skilled thing that we are trained to do, and to involve untrained people in that, well it seems like giving away our art in a sense. We're professionals for a reason. But we did involve them; we involved them firstly, and most importantly, in deciding the content of the brief, then we involved schoolchildren in mosaic making; we had two artists actually who did these mosaics with the children which were incorporated into the design. They designed a logo and some of the fencing. So I think there are ways of involving people in the detail. But the shaping . . . you get feed-back on the shaping of the space, after the briefing, which should tell you what the public are really after.

Peter Fischer believed that it was the landscape architect's responsibility to retain a degree of detachment and objectivity:

I think one has to be careful not to be driven by local interests or pressure from people who aren't that representative, or who – however well meaning – may not understand the longer-term problems with what they're suggesting. We should never abdicate our responsibility for saying 'Look, however unpopular what I'm saying to you is, I'm not just going to say "yes" because you want me to say "yes". You must realise that there are some unpalatable things. You may not politically like what is best for this area.'

Persuasion and consensus building

The ability to listen may be essential to good public consultation but the process is two-way and demands more active social skills on the behalf of the designer, who should bring his or her own experience, knowledge and ideas into play. Many interviewees told me that they had attempted to educate or persuade members of the public to what they considered a more enlightened view. But Heather Lloyd saw the process as a dialogue:

> It's a fine line between playing God ... because lots of times you talk to people and they say 'This is what we want', but in reality it's not really what they need ... and so you have to work on that, and it's not a case of making them come round to your way of thinking, so that you end up doing what you want in the end. It's sort of compromise and negotiation and discussion, and I think it's always good to bear in mind that there are plenty of completely nightmarish schemes out there designed by all manner of professionals and that you need to be a bit humble. Just because you've got a degree or a diploma and a few letters after your name doesn't mean that you've got all the right answers.

Dougal Thornton has been involved in a particularly sensitive piece of community consultation. In the aftermath of the tragic Dunblane shooting in 1996 where sixteen schoolchildren and one of their teachers were killed by an intruder, he became involved in designing a memorial garden which was to be constructed at Dunblane Cemetery. Whilst regretting the circumstances profoundly he told me that it had been a very rewarding piece of work to undertake and that his discussions with the bereaved parents had been very positive. However, he told me of a very difficult moment when it became clear that a headstone should be moved:

> There are all these gravestones ... and their parents wander up all the time ... and we had to move some of them which was quite ... because we couldn't get this kerb in ... and you can imagine going up to someone and saying 'We really need to move this gravestone' and one of the families said 'Well you're not moving it', potentially knackering the whole design! But I managed to meet them and I managed to talk them round to it. Again, just from experience, you tend to get more confident in communicating with them. I convinced them there was a benefit in moving it as well, because actually the stone wasn't very well mounted on its plinth and we could actually sort that out. You don't go away saying 'Well I won

Figure 7.8 and Figure 7.9 Memorial Garden, Dunblane cemetery: general view and one detail.

that argument'; you go away saying 'I'm really pleased they're co-operating', and they've since been back and said 'We're really pleased. We didn't realise it was just a little bit of adjustment that was needed.'

When dealing with large groups, such as the residents of a housing estate, the landscape architect may need not only to persuade but to facilitate the development of a consensus. Phil Moss of BDP has carried out public consultation in housing areas with multiple social problems in Liverpool. Ray Keeley undertook this sort of work when employed by North Tyneside MBC.[5] He offered a useful description of the dynamics of consensus building:

> You've got to get most people on board but you're not going to get everybody. Rather than trying to include everybody's wishes and get a complete hotch-potch that doesn't work, you get the majority – otherwise you've got no authority. You

can normally identify minority views that are a bit out of kilter then treat them very carefully.

This is skilful work! Landscape architects involved in these kinds of projects need to know as much about people as they do about soils or plants or paving slabs. As John Vaughan explained to me, his work often places him in the position of an arbitrator:

> There are inevitably differences of opinion about both what should be done and how it should be done. But I'm quite prepared, under those circumstances, to feel that that's a healthy option, and if we become the arbiters of debate and discussion, what comes out at the end of the day has a sort of broad consensus between people.

In order to perform this role, the landscape architect must overcome any resistance or apathy demonstrated by the community and somehow secure their trust. Both Heather Lloyd and Phil Moss recounted situations where they had been commissioned to work in areas with tremendous difficulties with communities which mistrusted authority. In both cases they succeeded in winning the trust of the residents only to find that circumstances outside their control undermined their good work. In Moss's case this was brought about by a change of administration in Liverpool from Liberal to Labour. In Lloyd's case it was the discovery of an asbestos problem on the estate in question, which diverted funding from the works she had been discussing with the residents. She told me that she had found this a particularly hard blow.

> It ended up very badly, like seriously badly. I put so much into it. It was the community consultation which I'd wanted to do all my working life . . . The estate had a notorious reputation and nobody caring at all and nobody coming to anything. The Tenants' Association meetings were really badly attended. We had a meeting before Christmas and nobody turned up and the Planning-for-Real exercise was scheduled for February, so to go from nothing to the Planning-for-Real day when 300 people turned up . . . I felt as though I'd really done something.

Unfortunately by this time the asbestos problem had been discovered. Having worked so hard to win people's trust, Lloyd felt very disillusioned:

I felt personally responsible because I'd said to people 'Get involved. It's up to you. You can change how this is', and they said 'No, the council will take the money away' and I said 'They can't take the money away' and then it all ends up like that . . .

. . . I thought it was wrong that we should spend money which we had told the community they could spend on whatever they wanted, trees and playgrounds, and now we turned around and said sorry, we're going to spend it on ground remediation works. I think that was totally wrong because we had got all these people out to Planning-for-Real,[6] the whole estate was totally revitalised by it, we had a revitalised TA,[7] we had people taking an interest and getting involved, and suddenly, the council's got no money, and that was quite, quite bad and I had a major falling out over it. But I won't do that again because, it sounds really shallow, but the amount of grief and aggravation I went through on that, I'm not going to go through that again, it's just not worth it. Until the next time!

Neil Mattinson was able to tell me of some happier outcomes. His work in Walker Park, Newcastle has already been mentioned. At the time of our interview he was also involved in two large community schemes in London, one of which, the Alexandra and Ainsworth Estate in St John's Wood, was one of the first 1960s housing estates to have been listed by English Heritage. This raised some particularly intriguing value conflicts between the demands of conservation and the needs of the residents – should the original planting scheme, which consisted mainly of ivy, be retained even though it was a headache to maintain? Mattinson explained that his goal was to empower the residents:

> One of the fundamental things is that the commissioning agent is actually the community. It's very important. It is they who make the final choice of consultant, so you're actually selling your skills and attributes to the people who live there, not the local authority . . . Once you're successful, the first meeting you have with them, you're there because they want you. That's jolly important . . .

This approach to empowerment continues throughout the ensuing meetings and discussions:

One thing you never do, we've found, is design something and ask for comments. We'd rather have the comments first. It's totally unstructured usually . . . So you take it all on board. That then gives you the framework for your revised brief, in effect, and therefore, when you go back with an idea, it's already on board . . . it's their idea you're selling back to them. And if they take ownership of that, you're off and running.

Mattinson told me that this close consultation would continue right through the construction period:

Then it's very important to go back and discuss any changes you want to make to it, even something as simple as a change of play equipment detail, or a change of paint colour, because, blow me, if you don't, and it goes on site differently, distrust is immediately back and 'You haven't conveyed that to us.' Often it's not a problem, but it's just the fact that you've missed them out of the process. So it's very important. Even minor issues, so they get sent copies of all Architect's Instructions, for instance, and they get to see them before they go out as a formal issue, so they really feel that they're part of it.

Case study 7.1: changing places: Groundwork's Millennium Projects

Background

Groundwork's Changing Places initiative seeks to involve communities in the reclamation of derelict land. In Britain the emphasis has been upon technical solutions to the complexities of restoring damaged and often contaminated land. In the process the landscape, wildlife and cultural values that may have accrued to the land over time have often been lost.[8] This £45 million[9] programme promotes a 'soft' approach to reclamation which may be more appropriate where the land is not seriously contaminated and where no 'hard' end-uses (e.g. sites for business or housing) are envisaged. The programme is supported by the Millennium Commission and covers twenty-one former industrial sites with a total area of over 1,000 hectares (equivalent to the area of the city of York).

Bold Urban Common, St Helens, Merseyside: Groundwork St Helens, Knowsley and Sefton

History

Bold Urban Common, near St Helens, Merseyside was one of the sites included in Groundwork's successful submission to the Millennium Commission. It comprises two main areas. The first is Bold Moss, where a 52-hectare colliery spoil heap had been tipped onto mossland (lowland peat) between 1955 until 1986. British Coal sold it to the Groundwork Trust for £1 in 1990 and it is one of Groundwork's prime examples of their alternative approach to reclamation. For reasons of public safety, the adjacent site, Bold Colliery itself, is being reclaimed in a more conventional way, but it will be linked to the Moss by a new bridge over the intervening railway line. The whole complex is situated on the urban fringe, near to a large housing estate which rejoices in the nickname 'Cement City'.

Community

At the outset of the Bold Moss project great emphasis was placed upon the need to find out what the local community wanted. This was not so easy, because initially very little community enthusiasm existed. Staff from the Trust had first to generate interest in the future of this large expanse of wasteland. Once this had been established, the Trust ran a 'Planning-for-Real' exercise,[10] but a conventional masterplan was eschewed in favour of a more evolutionary approach to design.

Community representatives were brought together to form the Bold Moss Forum, which reported to a Steering Group of councillors, local authority representatives and Groundwork staff. The detailed design evolved through the active involvement of community volunteers in physical works on site, under the energetic leadership of a ranger. Although these works have included the laying of paths and the planting of large numbers

Figure 7.10 Children on Bold Moss in 1992 in the early days of the project – notice the ornament in the stream behind them. (Courtesy of Groundwork St Helens, Knowsley and Sefton.)

Figure 7.11 'Planning for Real': local people build a model of Bold Moss. (Courtesy of Groundwork St Helens, Knowsley and Sefton.)

of trees, much of the work of reclamation is done by natural generation. The criticism that this process takes longer than conventional reclamation is easily countered by the observation that local people have been involved in every important decision on the site, with genuine influence over the design. Ultimately the Groundwork Trust intends to hand over the ongoing management of the site to a community based organisation.

Ecology

Bold Moss is fortunate in that it includes some remnants of original mossland which are of considerable scientific and educational interest. These have been protected throughout the pro-

ject. Although many young trees have been planted on the spoil tip, natural regeneration accounts for some 30 per cent of the vegetation to be found on site.

Various techniques for ameliorating the colliery spoil have been utilised. Currently sewage cake is being mixed with a fibrous by-product of waste-paper recycling and applied to the land. Where possible materials on site have been recycled. On Bold Colliery, for example, a large area of concrete is being crushed for use as a sub-base for the proposed paths.

In the long term, the ecological sustainability of the site is bound up with the social sustainability of the project. Groundwork is working towards the eventual handover of the site to a separate community based trust which will be responsible for its further development and management.

Delight

There can be little doubt that the ecologically diverse and visually interesting landscape which is emerging at Bold Moss is far more delightful than the neglected and unsightly pit heap from which it has developed, yet, while the development of the site has been informed by landscape science and management techniques, the role of conscious landscape design in this process has not been great. Admittedly one or two inadequacies of the path system might have been avoided if a designer had been involved sooner, and perhaps

Figure 7.12 Wetland area on Bold Moss. The bridge in the foreground was designed by local people and incorporates the winding wheel from the former colliery. (Courtesy of Groundwork St Helens, Knowsley and Sefton.)

a symbolic layer of meaningfulness could have been added, Jellicoe-fashion, to the whole, but landscapes like Bold Moss are something of a challenge to the design side of the profession, since they seem to grow in ecological, social and aesthetic value *without* drastic interventions by landscape architects. It will be interesting to revisit Bold Urban Common to compare the development of the Bold Colliery site with Bold Moss, since a landscape architect *is* involved in the day-to-day shaping of the former.

The Ridgacre Project: Groundwork Black Country

History

Situated to the north-west of West Bromwich town centre, the Ridgacre is remnant branch of the Wednesbury Old Canal. Last used for commercial traffic in 1966, the Ridgacre has not been navigable since the construction of a culvert in association with the building of the Black Country New Road in 1991. The neglected canal became a local liability, a site for dumping, vandalism and petty crime. In 1994 Groundwork Black Country were given the opportunity to develop the canal for recreation and as an educational resource.[11]

Community

Much of the effort on the Ridgacre has been put into people rather than into physical works on the site. One of the first steps which Groundwork took was to establish a Friends of the Ridgacre Group representing local residents. A series of community events, including barbecues, combined with surveys and leaflet drops helped to overcome initial scepticism and generate interest. The most active Friends are all local anglers for whom the canal is prized for its stocks of bream, carp and chub. There is also a Junior Friends of the Ridgacre Group led by a local Geography teacher.

Following a participatory workshop[12] in 1994 a development and management plan was produced. Its main aim was to improve the Ridgacre as a local fishery while managing the site for recreation and nature conservation. More detailed consultation has been carried out regarding

7.13 The Ridgacre Canal as it used to be. (Courtesy of Groundwork Black Country.)

the design of each of the five main access points. While a landscape architect has been involved in this process, the emphasis has been on helping people to design the site for themselves. Over the course of the project, responsibility for the management of the site has gradually shifted from the Groundwork Trust towards the Friends of the Ridgacre. They even have plans for a self-build community/educational resource centre on the canal embankment.

Ecology

While the original motivation of the Friends had been their shared interest in fishing, with support from ecologically trained staff at Groundwork they have become increasingly involved in the management of the site for nature conservation. With funding from the Civic Trust they have created a wildlife area on one bank for use by local schools. A management plan has been drawn up and three of the Friends are studying for NVQs in environmental conservation. By encouraging such initiatives, Groundwork believes that they can ensure the long-term sustainability of the project once their own involvement comes to an end.

Figure 7.14 Volunteers help to clean out the canal. (Courtesy of Groundwork Black Country.)

Figure 7.15 The Ridgacre Canal is much used by anglers. (Courtesy of Groundwork Black Country.)

Delight

To assess the visual improvement that this project has brought about, one really needs to compare before-and-after photographs. The canal had been such an eyesore that infilling seemed its most likely future. Through Groundwork's partnership approach a liability has been transformed into a very attractive and well-used urban greenway. Nature conservation is a strong influence upon the aesthetics of the scheme, but mown margins to the canal and the paths convey the message that the site is cared for and managed for human enjoyment.

Designed elements are low-key. Steel entrance arches have been designed by local schoolchildren for the main access points and there is a folly-like 'celebratory feature' in a similar style. These reinforce the identity of the area and the message that it is valued. The role of the landscape architect in all of this has been that of a facilitator rather than an artist-designer.

Figure 7.16 The Ridgacre Canal; entrance feature designed by local people. (Courtesy of Groundwork Black Country.)

Responsibility

Landscape architects often say that their discipline is concerned with four-dimensional design, in recognition of the temporal aspect of their work which is both its glory and its weakness. It is its glory because a landscape design, unlike a piece of architecture, will, if cared for, grow, develop and mature, rather than remain static; its weakness because it is so difficult for a designer to ensure that a landscape gets the maintenance and management that it requires. In the case of community schemes this is a particular problem, and it is one of the reasons why 'defensible space' strategies have been so popular. One way of coaxing people into taking responsibility for their surroundings is to create more private space, so that the duties are more transparent and clear cut.

It is now widely accepted that the residents of public sector housing should be encouraged to take responsibility for the open spaces around their homes, but it has been a long time in coming. Ivor Cunningham told me about an early attempt to do this. He was involved with the design of New Ash Green, a new village of some 2,000 houses built by the developer Span in Kent in the 1960s. He described attempts to get the residents to take responsibility for maintenance:

> The most revolutionary aspect was the residents' association . . . and you talk about hands-on . . . the maintenance of the ground was the very important contribution that Span made and that came out very early on and it came out for architectural reasons. We had to work out a method of looking after the space for the residents themselves to do, so the essence was that the residents' association looks after its own space.

At New Ash Green there was to have been local authority housing in the village, provided by the Greater London Council for tenants of Dartford Rural District Council. The idea was that these tenants should pay a subscription towards the maintenance of the grounds. At first Dartford resisted:

7.17

Figure 7.17 and Figure 7.18 (opposite) Two views of New Ash Green, a pioneering low-rise development of the 1960s by Span. The quality of the external spaces and planting is evident, but another innovatory aspect of the project was the (frustrated) attempt to involve local authority tenants in the management of their own environment.

7.18

'Oh can't do that . . . can't trust them!'. 'Well you can't come in then.' In the end they agreed. They'd do a bit of selective tenanting and we designed the first scheme of housing, we had a word with the municipal housing characters. We designed housing for them on local authority Parker-Morris standards. Twenty-five per cent of the village was going to be local authority housing and each of those was going to be represented in the village council. This was grass-roots democracy. At the last moment the Greater London Council pulled out . . . but this would have been the first time I know of where local authority tenants would have been responsible for their own environment. Now since then we hear nothing but . . . but at that time, no sign of it.

Some doubts

Several of the landscape architects interviewed expressed doubts about public consultation. Some of these were reservations about the efficacy of some approaches. One or two came out strongly against large public meetings where vocal minorities often dominate the proceedings. Nevil Farr expressed a preference for working with individuals or small groups. Others thought that consultation was a virtue but admitted that they did not feel qualified or skilled enough to do it properly, and one interviewee frankly admitted that although he thought it was important, he hated doing it and delegated it whenever he could. Another regretted the time it consumed and said that this limited the number of community-based projects her practice took on.

There were some more profound doubts. Cheryl Tolladay thought that there could be a degree of tokenism about efforts to consult:

The best schemes are when you can involve people. I mean this is the Groundwork theory. You know, they get ownership of the scheme . . . but I think often, and even in the way we do it, it is a bit tokenistic, and that for people to really feel that ownership, they've got to think of the idea themselves. And raise the money to get it created, and then they can say 'Oh, let's go to Groundwork. They'll design it for us'. And we design it and perhaps get it implemented.

But what happens a lot is that we have the money, we have the ideas, and we decide that we'll do it. And then we say 'Well let's see what people want', so we pull them in at a much later stage. I think they get what they want, because we'll say 'Look we're thinking of putting in a park here. What do you think about it?' We'll produce some sort of questionnaire and we'll say 'What do you like about it now? What don't you like about it?' And it's all a bit predictable, and what's often dissatisfying is that people often aren't interested or they're very pessimistic.

Tom Robinson thinks that there is a large element of political correctness about public consultation exercises and that they have little to do with good design:

They're generally political in intent. They're used by action groups opposed to the development and they are proposed by developers or by planning people simply to go through a difficult exercise because they believe they will be criticised if they do not. I won't say it's simply to go through the motions, because there is generally an opportunity to amend an aspect of the scheme. There's never a scheme that can't be changed. But so often with schemes that merit a public consultation, they're so complex that unless the public consultation exercise is itself sophisticated, the end result is very unsatisfying to the designer, because you rarely feel that the point has been got across. Having said that, it's . . . if nothing else . . . good manners, if you're going to affect the lives of some people, to bother to explain it and to listen to their response, but it's very hard to build it into the design, very hard indeed.

. . . to be perfectly frank, some of this is where the social work side of landscape design comes in. If you're doing housing work, which I remember doing when I worked at Newcastle . . . you know, at a public meeting – 'What kind of plants do you want?' That's to empower them. It's nothing to do with good design. It's nothing to do with good management of public housing. What it's to do with is good relations between citizens and local government. It's nothing to do with design.

Indeed, Robinson cautions against questionnaire-based approaches which are likely to favour lowest-common-denominator solutions, and thus prove inimical to good design.

There is a view, held to a greater or lesser degree by many of the people I talked to, which could be caricatured as 'designer-knows-best', but which, more charitably, could be called a belief in the empathetic powers of the good designer. As Pauline Randall pointed out, there are circumstances when the ability to put oneself in the shoes of others is the only possible approach:

> We're currently designing public landscapes for a private sector client within a new settlement. There, of course, the users don't exist yet, so the only thing we can do is say 'Well I'm going to pretend I'm living in this house, what do I want to see out there. Is that usable?; is it safe?; have I done something that I think is reasonable?' That is the only path you can use, your own experience as a human being.

Landscape architects as activists?

Although landscape architects may be aware of social issues it is rare to find one who has translated this concern into any kind of political stance. It did not seem appropriate, within the parameters of this study, to ask direct questions about political affiliations, but, of the twenty-six people interviewed, two volunteered that their politics were to the left of centre and another that he had voted for the Green Party. The rest hardly mentioned politics at all.

Peter McGuckin and Peter Fischer, both private sector consultants, referred to landscape architecture as a vocation, a term more commonly used in relation to the church, teaching or medicine. There is, in the broadest sense, a caring attitude inherent in landscape architecture, but that concern may be directed towards people, towards vulnerable landscapes, or, more abstractly, towards the global ecosystem. It is possible to identify a vein of small-c conservatism in those aspects of the profession which are most concerned with the protection of landscapes which are highly valued for cultural or aesthetic reasons, yet paradoxically it is only through interventionist policies that such assets can be safeguarded.

For my own part, I believe that such concerns sit more comfortably with a left of centre political ideology, but it is, of course, possible to define a concern about people in terms of their economic well-being and this is something which parties both to the left and the right would claim as a motivation. Tom Robinson and Peter McGuckin, both consultants working in the North East, took satisfaction in assisting the economic regeneration of the region. I asked Robinson whether he was ever troubled by the thought that landscape architecture was so often the handmaiden of commercial development:

> It doesn't bother me at all, because development is what pays for everything. It's part of the economic process and environmental design is a First World profession. Architecture may exist in the Third World, but I'm pretty certain that landscape architecture barely exists in the Third World, so I'm not going to kill the goose that lays the golden eggs. I'm a believer in economic reconstruction.

As John Vaughan indicated earlier in this chapter, it is easier for those in the public sector to take the moral high ground. Those in the private sector may have to face difficult ethical decisions because so much of their work is generated by development.

The picture of the profession which emerges is certainly not one of a radical body of individuals committed to large-scale social change. In Liverpool I interviewed Margaret Jackson, who had moved out of landscape architecture to work in community and local economic development work. It was very clear from the way the interview came alive when she started talking about the achievements she had helped the local community to realise that she had been very frustrated as a landscape architect and clearly regarded the profession as a poor vehicle for bringing about significant social change. However, there were those among my interviewees who saw greater possibilities. Rebecca Hughes, for example, finds it impossible to compartmentalise her professional and political values:

> I think my personal values guide my professional values quite closely. I don't think I could say that I could tease them apart completely. I have a very egalitarian approach to the issues concerning land or its ownership or its condition and that comes I think from being influenced and taught by people

who I have a high regard for professionally, who had a powerful effect on me at an impressionable age and I've continued those thoughts through, together with my own professional experiences.

Hughes has analysed the problems facing the upland areas of Scotland and reached some fundamental conclusions:

> In Scotland it is very evident that certain approaches to the way that land is managed has had an extensive effect on the natural heritage and the landscape quality. We all know of the old adage of 'Scotland – the wet desert[13] – that's because of land management for particular purposes or, in some cases, neglect, and allowing deer numbers to increase to unsustainable levels. Now deer numbers are being culled right back down, so that allows a heavily degraded landscape to repair itself in a natural way. This situation has come about through land management and land ownership, the land use intentions of using land as gaming or sheep grazing and not as a place for people to live and work and play. There is the whole political arena of land reform and still sensitive issues concerning the land clearances of previous centuries. It is very difficult to separate the land ownership issue in Scotland because it has affected the resource that we now have, and that won't change, I don't think, markedly.

A shared vocation

A profession is not a political party or a ginger group. Landscape architects hold a wide range of social attitudes and political beliefs, yet they appear to share a vocation, at the centre of which is a belief that they can improve people's lives. Landscape architects who work in local government are often attracted to this sector by a public service ethos, but private consultants often share these values, particularly if they have undertaken work on behalf of local authorities.

In the majority of instances there need be no conflict between social objectives and the various aesthetic and ecological ends which the profession also pursues. From time to time such clashes do arise, however, and then there may be no easy way of reconciling the different goals. My interviews suggest that social objectives will often, though not invariably, override other values in such cases. Ecological and aesthetic goals are often justified in terms of their beneficial effects upon people.

Notes

1 Stirling Council replaced Stirling District Council as part of the reorganisation of local government in Scotland in 1995.
2 I have not been able to identify the park in question.
3 This local landmark is a mock-Grecian temple built by public subscription in 1844 to the memory of John George Lambton, the 1st Earl of Durham. It stands on top of a scrub-covered hillock.
4 A town to the west of Salford, part of the Manchester/Salford conurbation.
5 North Tyneside Metropolitan Borough includes the towns of Whitley Bay, Tynemouth, North Shields and Wallsend.
6 See Chapter 6 for an explanation of this term.
7 Tenants' Association.
8 A report *The Post Industrial Landscape* was produced for the Groundwork Foundation by John Handley at the University of Manchester (1966). It presents the detailed case for a more community and ecologically oriented approach to land reclamation. It notes that many sites where contamination levels are not dangerously high have 'stressed' conditions which have encouraged the development of interesting plant communities. Such sites are often assets to their communities: the report argues that they should not be reclaimed in the traditional way unless the contamination presents a threat to controlled waters, health, ecological systems or property.
9 The Millennium Commission has provided £22.1 million, with matching funding from a variety of other sources including English Partnerships, the Welsh Development Agency, local authorities and the European Union.
10 See Chapter 6 for an explanation of this term. Originally the name for a specific methodology, I suspect that its meaning has broadened out in practice to cover a wide range of participatory design workshop activities. At Bold Moss a landscape architect was involved in the Planning-for-Real process.
11 The Ridgacre Project is a partnership venture between Groundwork Black Country, Sandwell MBC, British Waterways, British Trust for Conservation Volunteers, Black Country Development Corporation and Centro.
12 Once again the term 'Planning-for-Real' was used by the Groundwork staff involved.
13 Hughes is referring to the view that management practices in the Scottish Highlands, particularly over-grazing by deer, have, when combined with the high-rainfall factor, denuded many hills of the oak or pine forests they might otherwise have supported.

PART III
ECOLOGY

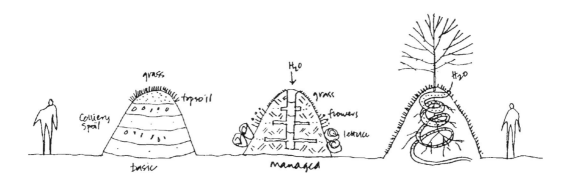

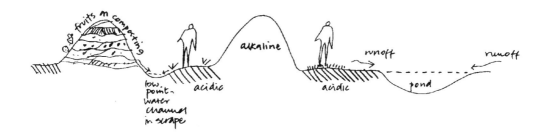

Earth Centre, Doncaster: concept sketches for the Pollution/Regeneration Garden. Situated on a primary footpath, this area will reveal the polluted nature of the ground and how it is being brought back to life (overleaf). (Courtesy of Grant Associates.)

8 Environmental ethics

In this section we must turn our attention to the third major source of values for landscape architecture which is to be found in the field of environmental ethics, which in turn draws heavily upon the science of ecology, although, as we shall see, there are contested models within ecology itself.

Landscape architects, increasingly, portray themselves as professional environmentalists. We must consider to what extent such a claim is justified, and how the moral values inherent in environmentalism correspond or fail to correspond with the aesthetic and social values considered thus far. This chapter will chart the emergence of an ecological perspective in landscape design and look in detail at some theories which, according to their proponents, have been expressly based upon ecological considerations. Just as we needed to explore aesthetic and sociological territory in previous sections, we now need to arm ourselves with a guidebook to ecology[1] and a map of the general ethical territory.[2]

Ecology: a science and a world-view

Ecology has entered into landscape architecture in two forms. As a science which has offered explanations of the manner in which plant species grow in association with one another, of how species relate to soil conditions and climate, and of the observable phenomenon of plant succession, it has had a direct influence on landscape architectural techniques. This influence was at its strongest during the 1970s when it became possible to talk of an 'Ecological Approach' to landscape design (which is described below). Ecology also enters into the landscape architectural

discourse as a rich source of metaphors and values. During the course of my interviews, many practitioners used the language of popular ecology to explain and justify their work. This was no surprise since the concepts of ecology have also swept through society as a whole to the extent that it is possible to talk of an ecological world-view.

But there are many ironies here. In particular it is striking that many of the metaphors that have made their way from ecology into the popular consciousness have been abandoned by the ecologists themselves. This suggests that some of the values which we label as 'ecological' are really nothing of the sort. It is just that ecology at various stages in its development has appeared to support ideas that were intrinsically appealing in their own right. To the extent that we hope to base our designs on good science, we must be wary of plausible explanations which may appeal to our common-sense view of the world, yet have no firm basis in observation and experiment.

De Jardins (1997) summarises some of the models that have been potent within ecology. First there is the name 'ecology' itself, coined by Ernst Haeckel in the 1860s by combining the Greek word *oikos*, meaning 'household' or 'home', with the word *logos*, meaning 'study of'. Thus ecology is the study of living organisms within their home environments. In one of the earliest metaphors to appear in this new subject, species were seen to relate to their environments in the way that organs are related to the body, a conception which opened the way for all sorts of associated imagery drawn from healthcare and medicine. De Jardins puts it in this way:

Just as an organism grows through developmental stages towards the mature level, so too do ecological 'households' grow, develop and mature. Ecological environments can therefore be described as healthy, diseased, young, mature, and the like, according to a natural developmental standard.

(De Jardins, 1997: 157)

The organic metaphor is anthropomorphic, as is the community metaphor. Two American ecologists, working at the end of the nineteenth century, Henry Cowles and Frederick Clements, first studied the waves of colonisation and displacement which we now know as plant succession. The facts of succession are readily observable in everyday situations. The farmer who does not cultivate a field will find that it is soon full of opportunistic weeds, which in time will be succeeded by tougher perennials, which in turn will give way to woody stemmed shrubs, and ultimately these will be replaced by trees. It is easy to slip into teleological ways of thinking about this process, whereby 'the hand of nature' prepares the ground for the trees, but there is a sufficient Darwinian explanation of the phenomenon which relies only upon the different reproductive strategies of the plants at different stages (Colinvaux, 1980: 111–113). Clements postulated that for any given location and climate there would be a relatively stable and permanent 'climax community'. However, he saw this community as a kind of superorganism. There is something comforting and orderly about the idea of succession leading inevitably to a climax community which is stable, unified, balanced and healthy, and this extremely powerful idea has persisted, even though ecologists themselves dropped the organic model early in the twentieth century, and even the idea that climax communities are stable has recently been questioned.

The community metaphor is also to be found in the work of the ecologist Charles Elton, who, in response to the Darwinian emphasis on competition between species, advocated a model of nature in which species are categorised by their function in the household of nature. Plants are producers, manu–facturing food through photosynthesis. Herbivores are primary consumers and carnivores are secondary or tertiary consumers. At the end of the food-chain come decomposers, mostly fungi and bacteria who feed on dead organic matter. It is interesting to note the use which the landscape architectural theorist Ian McHarg made of this metaphor (now superseded by explanations based on the language of energy flows in physical systems) in his book *Design with Nature*. For McHarg, mankind's special role in this household is to be the 'agent of symbioses' (McHarg, 1969), a poetic idea more than a scientific one.

In the 1930s the British ecologist Arthur Tansley introduced the concept of the ecosystem, which was to replace the organic model in mainstream ecological thinking. This did away with metaphysical notions of superorganisms. Ecosystems were to be understood in physical terms just like the systems which governed the behaviour of atoms and molecules or the motions of the planets. One advantage of this way of thinking was that it brought the abiotic elements such as soils, nutrients and climate into consideration in a way that the earlier models had not. Ecosystems were, however, still regarded in ways which were similar to the community model, in that they were seen as generally unified, balanced and stable. In the United States this view, which, while acknowledging competition between species, yet recognised emergent qualities of interdependence and co-operation at the ecosystemic level, was developed by Eugene Odum (1953) and was widely accepted. Aldo Leopold's '*Land Ethic*' (in Leopold 1949) suggested an ethical touchstone derived from these qualities. An act was right, he argued, if it preserved the *integrity, beauty* and *stability* of the biotic community, and wrong if it did otherwise.

Landscape architects, particularly those who wished to bolster the authority of the profession by placing it upon scientific foundations, took readily to the ecosystem model and even today it remains the most influential paradigm. This move also placed landscape architects in the same camp as those environmentalists who, believing that nature had an inherent tendency towards harmony and balance, tended to view the actions of humanity as the only serious threat to this order. Some of the possible responses to this threat are described later in the chapter. In general, landscape architects have taken the line that some *rapprochement* between humanity and nature is both possible and desirable and that it is their job to help to bring this about. This was a theme which often arose during the course of my interviews with practitioners.

However, while the world-view that has developed around ecosystem thinking has become a potent political force, within ecology itself a serious challenge to this paradigm has emerged.[3] In 1973, William Drury and Ian Nesbitt, drawing upon research in the north-eastern temperate forests of the United States, asserted that ecological succession does not invariably lead to the rise of a stable climax community. Indeed they found no progressive development of the characteristics which Odum had said were typical of a mature ecosystem. The forest was nothing more than an erratic, shifting mosaic of plants. This amounted to an individualistic account of nature in which each species did its own thing, without any emergent collective entities appearing.

Under intense scrutiny from within the scientific community, the idea that diversity and stability were positively related began to crumble. Computer simulations of 'random communities' suggested that diversity and stability might be *inversely* related (May, 1975). At the same time, the whole concept of 'stability' was questioned. It was seen that it could mean many different things – constancy (absence of change), persistence (length of survival), resistance to perturbation, speed of return after perturbation, and so on.[4] Robert Peters (1991) traces the origins of the diversity–stability hypothesis to pre-scientific notions of the 'balance of nature' which appealed to the conservationist inclinations of many ecologists. He concludes that the vagueness of the terms employed renders it unscientific:

> Despite its difficulties, the diversity–stability relationship cannot be said to be false. The ambiguity of the literature in its regard and the faddish swings of scientific opinion about it reflect the nebulosity of the terms. Unless these can be defined, the relation will never be falsified.
>
> (Peters, 1991: 97)

These ructions within ecology came at a time when the whole of science was moving towards a more chaotic view of nature.[5] In fields as diverse as climatology, physics, astronomy and economics, people were beginning to believe that the world is fundamentally discontinuous, erratic and unpredictable.[6] At the same time, a view of ecology in which there are no harmonious wholes but just raw competition can be seen to serve the political purposes of right-wing libertarians, for if there is no order in nature there is nothing for human activities to disrupt.

These are potentially worrying conclusions which could invalidate many of the landscape profession's core assumptions. While the 'mature ecosystem' view seemed to lend weight to the need for sound environmental management, what conclusions are to be drawn from a chaotic view of nature? Should we admit our incapacity to predict or control and withdraw from any sort of intervention? Does a chaotic world sanction any kind of exploitative behaviour? Or does the very unpredictability and volatility of the system make it all the more important that we act cautiously and responsibly?

Getting the science we need

These troublesome questions reveal how dangerous it can be to attempt to build an ethic upon science. Not only does this endeavour fall into what philosophers have called the 'naturalistic fallacy' of trying to derive values from facts (or to reason from *is* to *ought*), but science itself, far from being the value-free objective pursuit we were told it was in our schooldays, turns out to be just as subject to social influences as any other human institution. Not only does science not proceed by establishing unshakeable truths (but rather, as Popper and Kuhn have shown, by disproving shakeable hypotheses[7]), but in all sorts of ways, from the different levels of funding given to different sorts of inquiry, to the variety of metaphors that creep into scientific explanations, and the range of possible interpretations that can be given to any corpus of facts, the mirror which science holds up to the world is distorted by social influences.[8]

There are those outside the scientific community who seize upon evidence that nature is pure competition as a justification for their political beliefs, just as there are some who hope that ecology will demonstrate that mutualism and co-operation are the dominant characteristics of the natural world.[9] Scientists themselves may still cleave to the notion that they are distinterested observers, but at times scientific debates can appear to be just political fisticuffs about the nature of society transferred to a scientific venue.

Nevertheless, for all its failings, it is still rational to regard science as our best means for understanding the world. As Bertrand Russell wrote: 'Science is at no moment quite right, but it is seldom quite wrong, and has, as a rule, a better chance of being right than the theories of the unscientific' ([1959] 1995: 13).

What we need then is better, more useful science. In his powerful critique of contemporary ecology, Peters (1991) shows how ill-founded are many of its most influential concepts and models. His fundamental complaint is that ecology has not managed to turn itself into the predictive science that society most urgently needs. 'There is', he says, 'a disparity between the precision with which we can know past events and the crudity with which we can predict the future' (1991: 172).

Applied ecology shares a problem with medicine, in that both must address unique situations. A doctor must treat each of her patients as unique, although she seeks to bring her general medical knowledge to bear, as well as her knowledge of the patient's particular history. Each case is different, so there are no scientific controls or replication studies. If the patient gets better we cannot be sure if the doctor helped or not. It is similar in ecology. A management intervention into a forest or a lake will seek to apply the best available models to the unique circumstances of the situation, but the treatment must be monitored and changed if it does not seem to be working. Unfortunately ecological disturbances are often just the sort of novel circumstances in which models based upon previous observations are likely to break down. As Peters observes, the global models which suggest calamities like global warming or a lethal rise in ultraviolet radiation cannot be tested, so they remain plausible historical scenarios. They are so awful to contemplate, however, that we must keep their possibilities forever before our minds and manage the world in as cautious and conservative a manner as possible.

While we may lack certain information about the future we are still able to make choices about the need to optimise the well-being of a particular biological community or the biosphere; indeed, our situation is such that we *must* make such choices. We should be clear, however, about what we are doing. We are making value judgements rather than conducting empirical science. Science cannot spare us from the task of making difficult decisions, although we may still turn to ecologists for assistance and expert advice when considering such choices.

Gaia

Ecological science is of great importance to landscape architecture, and the cautionary tone of much of the preceding discussion has been aimed at those within the profession who, for the most laudable of motives, have seized upon ecological concepts uncritically and with too much eagerness. While it is reasonable to base one's practice on contemporary science, one must always remain aware that even good science provides only provisional knowledge. The same caution must apply to James Lovelock's Gaia Hypothesis (Lovelock, 1979, 1988) which in many ways is even more compelling than the notion of the stable climax community; yet its suggestion that the earth itself can be understood as a living organism is surely one of the most powerful and motivating ideas to have emerged in the twentieth century.

Lovelock's theory is, of course, metaphorical. In fact it embraces two images, a quasi-religious one which may have been responsible for much of the antagonism initially shown by scientists, and the more useful one of the biosphere as a kind of super-organism (the parallel with Clement's ideas of the 'climax community' is evident). It is this second metaphor which may turn out to be the most fruitful. Lovelock himself has amplified it by a series of analogies; the earth is like a termites' nest, where the insects shape their own house but could not exist without it, or like a great tree, which we would recognise as a living organism even though the only parts which are truly living are the leaves and a thin layer just beneath the bark. As with the organic model, Gaian terminology lends itself to medical analogies, for if the earth is a living organism it is reasonable to discuss its state of health.

Defending Lovelock's hypothesis, the philosopher, Mary Midgley, has written:

In short, [Lovelock] shows everywhere the tremendous continuity, the radical interdependence that links what we think of as living matter with the whole world around it.

Once understood, this reasoning debunks and displaces a deadening world-picture of which we were barely conscious – namely, the Enlightenment's vision of the world as an object, a meaningless mass of dead matter set over against us, something alien to us and properly viewed as a heap of resources. It shows that we, as living things, are natives of this earth, not alien colonists coming in from some distant intellectual sphere to subdue it by abstract thought. It shows that we are at home here – a vital insight which had been obscured by the two more specific world pictures which the Enlightenment has left us and which till now have been accepted as scientific.

(Midgley, 1998)

The two world-pictures to which Midgley refers in this passage are those of the world as a great piece of mechanism and the more recent picture of romantic individualism, expressed in what she describes as 'the myth of the Selfish Gene'[10] and in the competitive emphasis of some recent ecology. Gaia, conversely, suggests that while competition has its place, it can only work at all within a larger framework which is co-operative.

Landscape ecology

In 1986 Richard Forman and Michael Godron published their *Landscape Ecology*, establishing a sub-discipline which lies somewhere between the reductionism of the population ecologists and the quasi-mysticism of Gaia. Its focus is upon ecological processes at the scale of the landscape or region and it introduces concepts such as *patch, matrix* and *corridor* as analytical tools. This focus alone would make it particularly interesting to landscape architects, but the authors' determination to forge a useful applied science makes it even more so. Richard Forman has been developing the practical applications of his earlier theoretical work and his *Land Mosaics* (1995) attempts to answer the question 'how would you plan a sustainable environment and how would you recognise one?' (p. 486). The landscape he envisages is a mosaic of patches and corridors optimised to maximise the heterogeneity of ecosystems and the interactions between them. He throws out a challenge to all involved in landscape planning:

we hypothesise that for any landscape, or any major portion of a landscape, there exists an optimal spatial arrangement of ecosystems and land uses to maximise ecological integrity. The same is true for achieving basic human needs and for creating a sustainable environment. If so, the major, but tractable, challenge is to discover the arrangement.

(Forman, 1995: 522)

We will return to this challenge at the end of the chapter. First we must turn our attention to the related field of environmental ethics.

Typologies of environmental ethics

The perception that the world is fast approaching an environmental crisis has vastly increased the attention being paid by philosophers to questions concerned with humanity's relationship to its environment. Following the publication of Aldo Leopold's *A Sand County Almanac* (1949), a new branch of moral philosophy called environmental ethics developed, and this now substantial body of literature contains many insights which may be of value to the profession of landscape architecture as it strives to incorporate environmental obligations into a value system which has hitherto been concerned with matters of social benefit, amenity and aesthetics.

However, the proliferation of ideas within environmental ethics can seem bewildering and prolix. To progress we need a typology of the principal strands. There are two useful ways of approaching this daunting area. One is to consider the varieties of ethical theory in terms of the kinds of objects which they consider to have intrinsic worth, and, as such, to be worthy of moral consideration. Here there are two broad divisions, the anthropocentric and the nonanthropocentric, each of which may be subdivided. Anthropocentric theories include both egocentric and homocentric varieties, while nonanthropocentric theories can be classified as either biocentric or ecocentric (Table 8.1). The second approach, and this may be particularly fruitful for our investigation, is to follow Tim O'Riordan in classifying the policy outcomes, in terms of attitudes towards resource management, which emerge from different positions within environmental ethics (Table 8.2). These typologies are offered as useful conceptual tools, but it would be a mistake to regard any of the categories as hard-edged or mutually exclusive. There are infinite shades of environmental thought.

Egocentric, homocentric, biocentric and ecocentric positions

Anthropocentric theories place the human species at the centre of the moral universe. Human beings are not only the only moral agents in the world, they are the only creatures with moral interests or intrinsic

Table 8.1 A typology of theories within environmental ethics

Anthropocentric		Nonanthropocentric	
Egocentric	Homocentric	Biocentric	Ecocentric
Self-interest	Greatest good of the greatest number	Members of the biotic community have moral standing	Ecosystems and/or the biosphere have moral standing
Laissez-faire			
Mutual coercion (mutually agreed)	Stewardship of nature (for human use and enjoyment)		Duty to the whole environment
			Holism
Classical economics	Utilitarianism	Moral extensionism	Deep Ecology
Capitalism	Marxism	Animal rights	Land Ethic
New Right	Left Greens	Bio-egalitarianism	Gaianism
	Eco-socialism		Buddhism
	'Shallow' ecology		American Indian
Thomas Hobbes	J.S. Mill	Albert Schweitzer	Aldo Leopold
John Locke	Jeremy Bentham	Peter Singer	J. Baird Callicott
Adam Smith	Barry Commoner	Tom Regan	
Thomas Malthus	Murray Bookchin	Paul Taylor	
Garret Hardin			
	Most landscape architects?		

Source: Adapted from Merchant (1992).

worth. The rest of nature has no such interests, and has worth only to the extent that it is instrumental in meeting the needs of *Homo sapiens*. Anthropocentric theories can in turn be divided into egocentric and homocentric varieties.

Egocentric ethics are grounded in the self. What is good for individuals turns out to be good for society. Egocentric ethics, it is easy to see, sit uncomfortably with most theories of environmental ethics. They are more generally associated with *laissez-faire* liberalism, capitalism and free markets and are to be found in the work of Hobbes, Locke and Adam Smith. Garret Hardin's 'Tragedy of the Commons' (1968) can be said to be an environmental ethic which belongs in this company. Like Hobbes, Hardin believes that human beings are naturally competitive and that this leads inevitably to a capitalist form of economic life. Resource depletion and pollution are inevitable consequences, because there are no incentives for individuals, companies or nations to control their levels of exploitation. Like Hobbes he

believes that mutually agreed coercion is the only remedy for this predicament.

More commonly, anthropomorphic theories can be described as homocentric, in that they are grounded in notions of welfare and social justice. Both Utilitarianism and Marxism are species of homocentric theory. If Utilitarians came to regard the stewardship of the natural world as an important priority, it would only be because this in turn contributed to the greatest happiness of the greatest number (of humans!). Marx and Engels thought that science and technology could liberate mankind from the tyrannies of nature, but they also recognised the environmental consequences of the capitalist mode of production. Engels noted, for example, that the Italians who cut down fir forests in the Alps were simultaneously destroying the watersheds upon which their dairy industry depended (Parsons, 1977). Contemporary social ecologists like Murray Bookchin (1982, 1989) suggest that science and technology must be retained, but that they must be infused by a

Table 8.2 Contemporary trends in environmentalism

Technocentrism		*Ecocentrism*	
Belief in the retention of the *status quo* in the existing structure of political power, but a demand for more responsiveness and accountability in political, regulatory, planning and educational institutions.		Demand for redistribution of power towards a decentralised, federated economy with more emphasis on informal economic and social transaction and the pursuit of participatory justice.	
Intervention	*Accommodation*	*Communalism*	*Gaianism*
Faith in the application of science, market forces and managerial ingenuity	Faith in the adaptability of institutions and approaches to assessment and evaluation to accommodate environmental demands	Faith in the co-operative capabilities of societies to establish self-reliant communities based on renewable resource use and appropriate technologies	Faith in the rights of nature and of the essential need for co-evolution of human and natural ethics
Business and finance managers; skilled workers; self-employed; right-wing politicians; career-focused youth	Middle-ranking executives; environmental scientists; white collar trade unions; liberal-socialist politicians	Radical socialists; committed youth; radical-liberal politicians; intellectual environmentalists	'Green' supporters; radical philosophers
	Most landscape architects?	Some radical landscape architects?	Some radical landscape architects?

Source: Based on O'Riordan (1991)

new world-view which recognises the dependence of humans on non-human nature.

It is possible to hold a weak-homocentrist position which admits the intrinsic value of living things other than human beings. A distinction can be made between the belief that *only* humanity has intrinsic value and the belief that while humanity has the greatest value, other living things may have lesser, yet nevertheless intrinsic, values of their own.

Nonanthropocentrists start from a radically different position. They base their ethics on the view that all living things – and, in some theories, even non-living things like rocks or mountains – have intrinsic moral value and therefore we owe duties towards them.

Biocentric theories extend the boundaries of moral significance to include other members of the biotic community, i.e. plants and animals. Some philosophers advocate the principle of *biocentric egalitarianism* according to which human beings are not just a part of nature, they are an *equal* part of

nature. The Norwegian philosopher, Arne Naess (1973, 1989 with Rothenberg), suggests that all beings have 'the equal right to live and blossom'. At first sight this seems like an admirable principle, an extension of rights to the biotic community which parallels previous extensions to slaves, other races, women and so on, but humanists and homocentrists have been alarmed by the implication that the moral standing of human beings should be reduced to the same level as that of slime moulds or yeast cultures. Some deep ecologists (see below) have fuelled these fears by implying that humanity, far from being the crowning achievement of millennia of evolution, is instead some kind of planetary blight or disease.

Ecocentric theories are close in spirit to biocentric theories, but locate moral value in the larger ecosystem rather than the individual lifeforms that comprise it. Ecosystems are to be valued for their complexity, interconnectedness and persistence. Biocentrists also value ecosystems, but do so on the grounds that preserving ecosystems will ensure the protection of the plants and animals contained within them.

Support for ecocentric / biocentric viewpoints is often drawn from religious or spiritual traditions such as Buddhism or the land wisdom of the American Indians. These resonate with the ideas of unity, stability, diversity and harmony which, as we have seen, can be found in the scientific literature of ecology. Aldo Leopold is usually credited with the first modern formulation of a biocentric ethic. His 'Land Ethic', published as the final chapter of his posthumous *A Sand County Almanac,* includes this ethical test: 'A thing is right when it tends to preserve the integrity, beauty and stability of the biotic community. It is wrong when it tends otherwise' (Leopold, 1949: 240).

Closely related to biocentrism and ecocentrism is the idea of Deep Ecology, first coined by Arne Naess (1973). He proposes a new metaphysics, based to some extent on ideas found in the philosophy of Spinoza, in which all organisms, including people, are knots in the total field of existence. This paves the way for a close identification between individual humans and the cosmos. If this could be accomplished, Naess argues, there would be no need for an environmental ethics with its notions of rights and duties, because it would be self-evident that to harm nature is to harm ourselves. Some have wondered how this can possibly be achieved, while others have suggested that the demotion of individual human beings and their rights opens the door to some kind of eco-fascism. There is a temptation for deep ecologists to accept the Malthusian premise that excessive human numbers are at the root of all environmental problems and that scarcity and famine are therefore 'inevitable, irrevocable, even benign' (Bradford, 1989). Socially oriented ethicists are appalled by such suggestions.

Deep ecologists characterise anthropocentrically based environmental ethics as *shallow ecology.* 'Deep' is taken to mean more aware and more significant, so, by implication, 'shallow' has come to mean less aware and less significant. This might, however, be seen as an unfair characterisation of homocentric theories which have 'deep' philosophical foundations of their own. It also ignores attempts to reconcile classical humanistic ethics with the insight, now widely accepted, that there are intrinsic, non-instrumental values in nature and that these must be respected.

Attempts to reconcile the positions

While the differences between the anthropocentric and nonanthropocentric positions has produced a creative tension within environmental ethics, there have been many attempts to get beyond this division. Some, like Naess, try to transcend or dissolve the dilemma. Others seek a pragmatic compromise. Brennan (1988) has given the name of 'ecological humanism' to a position which recognises that most benign attitudes towards nature are ultimately human-centred. Pragmatically humans must be stewards of the environment because it is the capacity of ecosystems to provide resources that maintains human life, but non-material, non-pragmatic reasons, such as the spiritual and emotional satisfaction which humans derive from the contemplation of beautiful or unspoilt nature, are also of fundamental importance. Similarly Bryan Norton (1997) has advanced his 'convergence hypothesis' which claims that policies designed to protect the biological bequest to future generations will overlap significantly with policies that would follow from a clearly specified and coherent belief that nonhuman nature has intrinsic value. Norton points out that his hypothesis is an empirical one. He believes that policies designed to protect nature from an anthropocentric point of view will 'do as much good in protecting the moral commitment of deep ecologists as any other policy that could be undertaken given what we know now' (Norton, 1997: 99).

Of course, the pragmatists have their opponents and the argument probably has a long way to run, but let us provisionally side with the convergence camp, as they seem to offer us a way beyond the anthropocentric–nonanthropocentric division. Accepting Norton's hypothesis would seem to offer landscape architecture a means of reconciling its humanistic concerns with its ecological responsibilities.

Ecocentric and technocentric perspectives

O'Riordan (1991) proposes a terminology in which he contrasts ecocentric attitudes (he uses the word 'ecocentric' in a different sense to the one described above, although there are similarities) with the stance which he labels technocentric. Once again these broad categories can be subdivided (Table 8.2).

Ecocentrists have a mistrust of large-scale technology, but may believe in 'appropriate' technology. They abhor materialism and political centralisation and advocate forms of living based upon small-scale communities. They range from what O'Riordan calls the Gaianists (roughly equivalent to believers in Deep Ecology) to the communalists, whose underlying beliefs may be weak-homocentric.

On the other hand, technocentrists have faith in the capacity of science to solve environmental problems in the longer term. At the interventionist end of this spectrum are those who believe that our present form of society will be able to continue in its pursuit of economic growth while science and technology will be able to step in to cure any environmental difficulties that arise along the way. The accommodators are more cautious. They believe in careful economic and environmental management, including varieties of environmental assessment, cost–benefit analysis, environmental economics and risk assessment. O'Riordan recognises that the borders between the ecocentric and technocentric perspectives are fuzzy. Environmentalists often express views which amalgamate aspects of the two positions.

O'Riordan places most 'environmental scientists' into the category of 'accommodators', while 'intellectual environmentalists' are to be found on the opposite side of the ecocentric–technocentric division but within the 'communalist' camp. As we will see, great stress is placed within the landscape architectural literature upon the need to harmonise human activities with natural processes. This suggests a rejection of the interventionist position, but while individual landscape architects may espouse communalist or even Gaian values, it would seem that in the absence of any radical critique of societal organisation from within the profession, the most appropriate classification of landscape architecture would be among the accommodators. We will look more closely at this hypothesis when we come to examine some of the texts written by landscape architects considered to have been ecologically motivated and influential.

The development of an environmental perspective in landscape architectural theory

Having laid out maps of the scientific and ethical territory we are ready to consider the position occupied by landscape architecture. A historical perspective is required because just as society's cognisance of environmental issues has increased over the period in question, so the profession has assimilated

– or is assimilating – ethical values which reflect both this widespread concern and the emergence of ecology, from a relatively obscure branch of the biological sciences, into an influential world-view and belief system. To simplify the task, we will focus upon Anglo-American landscape architectural theory. The identification of eras is tentative and recognises that the boundaries between them are blurred.

Pre-1960: use and beauty

The early years of the Institute of Landscape Architects, which was established in Britain in 1929, were dominated by issues of aesthetics. Peter Youngman represented the mood of the times in an interview he gave for the book, *Reflections on Landscape* (Harvey, 1987):

> It was a time when Clough Williams-Ellis and others were writing polemical books (such as *Britain and the Beast*) and the Council for the Preservation of Rural England was increasingly active. People were becoming conscious of the damage being done to the rural landscape – ribbon development, trunk roads, advertisement hoardings, caravans. It seemed to me that designing herbaceous borders for Surrey and Sussex stockbrokers would scarcely be a worthwhile lifetime occupation. There were bigger concerns – more public.
>
> (Harvey 1987: 108)

The moral tone of this remark is evident, but note that the evils it condemns are essentially visual evils. The environmental damage depicted is primarily aesthetic.

Most of the influential books on British landscape design published around the middle of the century were centrally concerned with the visual quality of the British landscape. Brenda Colvin's *Land and Landscape* (1970), for example, first published in 1948, attempted to show that 'human use in itself is not incompatible with landscape beauty' (p. 150). She suggested, for example, that the needs for timber production, for raising the agricultural productivity of highland districts and for maintaining or increasing the recreational value of highland landscapes, are capable of being balanced by good design in a way that might actually improve the scenery. She offers advice on the design of forests, of new dams and reservoirs, of camp sites and caravan parks, of shelter belts, of allotment gardens, and so on, in a comprehensive survey of the British landscape and the social and economic pressures upon it. In similar vein, Sylvia Crowe's *Tomorrow's Landscape*, first published in 1956, has chapters on 'Open Country', 'The Farmlands' and what she calls 'The Townsman's Country' which are full of down-to-earth suggestions for removing or preventing visual ills. These topics were still alive in 1972 when Nan Fairbrother produced *New Lives, New Landscapes*, which covers similar territory, thematically and topographically.

For all of these writers it was important to establish that a visually attractive landscape could be a functional and productive one. This quotation from *Land and Landscape* indicates the tenor of such discussions:

> Planning at the present time is actuated by motives of efficiency and the needs of the future. But does it allow sufficiently for landscape beauty among those needs? And is the relationship between different functions, and the bearing of that relationship on efficiency and on landscape beauty, fully appreciated? We too readily discount as 'sentimental nonsense' any argument based on the appearance of the landscape, still reacting to the idea of use versus beauty. If we could once realise that in landscape they are fundamentally complementary we should suspect, profoundly, any line of action which clearly tends to destroy either.
>
> (Colvin, 1970: 178)

If we consider the sorts of work for which British landscape architects became recognised during this period we find that they reflect this concern for assimilating use with beauty. Practitioners became involved with the siting and visual amelioration of large industrial structures in the countryside, as did Geoffrey Jellicoe with the Hope Cement Works in Derbyshire (where he was appointed in 1942 to produce a fifty-year plan for the quarries), and Peter Youngman, whose involvement with the CEGB's controversial plans for a nuclear power station at Sizewell began in 1958. Sylvia Crowe's book, *The Landscape of Power* (1958), can be seen as a classic text for O'Riordan's accommodators. It shuns a preservationist stance towards the landscape and (as the dust-jacket notes state) 'she accepts the essential need for the construction of immense oil refineries, nuclear reactors, power stations and the network of the electricity grid'. Her later work for the Forestry Commission, which employed her in 1963 to advise on the aesthetics of plantation design, also comes under this description. This is a tradition which continues, Building Design Partnership's involvement in the visual mitigation of the Channel Tunnel Terminal being a contemporary example.

The issues which concerned authors like Crowe, Colvin and Fairbrother are still very much with us, but they tend now to be overshadowed by larger environmental concerns; what now appears to be at stake is not merely the preservation of a scenic rural England but the very continuation of human life, or

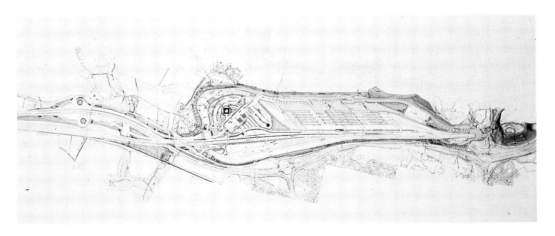

Figure 8.1 BDP's landscape masterplan for the Channel Tunnel is a sophisticated piece of 'technocentric accommodation', in the same broad tradition as the work done by Geoffrey Jellicoe for the Hope Cement Works or by Sylvia Crowe for the Central Electricity Generating Board.

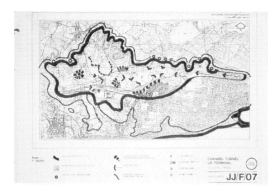

Figure 8.2 Visual analysis of the Channel Tunnel Terminal site undertaken by BDP as part of the Environmental Impact Assessment.

Figure 8.3 Landform model of the Channel Tunnel Terminal proposals. (BDP Landscape Ltd.)

life of any form, on the planet. In planning and designing the land it is no longer enough for use to be coupled with beauty; both must be wed to environmental sustainability. There is evidence to suggest that these early writers were becoming aware of this necessity. Colvin, for example, wrote: 'correct biological balance in the widest sense, comprising the whole life-cycle, through soil, plants, animals and man, must be applied to the whole land, if it is to remain beautiful' (1970: 83). Here she is equating the ecologically balanced landscape with the beautiful landscape, but interestingly beauty is still given the higher position in her value system. Ecological balance may be worth while in its own right, but it is also valuable because it is instrumental in creating landscape beauty.

And commenting upon *Tomorrow's Landscape* during her interview for *Reflections on Landscape*, Crowe observes:

> One of the points I made was that the future well-being of the land does mean you have to keep the full range of species and plant life going. I think the book covered it, but if I was writing it now, I would probably want to labour the point a bit more, because the dangers have increased since I wrote that.
>
> (Harvey, 1987: 40)

Elsewhere in the same book, Peter Youngman notes the effect that the publication of Arthur Tansley's *The British Isles and their Vegetation* in 1939 had upon his generation of landscape architects. Even in 1948 Colvin was able to describe ecology as 'the science of landscape' (Colvin, 1948: 65), and with the support of Sylvia Crowe and Brian Hackett it was included in the Institute of Landscape Architect's first examination syllabus. Moreover, when Hackett established Britain's first full-time postgraduate course in Landscape Design at the University of Newcastle upon Tyne in 1949, he expressly stated that it was to be a course based upon ecological principles of design. It is interesting to note that this development was taking place at the same time that Leopold was formulating his 'Land Ethic' (Leopold, 1949), although I found no evidence that British landscape architects of the time were aware of this work.

In claiming that a complex ecosystem has intrinsic value, one comes very close to saying that it has an aesthetic value, whether or not there are human beings around to appreciate it, but this is a problematic position and not one to which most aestheticians would subscribe. In general, when we talk about aesthetic values, we are talking about humanistic values. It is reasonable to conclude, therefore,

AERIAL VIEW FROM THE WEST   4.7.1990   BDP

Figure 8.4 Aerial perspective of the Terminal as viewed from the west. (Courtesy of BDP Landscape Ltd.)

that British landscape architects in the middle years of this century, while aware of the growing significance of ecology, were nevertheless very firmly in the homocentric camp in terms of their attitudes towards the environment. In terms of O'Riordan's terminology they could also be described as accommodators, with a belief in environmental planning and design but also a trust in the sorts of technologies represented by dams, nuclear power stations and large-scale extractive industries.

If we turn to American developments during the same period, we find different preoccupations, but they are, once again, dominantly anthropocentric. It is significant that when Peter Walker decided to write a chronicle of the achievements of post-war American landscape architects his chosen focus was upon modernism rather than environmentalism. (Walker and Simo, 1994).[11]

The American Modernists inherited Olmsted's twin concerns for aesthetics and for social questions. There is insufficient space within this volume to examine in depth the belief systems of such influential figures as Church, Halprin, Eckbo, Kiley and Tunnard, but Treib (1993: 36–67) has usefully identified six 'Axioms for a Modern Landscape Architecture' which, he believes, amounted to an implicit manifesto for the era. Briefly they are:

1 a denial of historical styles;
2 a concern for space rather than pattern;
3 landscapes are for people (i.e. a functionalist programme based on human use);
4 the destruction of the axis;
5 plants are used for their individual qualities as botanical entities and sculpture;
6 integration of house and garden.

This is a telling list. Note that the axioms can be classified into two groups – either they are concerned with aesthetics (1, 2, 4, 5) or with function (3, 6). Concepts like *ecology* and *sustainability* were not yet common currency, of course, but it is nevertheless striking how little attention the modernists paid to what we would now recognise as ecological issues.

In part this can be explained by the types of commission they received during the period. Looking back on his career, Garret Eckbo lists the following projects:

Gardens, north and south: 600–80[12]
Housing developments: 175
Community facilities: 76
Education, elementary to university: 81
Commercial: 62
Planning: 9

(Treib, 1993: 218)

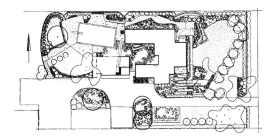

Figure 8.5 Californian garden in the modernist idiom by Eckbo, Dean Austin and Williams.

It can be argued that while the private garden was the perfect laboratory for experimenting with a modernist conception of landscape design, closely linked to architectural modernism, it was less suited to the development of an ecological awareness. Garden design is always undertaken for a client, who is most likely also the end-user. This sort of design is quintessentially homocentric, as the client's brief is paramount. Landscape architects of the period also looked over their shoulders at their iconoclastic colleagues in architecture and sought to assimilate their theories. At the garden scale, they found this easy to do. The key to this was to treat the garden as an additional room in the house, while regarding the house itself as 'a machine for living in'.

As we saw in Chapter 6, one of the most influential books of the period was Christopher Tunnard's *Gardens in the Modern Landscape,* first published in 1938, in which he suggests three sources for a creative renewal of landscape architectural design. The first is a functionalism straight from Le Corbusier and embracing such ideals as simplicity, the rejection of past styles, economy of expression and allowing function to determine form. This is closely linked with an aesthetic principle which relegates decoration and ornament, colour and pattern from being ends in themselves to being integral elements of an overall plan. These two principles are emphatically rationalistic and anthropocentric.

Only in the remaining principle, which Tunnard calls the 'empathetic' and which is strongly influenced by traditional Japanese architecture and garden design, does he betray sentiments which might be considered ecocentric, for he says that 'nature is therefore not to be copied or sentimentalised, neither is she to be overridden.' (1948: 105). He wishes to banish 'the antagonistic, masterful attitude towards Nature'. In Japanese design he finds the truth that Western man's 'much vaunted identity is an illusion, and the truth which the Orient now reveals to him is that his identity is not separate from Nature and his fellow-beings, but is at one with her and them'. This almost sounds like something that a deep-green follower of Arne Naess could espouse. It is not, however, the dominant theme of Tunnard's book.[13]

1960–80: The era of environmental awareness

Choosing a particular date as the point at which an environmental or ecological ethos emerged is diffi-

cult and almost certain to misrepresent what was a gradual process. Peter Walker recounts that it was in 1950 that Hideo Sasaki persuaded Stanley White to reorganise landscape teaching at the University of Illinois on the basis of natural science, and that when the NCILA met at Harvard in 1951 one of the topics discussed was the ecological approach to analysis and design. As we noted at the beginning of this chapter, the development of environmental ethics began with the publication of Leopold's *A Sand County Almanac* in 1949. Walker recognises that this was an important moment, but also that it took time for the new thinking to percolate through the discipline: 'Even if few landscape architects had read Leopold's wonderful book in the 1950s, the profession would soon inherit Leopold's concern for ecological balance and stewardship of natural resources' (Walker and Simo, 1994: 262).

Nevertheless there are good reasons for selecting the 1960s as the decade in which ecological ideas took hold. The event which got things moving was the first publication in 1962 of Rachel Carson's *Silent Spring* (1963) which aroused the general public to the threat posed by pesticides to all life on earth. Environmental concern continued to mount throughout the decade. When the first pictures of the earth from space were beamed down from Apollo VIII in 1968, it was revealed to be a uniquely beautiful planet, and seen against its vast empty backdrop it also appeared bounded and vulnerable.

During the late 1950s, Philip Lewis, working at that time from the University of Illinois,[14] had started to develop an approach to large-scale landscape planning which recognised a relationship between visual quality and underlying environmental factors (Lewis, 1996), but the landscape architect whose name is most widely known in this context is Ian McHarg, whose seminal book *Design with Nature* (1969) had a profound influence upon a generation of practitioners and it still widely used in landscape education today. Lance Neckar observes that McHarg paid tribute to the ideas of both Tunnard and Eckbo, but that his fundamental departure was to recognise that: 'The client took a tertiary position within a larger matrix of problems, the bases of which were the bio- and geo-physical orders of the landscape' (Neckar, 1990: 243).

In *Design with Nature*, McHarg attempts to establish an entire system of values upon natural science, and in particular upon the concepts of entropy and negentropy. He expresses his world-view through an imaginary people, the Naturalists, who live close to nature, believing that 'the earth and its denizens are involved in a totally creative process and that there is a unique and important role for man. It is agreed that evolution is directional, that it has recognisable attributes and that man is involved in its orderings' (McHarg, 1969: 117). This hints at a teleological view of evolution and at a homocentric view of humanity's position. However, elsewhere McHarg likens mankind's role to that of a 'planetary enzyme' and this image is more consistent with an ecocentric position:

> If one can view the biosphere as a single super-organism, then the Naturalist considers that man is an enzyme capable of its regulation, and conscious of it. He is of the system and depend-ent upon it, but has responsibility for manage-ment, derived from his apperception.
>
> (McHarg, 1969: 124)

McHarg justifies his value system with an argu-ment that commences with the thought that in living processes energy is trapped on its path from the sun down into entropy. He defines this as 'creation – the raising of matter from lower to higher order, negentropy' (1969: 118). He contrasts a sand dune, which is simple, unstable and not very ordered, with a forest, which is diverse, stable, highly ordered and therefore possesses high 'negentropy'. If this were all that there is to McHarg's system, it would follow that plants are the supreme creators of value, since they are the primary creators of negentropy. Other lifeforms, including humans, would have far less value.

However, McHarg takes a further step by equating energy with information:

> If we consider energy as information and use apperception as value, then quite different creatures assume ascendancy. The evolution of more complex perceiving creatures reflects this value, and here man ranks very high indeed.
>
> (McHarg, 1969: 121)[15]

This is a dubious move because there is no strict equivalence between an amount of energy and an amount of information; the best that can be argued is that information is structured energy. McHarg seems to be suggesting two polarised value systems:

one is essentially ecocentric, the other homocentric, for it could be argued that the value of planktons, lichens and the rest of the vegetable kingdom is purely instrumental – they only have value because they allow sentient organisms, particularly man, to exist.

McHarg's route out of this apparent contra-diction is to introduce the idea of symbioses, co-operative arrangements which play an essential part in sustaining the biosphere and thus in adding value through increased negentropy. *Homo sapiens*, he argues, is a uniquely perceptive creature and it is his place to become 'the agent of symbioses'. In other words, apperception is only of value because it allows man to be the steward of the biosphere. Ulti-mately then it is the whole biosphere and its contin-uing evolution that has intrinsic value.

McHarg's broad thesis is, therefore, pointedly eco-centric, but in many passages he reveals himself to be less than consistent – humanistic concerns are always breaking in. For example, in the chapter titled 'The Plight', McHarg writes:

> Clearly the problem of man and nature is not one of providing a decorative backcloth for the human play, or even of ameliorating the grim city: it is the necessity of sustaining nature as a source of life, milieu, teacher, sanctum, chal-lenge and, most of all, of rediscovering nature's corollary of the unknown in the self, the source of meaning.
>
> (McHarg, 1969: 19)

The emphasis here would seem to be upon human spiritual development, and the contribution that nature can make towards this, rather than mankind's role as a planetary enzyme.

One of the remarkable features of *Design with Nature* is that it does not just set out a cosmology (though that would be ambitious enough!); it also provides a methodology whereby planning decisions based upon this value system can be made. But in the chapters which draw upon McHarg's own planning experience, we discover examples of least-social-cost/maximum-social-value analysis, which are essentially socio-ecological and can therefore be classified as essentially homocentric. It would seem that where real landscape planning is concerned there is less room for talk of mankind as steward, and still less for the idea of humanity as the agent of symbioses.

In Britain too there were those who called for an ecologically based landscape architecture. Prominent among them was Brian Hackett, who established a landscape design course at Newcastle University in 1949 and taught there until 1977. This course was only the second landscape architectural course to be created in Britain (the first was at Reading) and Hackett's ambition was to base it upon sound ecological principles. His main theoretical contribution is to be found in his *Landscape Planning: an Introduction to Theory and Practice* (1971). As its title suggests, this book is concerned with large-scale planning rather than small-scale design, and Hackett believes that all such work must proceed from ecological principles; indeed he expressly states that:

> The involvement with large areas of land in most landscape planning precludes the likelihood that techniques based on the visual/functional approach often applied for small scale landscape design can be successful.
>
> (Hackett, 1971: 26)

Writing before the word 'sustainability' had reached its contemporary voguishness, Hackett utilised some of the then current concepts, such as stability, balance and diversity, to create a paradigm for the healthy landscape, and it is one which, with its emphasis on self-renewal, we might today call sustainable. Hackett thinks that the aesthetic satisfactions a landscape may provide are a by-product of its health, and therefore, if landscape planning is undertaken along ecological lines, the visual aesthetics will, more or less, take care of themselves. He writes;

> If an onlooker holds to the doctrine that the creation of beauty in a landscape can only be arrived at by a personal intuitive quality that he possesses and which cannot be described in simple terms, then the technique with its physical basis will almost certainly fail to produce a landscape that will satisfy him. But if it is believed that the natural landscape is the basis upon which an onlooker establishes his criterion of beauty, then the technique will go a long way towards achieving a beautiful landscape because the aim is to express the natural landscape in terms adapted to man's needs.
>
> (Hackett, 1971: 40)

As an afterthought, he adds,

> This does not mean that matters of form, balance and proportion should be ignored whenever aesthetically pleasing alternatives are practicable and minor adjustments can be made to boundaries and the planting details.
>
> (Hackett, 1971: 40)

Clearly Hackett is exalting ecological values above the kinds of aesthetic values we explored in Part I.

On the other hand, while Hackett often writes as though 'healthy' or 'balanced' landscapes have ultimate value in his system, elsewhere it is very clear that his ideal landscape is one in which human purposes, as manifested in various types of land use, are accommodated. We find him talking, for example, in utilitarian terms about 'the highest state of landscape health and the greatest total benefit' (1971: 46), where the latter refers to the maximisation of productive land uses. It is clear that the highest-order values in Hackett's system are concerned with the welfare of human beings, who should be able to enjoy the benefits of an ecologically stable, yet productive landscape.

Leaving aside some of their rhetoric, it would seem that for both Hackett and McHarg the task of landscape planning does, after all, come down to one of reconciling humanistic values with ecological values. It is not a question of the latter subsuming or replacing the former. In the profession of landscape architecture (in both its planning and design roles) the idea of service to clients and end-users has always been prominent. This is an *essentially* homocentric concern, and it is difficult to see how it could be maintained in an ethical system rigorously based on biocentric or ecocentric principles. In terms of O'Riordan's classification, both McHarg and Hackett are accommodators, since both would put their faith in the adaptability of existing institutions to accommodate environmental demands.

The 'Ecological Approach' of the 1970s

During the 1970s there was a great deal of interest in Britain in what became known as the 'Ecological Approach' to landscape design, planting, maintenance and management pioneered largely in Holland.[16] Alan Ruff (1979) set out the principles behind such an approach, which can be summarised thus:

1 Planting ceases to be a decorative feature and becomes a functional structural element in the external environment.

2 The planting is not designed for visual effect but to achieve the status of woodland in the shortest possible time.

3 The landscape is a low-cost/high-return land-scape. Maintenance costs decrease as social benefits rise.

4 The landscape's users determine its form. It is a place for using rather than looking at.

5 The scheme moves towards greater ecological stability, therefore requires less and less human intervention.

This approach found favour with many practitioners. Its most articulate proponents were the designers and managers working for Warrington New Town. During the early 1980s, the professional magazine *Landscape Design* ran a series of technical articles related to experience at Warrington and elsewhere under the general title 'New Directions' (Manning, 1982; Greenwood, 1983; Gustavsson, 1983; Tregay 1985). Many of the lessons learnt during this innovative period were collected in *Ecology and Design in Landscape* (Bradshaw *et al.*, 1986).

In technical terms the ecological approach was an undoubted success. In many ways it was the precursor of today's interest in sustainability. The landscapes it sought to create were intended to be sustainable, in the sense that they worked with natural processes rather than against them, and maintenance inputs, whether in the form of energy or chemicals, could be minimised.

Considering that this approach was more ecocentric than anything that had preceded it, it is interesting to note that it was most often justified in social and financial terms. People, it was argued, had a deep-seated need for more contact with a natural world, and it just so happened that such naturalistic landscapes were also cheaper to establish and manage. These are both good anthropocentric arguments. As Goode and Smart (1986) observed, nature conservation was not the prime motivation for ecological planting; indeed, the latter was sometimes no more than a 'green veneer' which gave people the impression that there was nature in their towns and cities but did little to support genuine species diversity. On the other hand there were landscape architects like Rettig (1983) who protested that by

elevating the physical and biological components of the site in determining the ultimate form of the landscape, other social, aesthetic and functional requirements are correspondingly downgraded. In other words, for landscape architects of this persuasion, the approach was not humanistic enough.

If the Ecological Approach is seldom mentioned in the current literature it is because its technical lessons have been absorbed into general landscape practice. Any qualified landscape architect should now understand how to go about establishing structural mass plantings of native trees and shrubs or creating a wildflower meadow. A second reason for the apparent demise of the ecological approach is more paradoxical. It is because environmental concern has grown deeper and more widespread. In the face of threats such as global warming, ozone depletion and the greenhouse effect, an approach which seems to concentrate upon the establishment and management of planting has come to appear rather parochial. It may be part of the solution, but it is not the whole solution.

Yet the intuition that an ecologically centred approach is needed persists. It can be argued that the Ecological Approach achieved some convergence in practice between humanistic and ecological concerns, but the ethical principles embodied in such an approach need to be made more explicit.

Post 1980: challenges to complacency

During the 1980s the landscape architect's comfortable technocentric accommodation started to be challenged. For example, in 1989, John Whitelegg, a prominent campaigner against society's over-dependence on the motor car, wrote an editorial for *Landscape Design* entitled 'The Nightsoil Profession', in which he attacked the profession for playing a merely cosmetic role in the development process – 'hence the use of the term "nightsoil"; cleaning up the foul messes left behind by others while failing to prevent the mess being produced in the first place'. He suggested that from time to time landscape architects 'might stand up and state that a particular development can never be justified because of the damage it does to that environment'. It is worth quoting his editorial at some length:

Too many road schemes have been pushed through with the help of a hefty shove from the landscape architectural profession and justified or excused on the grounds that the environment will be improved by the scheme. This approach can become very arrogant as in the case of the Oxleas Wood route for the East London River Crossing. At this inquiry the Department of Transport argued that it would improve the several thousand year old woodland by its imaginative planting after road construction.

(*Landscape Design*, No. 185: 2)

And a few paragraphs later:

The profession of landscape architecture is uniquely placed to comment on the inter-relationships between physical planning, protecting landscape and environment and improving the quality of life in a way which respects the integrity of places. But clearly it does not do this.

A month later, in a letter to the same publication, Chris Baines condemned those landscape practices which were, in his view, aiding and abetting the destruction of unique habitats in their role as consultants to the Cardiff Bay Development Corporation. The proposal that had angered him so much was the Barrage which would create a fresh-water lake in the place of tidal mudflats, a scheme also opposed by the Royal Society for the Protection of Birds and the Royal Society for Nature Conservation. 'One thing which might bring the government to its moral senses', he protested, 'is a refusal by the landscape profession to play a part in this destructive project' (*Landscape Design*, No. 186: 3).

The correspondence continued for several more issues and included an impassioned piece from Kevin Patrick, suggesting that the Landscape Institute needed a code of ethics which would debar its members from working on projects 'which, set against published and objective criteria, are detrimental to the long term interests of the biosphere'. He accusingly suggests that the real role of the contemporary landscape profession is 'the cosmetics of environmental degradation', and that all issues are 'trivialised down to the level of visual landscaping' (*Landscape Design*, No. 187: 3).

Predictably perhaps, there was a backlash. Peter Youngman entered the fray with a letter captioned 'In Defence of Beauty'. In this he deplored the 'emotive terminology' used by Whitelegg and Baines. Planning issues are complex, he argues, and the profession's role is to provide clear thinking and objective analysis in the interests of 'the reconciliation of the inevitable conflicts between genuine interests'. Youngman then succinctly states his own value system:

For me reconciliation comes first; but where it is unattainable people matter more than birds and beauty more than scientific interest.

(*Landscape Design,* No. 192: 3)

This is a clear statement of a homocentric ethics. Not only are human beings more important than the rest of nature, but beauty (as appreciated by human beings) is more important than the abstractions of ecology. It is apparent from this flurry of letters alone that the British landscape profession contains both those who would employ aesthetics as the keystone of their value system, and those who would prefer to see environmental values in that position. Still others would adopt some form of humanistic value system, which would make both aesthetics and environmentalism subservient to some notion of human good or well-being. Moreover, there are those who shift between these various positions, depending upon the audience they are addressing.

In view of the prominence given to environmental issues in contemporary society, there is certainly no way that the landscape profession can overlook environmental ethics. The question is how to build them into the professional value structure. Are environmental considerations to be secondary to aesthetic or social ones, a sort of additional filter applied to schemes that have been devised for other ends? Or should they be the primary, overriding and motivating concerns of the landscape architect? And if the latter, what brand of environmental ethics should the profession adopt? Prima facie it would seem far easier to combine a homocentric version with the social and aesthetic goals that landscape architects have often in the past espoused, although this may be seen as a conservative attitude by the more ecologically inclined. This book takes the view that there are three overlapping sources of values in landscape architecture – the aesthetic, the social and the ecological – but that these cannot be ordered into a universal hierarchy. For different projects, different emphases will be appropriate. This view will be amplified in the final chapter.

A new paradigm for landscape architecture?

We have seen that landscape architects have striven to accommodate what they have perceived as socially necessary forms of development into the landscape. If we consider the needs of only the present generation, then the power stations and large-scale extractive industries with which they have been involved might be regarded, in a utilitarian sense, as socially benign or beneficial. However, if we enlarge the scope of our moral concerns to include generations as yet unborn, some of these activities must take a negative value. This is the essential insight captured in the principle of 'sustainable development',[17] first coined in the World Conservation Strategy (IUCN, 1980). In 1987 the United Nations-sponsored World Commission on Environment and Development, headed by the Norwegian Prime Minister Gro Harlem Brundtland, defined it to mean 'development that meets the needs of the present without compromising the ability of future generations to meet their own needs . . . Sustainable development requires meeting the basic needs of all and extending to all the opportunity to fulfil their aspirations for a better life' (UN, 1987: 46). In this bare form, the environmental ethic encapsulated here is still resolutely homocentric. Its main thrust is to insist that our moral responsibilities extend to future generations of human beings. However, much energy has been devoted to working out the moral and practical implications of such a requirement. The WCS document emphasised three fundamental objectives:

1 that essential ecological processes and life-support systems must be maintained;
2 that genetic diversity must be preserved;
3 that any human use of species or ecosystems must be sustainable.

A sustainable activity or use is one which, in practice as well as principle, can continue forever. It can be argued that sustainability is essentially a homocentric concept, since the touchstone of moral value remains the effect that actions will have upon the quality or continuance of human life. The idea of sustainable development is ambiguous in that it can be given a technocentric slant, in which environmental conservation criteria are traded-off against economic development criteria, or a more radical, ecocentric spin, which emphasises the constraints on human activity that must be accepted if biospheric systems are to be protected against further life-threatening deterioration (Healey and Shaw, 1993). The Brundtland Report is inclined to regard species and ecosystems as resources for humans rather than things which have intrinsic value. However, it recognises that the quality of human life can only be guaranteed if it does not put excessive demands upon the carrying capacity of the supporting ecosystems. Following Callicott and Mumford (1998), we may prefer the term 'ecological sustainability' to the term 'sustainable development'. The latter is often taken to imply (or at least condone) continued economic growth, whereas the former encourages a vision of steady-state economic development in which human wants are met through greater efficiency rather than an increased consumption of resources.

Following Brundtland, the principles of sustainability received further definition in *Conserving the World's Biological Diversity* (IUCN, WRI, CI, WWF, World Bank, 1990). Of particular interest is the set of ethical principles suggested by the authors of this document, which represent an attempt to get beyond 'resourcist' thinking. They are based upon the idea of interdependence: 'humanity is part of nature, and humans are subject to the same immutable ecological laws as all other species on the planet', from which it follows that sustainability must be 'the basic principle of all social and economic development. Personal and social values should be chosen to accentuate the richness of flora, fauna and human experience.' So far these principles could be construed as homocentric, as could the report's insistence that the well-being of future generations is a social responsibility of the present generation. However, the document also embraces Naess's principle of *biocentric egalitarianism* when it states, 'All species have an inherent right to exist. The ecological processes that support the integrity of the biosphere and its diverse species, landscapes and habitats are to be maintained.'

The report's attempt to balance the ecocentric with the homocentric is valiant. It attempts to draw a parallel between conserving species diversity and encouraging diversity in ethnic and cultural outlooks towards nature. In doing so, it inevitably ducks some of the difficult, maybe even intractable, conflicts that are sure to arise when the effects of particular cultures or lifestyles are examined closely. Nevertheless, its overall thrust is surely right; it acknowledges ecological limits within which human society must work, but emphasises that these are not limits to human endeavour; 'instead, they give direction and guidance as to how human affairs can sustain environmental stability and diversity'. If Norton's convergence hypothesis is right, the steps taken to implement such a policy of sustainable development should also meet most of the concerns of the deep ecologists. What the landscape architectural profession requires, at this stage in its development, is a revised system of values which places sustainability alongside the more traditional interests in aesthetics and utility, together with credible visions of how these three value areas may be combined in realisable landscapes.

Case study 8.1: The Yulara Resort, Northern Territory, Australia

In architecture, sustainable design is the antithesis of the International Style. It must respond to the particularities of geology, climate, ecology and culture. The Yulara Resort, developed in the 1980s to accommodate the growth of tourism at Ayers Rock in Australia's red desert, is such a project. It was planned to replace the haphazard shanty town that was burgeoning around the base of the rock. A new town was conceived some 17 kilometres away from the monolith, a site chosen in part for its accessibility to the airport, but also for the ability of the landscape to absorb the development.

The architects Philip Cox and Partners Ltd of McMahon's Point, New South Wales, utilised many features of the Australian vernacular, including covered ways and bull-nosed verandas but introduced striking sail-cloth canopies to provide shade. The harshness of the climate and the remoteness of the site meant that energy conservation was an important guiding principle. Vented pitched roofs aid the circulation of air through the buildings, and the roofscape was designed to accommodate gantries of solar collectors. The sails reduce the heatload on walls and roofs, reducing the energy needed for cooling, which is achieved by ice produced in three 71,000-litre ice-making tanks which operate at times of low energy demand. Water for the complex is pumped from artesian wells.

The landscape architects for Yulara were Environmental Landscapes of Sydney. At their

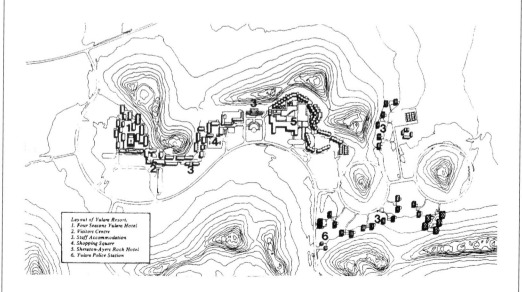

Figure 8.6 The plan for the Yulara Resort at Ayers Rock shows how the sinuous form of the development has been shaped by the topography of the sand dunes.

Figure 8.7 Striking sail-cloth canopies and native desert planting define the aesthetics of the Yulara Resort close to Australia's Ayers Rock. (Courtesy of John Hopkins.)

prompting 25 kilometres of temporary fencing was erected during the construction of the resort to prevent damage to the sensitive desert surroundings. Areas that were damaged were reinstated using soils and vegetation which had been carefully 'harvested' from the desert before building began. Within the complex, with the benefit of irrigation and special soils they created an 'Australian Oasis' using the best of native Australian flowering plants. Additionally, salt-tolerant species were selected to provide extra shade and to act as an aesthetic foil to the architecture.

I am grateful to John Hopkins, who worked on this project, for bringing it to my attention.

The implications of sustainability

If sustainability is adopted as a guiding principle it has both ethical and aesthetic consequences for landscape architects.

For planners, sustainable development seems to suggest the need for more compact and contiguous growth patterns at higher densities and for greater reliance on mass transportation.[18] From science it demands new technologies which minimise resource consumption and promote recycling, but which in their turn will need to be accommodated in the landscape just as were the previous generation of power stations and dams. From landscape architects/planners it requires not just the avoidance of devel-opment on ecologically sensitive lands but also new visions of the landscape informed by the emerging discipline of landscape ecology. Many landscape architects have started to think along these lines and two have already published important books which consider some of the possibilities just mentioned. These are John Tilman Lyle's *Regenerative Design for Sustainable Development* (1994) and Robert Thayer's *Gray World, Green Heart* (1994).

Lyle addresses the twin problems of resource depletion and environmental degradation. His thesis is that industrial society is a world-wide one-way throughput system in which materials are taken from the earth at rates far greater than those at which

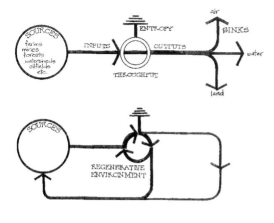

Figure 8.8 These diagrams from John Tilman Lyle's Regenerative Design for Sustainable Development illustrate the difference between 'paleotechnology' (**top**), in which resources are depleted and waste products dumped, and 'neotechnology' or 'regenerative systems' where energy and materials are recycled.

they can be replenished, and waste products are deposited in sinks – the atmosphere, lakes, rivers and the sea – which are loaded beyond capacity. His remedy is 'regenerative design'.[19] 'A regenerative system provides for continuous replacement, through its own functional processes, of the energy and materials used in its operation' (Lyle, 1994: 10).

Lyle's compendious book bulges with examples of such technologies, ranging from the anaerobic digestion of biomass to zero runoff drainage systems and from polyculture agriculture to the use of wind scoops and thermal chimneys for natural air-conditioning. He notes that because regenerative technologies are often very specific to their locality, they can, like older technologies, have a considerable visual impact.[20] He cites the case of wind-farms which some people regard as intrusive. This is a point which is central to Thayer's book. He urges us to find a new aesthetic, arguing that much landscape practice has been devoted to the camouflaging of inappropriate technologies, whereas in the new sustainable landscape (which we must all play our part in creating) this will be unnecessary. Our technologies will be 'transparent' because they are a source of pride rather than guilt (in the case study of the Earth Centre in Chapter 10 we will see a good example of this – the Living Machine for waste-water recycling). Thayer's ecotopia is a decentralised one based on small communities. He also goes further than most landscape architects have done in advo-

cating fundamental changes in the way society is organised. This places him on the ecocentric side of O'Riordan's ecocentric–technocentric dichotomy.

A corollary of the sustainability principle is that we must be on our guard against irreversible actions. This principle has been to the fore in recent British planning battles. It won the day in the case of Oxleas Wood, when in 1993 the government cancelled a proposed trunk road which would have damaged a Site of Special Scientific Interest (SSSI), but was overruled in the regrettable case of Twyford Down, where a hill of enormous landscape significance was bulldozed to make way for the M3 motorway, and also in the case of the Newbury Bypass which went ahead in 1996 despite the damage it would cause to two SSSIs and twelve sites of archaeological interest. Adopting a technocentrist stance, the landscape profession has seen itself as offering objective advice in such circumstances. In a quasi-legal situation landscape architects often appear as expert witnesses on both sides of the argument, leaving the profession open to the charge of aiding and abetting damaging developments. This charge carries some force if landscape architects confine themselves to commenting on the aesthetic implications of proposed developments. It can be defused if practitioners also regard themselves as ethically responsible for evaluating proposals objectively in terms of their contribution towards sustainability.

Planning for sustainability requires that some priorities should be reversed. Rather than planning the human habitat first, by allocating land for housing, industry or recreation, and only then seeking to preserve what remnants of other habitats remain, we should be putting the best habitats first whilst also taking steps to ensure that the hydrological cycle is disturbed and polluted as little as possible (Punter and Carmona, 1997). Only by reordering our priorities in this way can we hope to protect the natural processes upon which our continued existence ultimately depends.

To say that landscape architects are against environmental degradation is a little like saying that they are against sin. It is an assertion which is too broad to be meaningful. The planning theorist Tim Beatley (1994) has suggested that, as a mid-range principle, such degradation is only to be tolerated if it is unavoidable in order to meet *basic* human needs, and not to be tolerated if only to meet *non-basic* needs. Of course, there is still room for debate about what is to count as basic, but this principle, if coupled with the requirement to exhaustively consider less damaging alternatives, would seem to provide a reliable ethical touchstone.

The move towards sustainability and away from damaging forms of development would seem to involve a rejection of consumer-oriented lifestyles in favour of ones which emphasise community, inter-personal links, and connection with the environment. In his suggested checklist for ecovillage development, Ted Trainer (1998) describes the features of an ideally sustainable settlement. He divides his list into things which are 'simple and easy' because they involve the adoption of new technologies or new approaches to town planning, and things which are difficult because they involve changes in people's fundamental attitudes and lifestyles. At the 'simple and easy' end of the continuum we find all sorts of initiatives in which landscape architects are already involved such as greening cities, the creation of wildlife corridors and urban commons, the provision of cyclepaths, site planning for solar efficiency, permaculture and alternative water collection and sewage systems.

The more socially engaged members of the profession are also engaged in activities which attempt to transform society at the 'difficult end' of Trainer's checklist. These range from environmental education and the improvement of school grounds to the creation of sustainably and locally managed neighbourhood parks (see, for example, the Ground-work's Changing Places programme, reviewed in Chapter 7). All of these activities can be said to foster the kind of social cohesion which seems to be the necessary condition of any shift towards more sustainable lifestyles. To balance this, it is equally clear that landscape architects are also involved in activities which are easily identified as technocentric impositions from centralised agencies and deserve to be questioned because they seem to promote non-sustainable development. The road-building programme is a good example.

To be credible the ethical realignment needs to be accompanied by visions of what sustainable land-scapes could look like. The move towards sustain-ability requires an innovatory aesthetics. Landscape ecology, as suggested earlier in this chapter, would seem to have the potential to place the new aesthetics on a sound theoretical footing. Dramstad, Olson and Forman (1996) have sought to interpret the principles of landscape ecology diagramatically for use by designers and planners. Some very useful work in this direction has also been done by Ann Rosenberg (1986) who suggests in her paper 'An Emerging Paradigm for Landscape Architecture' that:

> Instead of admiring a landscape that is orna-mental, paved, groomed, and relatively static, an alternative design language would empha-sise a diversity and complexity that the human component can interrelate with – water resources, wildlife habitats, edible landscapes, and urban woodlots.
>
> (Rosenberg, 1986: 81)

Similarly, in her aptly titled 'Messy Ecosystems, Orderly Frames', Joan Nassauer (1995) observes that many indigenous ecosystems and wildlife habitats violate cultural norms regarding tidiness and order when retained or introduced into the urban fabric. She suggests that designers should provide 'cues to care' which tell the public that an apparently 'untidy' landscape is part of a larger intended pattern. 'Orderly frames', she says, 'can be used to construct a widely recognised cultural framework for ecologi-cal quality' (p. 169). (The Ridgacre project reviewed in Chapter 7 uses just this approach.)

If the advocated paradigm shift is to happen, there will be aesthetic casualties because our admiration of formal landscapes and architectural grand gestures, whether classical, modern or whimsically postmodern, will be necessarily tempered by con-sideration of their ecological suitability. On the other hand, the development of a new ecologically in-formed aesthetic is the most exciting challenge facing the landscape design profession. As Lyle (1991: 41) has suggested, this is 'a task for a truly exploratory avant-garde'.

Notes

1 I have found two books very useful in this regard. One is Colvinaux (1980), which is a very readable introduction to ecology which stresses its Darwinian credentials. The second is De Jardins (1997), particularly Ch. 8 which explores the linkages between ecology and ethics.

2 In addition to De Jardins (1997), Carolyn Merchant's *Radical Ecology*, Routledge, London (1992), contains an excellent summary of the various ethical positions within environ-mentalism.

3 For an excellent discussion of these developments and their

implications see Donald Worster's *The Wealth of Nature*, Oxford University Press, Oxford, 1993, particularly Chs 13 and 14.

4 For a good summary of this interesting topic see R.H. Peters, *A Critique for Ecology,* Cambridge University Press, Cambridge, Ch. 4.

5 This is dangerous territory for a layman. As Alan Sokal and Jean Bricmont point out in Ch. 7 of their *Intellectual Impostures* (Profile Books, London, 1997), ideas from chaos theory have been widely misinterpreted and misunderstood. Some systems, such as the weather, while governed by deterministic laws and therefore predictable in principle, are nevertheless so complex and so 'sensitive to initial conditions' that in practice they are unpredictable.

6 Matters of spatial and temporal scale are important here. The British, for example, are aware of the unpredictability of their climate and agonise about whether to wear shorts, a pullover or a raincoat, but their climate fluctuates within a fairly constant range.

7 Alan Sokal and Jean Bricmont, in their *Intellectual Impostures* (see note 5), argue that science is not just about the falsification of hypotheses but about the establishment of theories with 'high subjective probability'. Certainly it is upon such probabilities that most technological enterprises, including medicine and engineering, ultimately rest.

8 Emphatically, science is not *just* a 'social construct'. It does give us information about nature which can be taken at least as approximate and provisional truth.

9 The concept of the 'ecological niche' suggests a mixture of these world-views, for while species may compete to occupy niches, the niches themselves form part of more co-operative communities.

10 Dawkins's notion of the 'selfish gene' seems to be a prime example of the 'pathetic fallacy' whereby human emotions or desires are attributed to non-human entities.

11 This observation must be balanced by noting that the foundations of ecologically aware landscape planning were laid down in the United States as early as 1864 with Frederick Law Olmsted's involvement in the creation of Yosemite National Park. We should also note that in the aftermath of the Dust Bowl, the Soil Erosion Service was established in 1935 recognising the need to conserve natural resources.

12 This is ambiguous. I take it to mean a total of 1,400 gardens, but it could mean somewhere between 600–800, still a high percentage of Eckbo's total workload.

13 In the second edition of *Gardens in the Modern Landscape* (1948) Tunnard qualifies the strident modernism of the first edition. He had become disillusioned with the mannered stylism of some Modern architecture, and was more respectful of historical styles. Tunnard's ambivalence is reflected in the unevenness of the book.

14 Lewis moved to the University of Wisconsin in 1960 where he continued to develop his 'Regional Design Process'.

15 There are striking parallels between McHarg's theory, first offered in 1967, and the manner in which the contemporary architectural theorist Charles Jencks has interpreted ideas from Complexity and Chaos theories in architectural terms in his book *The Architecture of the Jumping Universe* (Academy Editions, London, 1995).

Growing life and complexity have always been intuitively understood as countering the basic Second Law of Thermodynamics, which holds that a closed system must always run down, become more disorganised, suffer dissipation and die. In fact the primary search of Complexitists is for the "New Second Law", which will explain the spontaneous growth of the universe towards higher levels of what is ridiculously called negentropy, negative entropy.

(Jencks, 1995: 37)

Jencks suggests that complexity is opposed to both simplicity *and* entropy or disorder. Like McHarg, he claims to have discovered a 'cosmic axiology (or natural system of value)' in which 'entropy, the necessary unravelling of time can be considered "bad", "evil", "sinful" in the sense that most theologies condemn destruction, boredom, dissolution, decline, killing and kitsch (cultural entropy)' (p. 37).

Jencks extends his cosmic axiology to include both natural and cultural systems. Whether we are considering a developed ecosystem, the structure of the human brain, a fine wine, or Le Corbusier's *Ronchamp,* what we spontaneously value in each case are their complexity and depth of organisation. In effect Jencks is evoking these as higher order values which can be applied across the nature/culture divide, and in doing so offers us a way out of the homocentric versus biocentric debate.

16 Of course this approach did not appear overnight. As long ago as the 1920s and 1930s the American landscape architect, Jens Jensen, was advocating the use of native plants in a way which reflected the local landscape (Jens Jensen, *Siftings* (Chicago, Ralph Fletcher Seymour, 1939). At the same time in Holland, Jaques Thijsse was pioneering a new type of urban park which brought the plant communities of the polders into town. His 'instructive gardens' recreated habitats such as hornbeam woodlands and heather moorland from the Utrecht Hills.

17 A cautionary note is needed because the word 'sustainability' is used in different contexts, and similar sounding phrases can have almost opposite meanings. A sustainable activity is one which can be maintained or prolonged. Something is 'environmentally sustainable' if it can continue without causing damage to ecosystems. However, economists use the expression 'sustainable growth' which implies a steady increase in economic activity, which some believe is not environmentally sustainable. 'Sustainable development' seems to carry with it the idea that economic growth can continue but only within limits set by the carrying capacities of ecosystems.

18 This is the general thrust of a large body of literature, but many of the implications of sustainability for strategic planning are still contested. See H. Barton (1998) 'Eco-neighbourhoods: A Review of Projects', *Local Environment*, 3(2): 159–177.

19 Following Patrick Geddes, Lyle uses the term 'Palaeo-technic' to describe a society based upon linear, non-

regenerative technology, and 'Neotechnic' to describe one based on cyclical, regenerative processes. The parallel is with Palaeolithic and Neolithic societies.

20 In some ways a greater impact, for whereas a power station is a concentrated source of visual impact and can be hidden away, disguised and mitigated in various ways, regenerative design will distribute smaller but more localised impacts far more widely.

Bibliography

Beatley, T. (1994) 'Environmental Ethics and the Field of Planning: Alternative Theories and Middle-range Principles', in H. Thomas, *Values and Planning*, Avebury, Aldershot.

Bookchin, M. (1982) *The Ecology of Freedom*, Cheshire Books, Palo Alto, Calif.

Bookchin, M. (1989) *Remaking Society*, Black Rose Books, New York.

Bradford, G. (1989) *How Deep is Deep Ecology?*, Times Change Press, Hadley, Mass.

Bradshaw, A.D., Goode, D.A and Thorp, E.H.P. (1986) *Ecology and Design in Landscape*, Blackwell Scientific Publications, Oxford.

Brennan, A. (1988) *Thinking about Nature: An Investigation of Nature, Values and Ecology*, Routledge, London.

Callicott, J.B. and Mumford, M. (1998) 'Ecological Sustainability as a Conservation Concept', in J. Lemons, L. Westra and R. Goodland, eds, *Ecological Sustainability and Integrity: Concepts and Approaches*, Kluwer Academic Publishers, Dordrecht, Netherlands.

Carson, R. (1963) *Silent Spring*, Hamilton, London.

Colvin, B. ([1948] 1970) *Land and Landscape: Evolution, Design and Control* (2nd edition), John Murray, London.

Colinvaux, P. (1980) *Why Big Fierce Animals Are Rare*, George Allen and Unwin, London.

Crowe, S. (1956) *Tomorrow's Landscape*, Architectural Press, London.

Crowe, S. (1958) *The Landscape of Power*, Architectural Press, London.

De Jardins, J. (1997) *Environmental Ethics* (2nd edition), Wadsworth Publishing Company, Belmont, Calif.

Dramstad, W.E., Olson, J.D. and Forman, T.T. (1996) *Landscape Ecology Principles in Landscape Architecture and Land-Use Planning*, Island Press, Harvard.

Eckbo, G. (1994) 'Pilgrim's Progress', in M. Treib, *Modern Landscape Architecture: A Critical Review*, The MIT Press, Cambridge, Mass.

Fairbrother, N. (1972) *New Lives, New Landscapes*, Architectural Press, London.

Forman, R.T.T. (1995) *Land Mosaics: the Ecology of Landscapes and Regions*, Cambridge University Press, Cambridge and New York.

Goode, D.A. and Smart, P.J. (1986) 'Designing for Wildlife', in A.D. Bradshaw, D.A. Goode and E.H.P. Thorp, eds, *Ecology and Design in Landscape*, Blackwell Scientific Publications, Oxford.

Greenwood, R. (1983) 'New Directions 5: Gorse Covert, Warrington – creating a more natural landscape', *Landscape Design*, 143: 35–38.

Gustavsson, R. (1983) 'New Directions 2: Nature on the Doorstep', *Landscape Design*, 143: 21–23.

Hackett, B. (1971) *Landscape Planning: an Introduction to Theory and Practice*, Oriel Press, Newcastle upon Tyne.

Hardin, G. (1968) 'The Tragedy of the Commons', *Science*, 162: 1243–1248.

Hardin, G. and Baden, J., eds (1977) *Managing the Commons*, W.H. Freeman, San Francisco.

Harvey, S. (1987) *Reflections on Landscape: the Lives and Work of Six British Landscape Architects*, Gower Technical, Aldershot.

Healey, P. and Shaw, T. (1993) *The Treatment of 'Environment' by Planners: Evolving Concepts and Policies in Development Plans*, Working Paper No. 31, Department of Town and Country Planning, University of Newcastle upon Tyne.

IUCN (1980) (with assistance from UNEP, WWF) *World Conservation Strategy*, Gland, Switzerland.

Leopold, A. (1949) *A Sand County Almanac*, Oxford University Press, London.

Lewis, P.H. (1996) *Tomorrow by Design: A Regional Design Process for Sustainability*, John Wiley and Sons Inc., New York.

Lovelock, J. (1979) *Gaia: A New Look at Life on Earth*, Oxford University Press, Oxford.

Lovelock, J. (1988) *The Ages of Gaia: A Biography of Our Living Planet*, Oxford University Press, Oxford.

Lucardie, P. (1993) 'Why Would Egocentrists Become Ecocentrists?', in A. Dobson and P. Lucardie, eds, *The Politics of Nature*, Routledge, London.

Lyle, J.T. (1991) 'Can Floating Seeds Make Deep Forms?', *Landscape Journal*, 10(1): 37–47.

Lyle, J.T. (1994) *Regenerative Design for Sustainable Development*, Wiley, New York.

McHarg, I. (1969) *Design with Nature*, The Natural History Press, Garden City, New York.

Manning, O.D. (1982) 'New Directions 3: Designing for Man and Nature', *Landscape Design*, 140: 30–32.

May, R.M. (1975) 'Stability in Ecosystems: Some Concepts', in W.H. Van Dobben and R.H. Lowe, eds, *Unifying Concepts in Ecology*, Dr W. Junk, The Hague.

Midgley, M. (1998) 'The Fear of Gaia', *Gaia Circular*, 1(2), Winter.

Merchant, C. (1992) *Radical Ecology, the Search for a Liveable World*, Routledge, New York.

Naess, A. (1973) 'The Shallow and the Deep, Long-Range Ecology Movement', *Inquiry*, 16: 95–100.

Naess, A. and Rothenberg, D. (1989) *Ecology, Community and Lifestyle*, Cambridge University Press, Cambridge.

Nassauer, J.I. (1995) 'Messy Ecosystems, Orderly Frames', *Landscape Journal*, 14(2): 161–170.

Neckar, L.M. (1990) 'Strident Modernism/Ambivalent Reconsiderations: Christopher Tunnard's Gardens in the Modern Landscape', *Journal of Garden History*, 10(4): 237–246.

Norton, B.G. (1997) 'Convergence and Contextualism: Some Clarifications and a Reply to Steverson', *Environmental Ethics*, 19: 87–100.

Odum, E. (1953) *Fundamentals of Ecology*, Saunders, Philadelphia.

O'Riordan, T. (1981) *Environmentalism*, 2nd edition, Pion, London.

Parsons, H.L. (1977) *Marx and Engels on Ecology*, Greenwood Press, Westport, Conn.

Pepper, D. (1996) *Modern Environmentalism*, Routledge, London.

Peters, R.H. (1991) *A Critique for Ecology*, Cambridge University Press, Cambridge.

Punter, J. and Carmona, M. (1997) 'Cosmetics or Critical Restraints? The Role of Landscape in Design Policies in English Development Plans', *Journal of Environmental Planning and Management*, 40(2): 173–197.

Rettig, S. (1983) 'The Rise of the "Ecological Approach" to Landscape Design', *Landscape Design*, 143: 39–41.

Rosenberg A. (1986) 'An Emerging Paradigm for Landscape Architecture', *Landscape Journal*, 5(2): 75–82.

Ruff, A. (1979) *Holland and the Ecological Landscapes*, Deanwater Press, Stockport.

Russell, B. ([1959] 1995), *My Philosophical Development*, London, Routledge.

Shrader-Frechette, K. (1998) 'Sustainability and Environmental Ethics', in J. Lemons, L. Westra and R. Goodland, eds, *Ecological Sustainability and Integrity: Concepts and Approaches*, Kluwer Academic Publications, Dordrecht, Netherlands.

Sterba, J.P. (1994) 'Reconciling Anthropocentric and Nonanthropocentric Environmental Ethics', *Environmental Values*, 3: 229–244.

Steverson, B.K. (1996) 'On the Reconciliation of Anthropocentric and Nonanthropocentric Environmental Ethics', *Environmental Values*, 5: 349–361.

Thayer, R.L. (1994) *Gray World, Green Heart: Technology, Nature and the Sustainable Landscape,* John Wiley and Sons, New York.

Trainer, T. (1998) 'Towards a Checklist for Ecovillage Development', *Local Environment*, 3(1): 79–83.

Tregay, R. (1985) 'New Directions: A Sense of Nature', *Landscape Design*, 156: 34–38.

Treib, M. (1993) *Modern Landscape Architecture: A Critical Review*, The MIT Press, Cambridge, Mass.

Tunnard, C. ([1938] 1948) *Gardens in the Modern Landscape*, The Architectural Press, London.

United Nations. World Commission on Environment and Development (1987) *Our Common Future* (the 'Brundtland Report'), Oxford University Press, Oxford.

Walker, P. and Simo, M. (1994) *Invisible Gardens: The Search for Modernism in the American Landscape*, The MIT Press, Cambridge, Mass.

Williams-Ellis, C. (1937) *Britain and the Beast*, Dent and Sons Ltd, London.

9   In practice: saving the planet?

Grown-up hippies

We hear so much about ecological issues and environmental crises today, both within professional circles and in the wider media, that it is easy to forget that these are relatively recent concerns. Within landscape architecture, as we saw in the previous chapter, ecological values have risen to take their place alongside longer-standing concerns about aesthetics, amenity and utility. Mid-career landscape architects can look back upon a time when the profession's environmental concerns were embryonic. When deliberating about his choice of career John Hopkins had some premonition of the importance they would one day assume:

> I started to do some research into architecture and town planning, went to visit town planning offices in the local authority and also Mary Mitchell, a landscape architect, and got much more interested in landscape architecture. It seemed much more akin to what I wanted to do. This was in 1969–70, so it was really before the oil crisis of 1973, and before ecology and the issues of conservation and pollution had really come to the fore but were there but not publicly acknowledged and certainly not politically or economically acknowledged, but I could see, or just intuitively felt, this was an area that I wanted to work in.

In fact the 1970s, formative years for many of my interviewees, was the period when environmentalism began to make the headlines and youthful ideal-ism abounded. In retrospect Tom Robinson thinks that some of this was naive and misplaced:

> And there was a hardly defined at all good feeling about the Environment with a capital E, or Earth as we would have called it then, and although I'd never been interested in the theory of that – Gaia theory or anything – I accepted it, along with long hair and west-coast bands. An utterly frivolous reason but it's true. It was an utterly unintellectual reason or a cultural reason . . .
>
> There was an anti-progress, anti-modern-world, 'Good Life' idea, associated with some ill-defined idea of back-to-nature, so it was the sort of stuff you would pick up in the magazines of the period and texts – counter-culture thought, like the alternative 'Whole Earth' catalogue. A lot of the rubbish in there all stems from a benign attitude towards the planet. Not so much its appearance, but more its fitness, so to a certain extent there was a moral attitude, but I wasn't really exercised by all that.

Tim Gale recalled the same period:

> I'm trying to think when the first Stockholm conference on the environment took place . . . I would think that was a little later actually . . . but no, students were already in the early 1970s taking the wrappers off everything at Tesco before leaving the shop, so there was already an interest in fairly basic things. In fact I think it's slightly sad because I don't think it's moved on very much. It's moved on strongly within the public consciousness, but I'm not sure whether it

has in any particular way with landscape architects . . . perhaps it has.

Gale's uncertainty about the extent to which environmental thinking has taken root in the landscape profession is borne out by my research, because the responses to questions on this topic were very uneven. Some practitioners, as we shall see, thought that issues of ecological design and sustainability were absolutely central. Others thought that they had their place, but were simply not relevant in certain kinds of project. Some paid lip-service to environmental sentiments, but showed little depth of understanding and in practice applied ecological ideas in a superficial way. One or two regarded ecology with something verging on hostility.

In general, practitioners linked the concept of *ecology* to the idea of using native species in planting designs, and interpreted the concept of *sustainability* in terms of low-maintenance designs which would be enduring. Some viewed sustainability as a matter of specifying the right products – not using tropical hardwoods, for example. On a more subtle level, the language in which landscape architects discuss their work has been profoundly influenced by concepts and metaphors which have come from ecology. Their conversation is peppered, not so much with scientific terms like succession, ecotype or ecotone (although these do appear occasionally), but with more general, value-laden words from popular ecology like harmony, balance, species richness, and diversity.

Anthropocentrists or ecocentrists?

The debate in environmental ethics between the anthropocentrists and the ecocentrists, described in Chapter 8, does not seem to have engaged landscape architects at all. No doubt this is because people in practice do not have the time or inclination to read scholarly journals – and this debate has not been given much coverage in professional magazines – but it may also be because, given the profession's deep involvement in social matters and the fact that, as a designer, one is always working on behalf of a client, whether an individual, a corporation or a community, the question hardly arises. Practising landscape architects are generally anthropocentrists by default, though the more environmentally concerned may flirt with more radical

positions. Of the people interviewed, only John Vaughan offered a thought-out position on this issue. His position is an interesting mixture of broad-scale, long-term ecocentrism and short- or medium-term anthropocentrism:

I don't see the two things (homocentrism/ ecocentrism) as incompatible. It seems to me that real progress will be made in terms of the environment when people begin to genuinely understand and behave as if they are part of the environment instead of separate from it. In global terms I take an ecocentric view. I have a much bigger philosophy which has a very harsh view of people, that people are the most destructive element that the world's environment has ever seen in a short space of time, but in comparison with other elements we're only relative non-entities. We'll be come and gone in the blink of an eyelid in terms of geological time . . .

I find it natural to assume that we are a transitory phase. It gives me a sense of proportion. It makes me actually think that although people are amazingly destructive things will essentially continue. If we do things right we'll succeed, if we do things wrong we'll be wiped out, but, in a sense, species have come and gone and the world has drifted on, and the world is no different . . . you know, tectonic plates are still moving and mountains are still growing, and these are all part and parcel of the processes of the cosmos . . .

But within that system it seems to me that it is not possible for us to take an ecocentric view. By our nature we will always take a view that is based on human judgements, human values and human experience. That's not wrong, but the key is to recognise that there are greater forces and that there are things that are beyond our control. There are greater goods of which we know nothing and which we are not capable of influencing. And within that we have to say that we have a defined time and space, and that defined time and space is for people as they are now.

The politics of the environment

As already indicated in Chapter 7, landscape architects do not appear to be a radically politicised group. Very few of the people interviewed volunteered any political opinions whatsoever. Some of the exceptions have already been mentioned. Not only was there little comment in terms of traditional left–right divisions, but Green politics, which might reasonably have been expected to appeal to many landscape architects, were only mentioned by a handful of interviewees. Rebecca Hughes, as we saw in Chapter 7, could not make a separation between her values as a landscape architect and her political beliefs, which might best be described as red–green or socialist/environmental, but only Dougal Thornton declared a completely Green affiliation:

> Yes, if you want to know my political leanings, at the last two opportunities I've had to vote I've voted Green. I know that I'm in a tiny minority, but it's not a wasted vote to vote the way your conscience says, and it's only the Green Party that's coming up with the really radical policies, saying 'we've got to stop this' before we choke ourselves to death.

Local Agenda 21

In fact Thornton's involvement in environmental issues goes considerably further than voting for a particular political party. He also believes that his involvement in such matters is something over and above his specific professional role:

> Latterly I've got much more interested in Local Agenda 21,[1] and for a while I took on, within Stirling District Council, the mantle of being the Local Agenda 21 person as well as the landscape team leader, because I did feel that it was really important. I do feel quite strongly that we should have much stronger environmental policies than we've got, and I think the main blame is central government, but I don't know if local government is very good either. So that is quite high on my agenda, and I'm quite happy going into meetings and arguing about traffic objectives and getting well beyond the spheres of what I was trained to do, because I feel strongly.

Thornton was willing to become involved in wider issues than those which had traditionally concerned the landscape architect. He also believed that his landscape architectural training had given him a practical slant on environmental problems which was sometimes lacking in others in the council who looked at the same issues from a policy perspective. He tried to apply the principles of sustainability to landscape management for example:

> We've got an environmental officer. He's up there doing the policy work, but we need to have other folk bringing it through into the practicalities of what we're actually doing, how we're maintaining our open spaces, and could we be maintaining them in a way that's better, in the long term, for the environment.

At the same time, though Thornton held firm views on environmental issues, he balanced these against the more immediate, more pressing concerns of the community:

> If we changed our mowing regimes drastically you might get a bloody outcry from the public. Now you have to address that. You can't say 'Ah, well, you've got it all wrong . . .' And by not mowing do you create problems? I'm not sure about that. It's easy to say we'll cut the grass less times and [then] you get more accidents with kids cutting their hands on broken glass because they didn't see it because the grass wasn't cut. Life's a series of compromises isn't it?

While interviewees seldom mentioned Green politics directly, a significant number expressed interest in or a commitment to the ideals expressed in Agenda 21. Margaret Jackson, the landscape architect who has moved into community and local economic development work in Liverpool, became much more animated during our discussion of the potential of Agenda 21 than she had been in our earlier conversation about aesthetics and design. It emerged that this was because she saw possibilities for local employment:

> Our consultancy undertook action research and prepared a successful submission for an Article 10 action research pilot project funded by the European Commission on behalf of the five local authorities on Merseyside. This project researched seventeen new areas of potential employment, the object being to identify where there was urgent demand for particular services. Recycling constituted one area of research for which a need was identified. However, until legislation means that recycling becomes more profitable, then this area of potential employment is not reaching its full

potential. The pilot project, which is currently underway in each of the five local authority areas, is seeking to generate new sustainable employment opportunities for long-term unemployed people over 40.

Jackson saw a great opportunity for the landscape architectural profession to seize Agenda 21 and take a leading role, but, with the recent experience of the Job Creation initiatives of the 1980s in mind, where a great number of poorly designed and executed 'environmental improvements' were undertaken in inner city areas, she suggested that lobbying would be required to ensure that other values – aesthetic and design values – were not overlooked:

> With the introduction of the 'New Deal', including as one option the 'Environmental Task Force', there is a concern that the quality of landscape improvements may not always be up to scratch. In the recent past the community programme produced mixed-quality products. There may be a role for the landscape profession to lobby to ensure that quality and aesthetic issues are as important as the training and employment outputs.

Interestingly, John Vaughan, whose work for the Great North Forest could also be described as a form of community development initiative, was also very enthusiastic about Agenda 21:

> Agenda 21 ought to be a process whereby people become deeply enmeshed again in the shaping of the environment, in the determining of principles and processes, not just tinkering with the postage stamp outside the door. One of the great things that landscape architecture could do would be to grab hold of that process. We would become the facilitators and enablers of the process, and we would ensure that in the development of Agenda 21 design is a component . . .

Vaughan linked Agenda 21 to the call for local distinctiveness, about which, as we saw in Chapter 3, landscape architects often feel passionately:

> People are beginning now to reassert small-scale human values – not small in terms of their importance, but more local yet longer-term values in all these processes that shape the environment around them. And the real trick is to get people to

appreciate the value of design in that process, and to feel that they understand it, to feel that they value it in some way, that it contributed to their lives, not just as they are now, but that it will contribute to how future generations will develop. It will contribute to their children's lives. That they will be leaving behind something that they can be proud of and they feel will be of value to future generations.

The rise of environmental planning

There is a radical, campaigning tone to some of the remarks quoted in the previous sections, but many landscape architects, particularly those involved in landscape planning, now regard the consideration of environmental issues as a routine aspect of their everyday work. This is hardly surprising when the larger part of many landscape practices' workloads consist of fighting planning inquiries, producing environmental impact assessments, suggesting amelioration measures, and so on. In O'Riordan's terms this work could be described as 'technocentric accommodation'. In terms of its ethical basis, landscape planning serves public policy purposes which are generally shaped by utilitarian ideas of resource management, though there may be instances when a preservationist stance based upon consideration of the intrinsic qualities of a particular place takes precedence. Such work is generally regarded as essential, potentially lucrative, but also, for the design-minded, decidedly unglamorous. Tim Gale looked back at a time when it all seemed more radical and challenging than it does today:

> As far as McHarg was concerned, I supposed what hit the button as far as I was concerned, and students of that generation were concerned, was that it gave you a philosophical base from which to work and also a scientific base. A lot of us were worried that what we were doing was all a bit airy-fairy and we got sick of being called 'gardeners' and so on. And here was a real philosophical basis: 'You're going to go out there and save the world!' That's what it seemed like, and that's a good position to go forward from.

These sentiments were echoed by John Hopkins, who, having studied both in the United States and in

Britain, was well placed to comment on the development of landscape architecture, and specifically the development of landscape planning, in the two countries:

> I think at the beginning of the century landscape practice was mainly coming out of two strands. There was Law Olmsted and park planning and urban issues, and there was a very strong garden design tradition as well. And then, through the Modern era, for landscape architects there was a hiatus for the profession. Then, through the '60s and '70s there was a massive growth, through the work of Sasaki, Eckbo and the big American firms . . .Wallace, McHarg, Roberts and Todd . . . all those firms . . . and they were doing that on the back of looking at the public realm, in and of itself, with its own value systems separate from architecture. So that became landscape strategic planning. That became the realm of landscape architects, because there were figures in the United States who could understand and work in that scale. And underlying it was ecology, nature, the environment, because working at that scale they had to take account of nature and the environment . . .
>
>   I think what happened after that was that McHarg came to the fore with his *Design with Nature* . . . which is an absolutely seminal text, and that is where ecology really did start to make a difference. Ecology is a twentieth-century discipline as is landscape architecture. And I think that it took landscape architecture in a different direction. What it did was it took it away from its roots in design, and I think we're starting to recognise that now.

Hopkins went on to explain his own view that the profession needed to be rebalanced in terms of three intersecting systems of values. He gave these the labels Ecology, Community and Art. This is a view which I very much share, to the extent that I have used a tweaked version of his formulation as the title for this book.

   When wedded to a programme of implementation works, a strategically planned approach to landscape issues can be enormously effective, and this is perhaps best exemplified by the work carried out by the metropolitan councils like the Greater London Council, Greater Manchester Council or Tyne and Wear County Council before their abolition in 1986 by Margaret Thatcher's Conservative government. Often this work was unglamorous and perhaps it lacked some of the aesthetic finesse to be found in contemporary practice, but it was solid, enduring and made a difference to people's lives. Several of my interviewees had worked for these organisations and lamented their passing. David Appleton regarded the large-scale work he had been able to undertake at GMC as some of the most significant of his career. A large part of the reason is that this is work which has survived. It has been enduring, which is almost (though not quite) a synonym for sustainable. I asked him what his most rewarding piece of work had been:

> I suppose I would be looking for something that endured. So that you could come back in ten years and you could still read the bones of it. Now on that basis I suppose I would probably have to go back to my days in the GMC where people were creating woodlands, because it doesn't matter what happens to them. If the woodland is there and you've created space, it doesn't matter if people can alter them by management afterwards. They are there and they endure. Even urban design that can look so crisp the day after it's been constructed, you can come back ten years down the line and the thing is totally and utterly destroyed and changed by other people.

It was at this point in the interview that Appleton used the expression 'Commodity, Firmness and Delight', a reference from Henry Wotton's *Principles of Architecture*. 'Commodity' is a synonym for utility, while 'firmness' refers to the robustness of the construction, which can easily be given an ecological or sustainable interpretation in the case of landscape architecture. Sharp-eyed readers will recognise that Wotton is the second source for my compound title; I have borrowed the word 'delight' because it seems to encompass all aspects of the aesthetics of landscape – not only the natural beauties of the countryside but also the contrived beauties of the designed park.

Ecological design

Consideration of commodity, firmness and delight brings us appropriately to the place of ecological principles in design, as opposed to large-scale planning. Appleton has given us the key to one way of understanding this. If good design is design which endures (and this was a common thread in several interviews), then ecological design, which ought to be easier to manage and therefore more enduring, must be regarded as good design. Firmness in terms of landscape could be seen as sustainability. Another way of putting this is to say that ecological designs work. Coming from a background in fashion design, Heather Lloyd was not initially enthusiastic about science-based approaches to design, but her attitude has changed with experience:

> the more you are involved in it, the more you realise that the better designs, the ones that work, are ones that take notice of the environment . . . they aren't just a load of pretty schemes arbitrarily flung into the environment.

John Hopkins takes this intuition much further:

> To me ecology is at the core of landscape architecture, and in all the debates about 'what is landscape architecture?' I think nobody would deny that at its core is ecology and at its core is sustainability.

In fact the profession, at least in Britain, is not as homogeneous as Hopkins imagines. One or two of the people I spoke to had little enthusiasm for ecology and for the majority ecological values had to take their place alongside, or in some cases below, social or aesthetic values. These are the facts as observed, but the more interesting question is whether ecology ought to be the primary value and the foundation stone of all landscape design. This is something which calls for much debate and discussion and which, ultimately, cannot be decided by conducting an opinion poll. It is a question to which we will return in Chapter 10.

There are three areas of recent landscape practice where considerations of ecology have been prominent. The first is the reclamation of derelict land, which can be regarded as design at a very broad scale where the ultimate goal is often to restore the land to something akin to its condition before it was disturbed. As thinking about reclamation became more sophisticated, and physical techniques improved, more thought was given to the establishment of worthwhile end-uses. The latter need not be agricultural; indeed, under contemporary

policies they are more likely to include some form of nature conservation objectives. The second ecological theme in recent landscape architectural practice has been the influence of the Ecological Approach pioneered in Holland and adopted by many public bodies in Britain. The third, growing out of and related to the previous two, has been an interest in habitat creation. All of these were mentioned during the interviews so we will consider them in turn.

Reclamation

Some of the most powerful and motivating metaphors in landscape architecture are to be found in relation to the reclamation of derelict land. The landscape architect is seen as a healer, a mender or even a redeemer. Here, for example, is the way in which Cheryl Tolladay described the idealism of her college days:

Figure 9.1 Festival Park, Ebbw Vale in 1998. The park was created as part of Garden Festival Wales in 1992 on a site reclaimed after the closure in 1978 of what had been Europe's largest steelworks.

You saw everywhere the impact upon the environment and you were going to go out there and sort things out. And of course, when you are doing paper landscape, that is what you do. You turn pit heaps into leisure parks and so on . . . rescuing decaying woods, getting the management plans all sorted out . . . and you just presume that's what you would be doing in practice. You'd be mending . . . making things right again.

Tolladay felt that her subsequent career had fallen some way short of this messianic ideal, and even that during the development boom of the 1980s there had been much get-rich-quick cynicism within the profession. Only since starting to work for a Groundwork Trust has she recovered some of the early idealism:

It's only really now that I'm working in the east Durham coalfields that we're doing what I had always thought landscape architects should do, which is really improving a terrible environment, you know, an environment that is absolutely degraded.

She was very ambivalent about some of the work she had undertaken while working in private practice. Even though she had asked to be given landscape impact assessment work to broaden her experience, she sometimes found, as she became more deeply involved with the projects, that she began to have feelings of disquiet about the possibly detrimental effects of the proposals upon the landscape and the local community.

You know, creating some business park on Grade II agricultural land, when there's a whole pile of brown sites in Hartlepool[2] it could have been put on. That's destroying the environment, as is . . . you know, landscape architects who work on highways and these sorts of things.

Tolladay believes that this can be a quandary for many landscape architects, and that they resolve the problem in different ways. Hers was to leave private practice.

Interestingly, John Vaughan, who held a degree in ecology before he began his landscape training, had an apparently very different metaphor for the landscape architect's role at the outset of his career:

I think the direction I came from was 'Is there a practical problem to be solved?' and 'Is there a way in which you can use ecological principles to solve it?' It was very much to do with plant colonisation, difficult habitats, reclamation schemes, the problems of tackling problem environments, so it was very much a technical role rather than an aesthetic one, and I don't think I saw myself getting involved at that time in being the person that produced the shape of the environment. I think I saw myself as being the technician, in terms of advising on practical solutions to a difficulty. I don't suppose there was any contemplation of design ideologies or aesthetics or anything like that.

The difference between Vaughan's imagery and that of Tolladay is not as great as it first seems. There is something surgical about Vaughan's technician. It is not hard to imagine him in a white coat, diagnosing the ills of the landscape and setting out to cure them through science. Rebecca Hughes, another ecologically trained practitioner, also evoked a medical metaphor when she explained the characteristics she admired in a landscape:

I value health. The condition of the biophysical processes going on in a landscape that impart an element of well-being or optimal state contribution. That it's not dying on its feet. Then it has a future. You can see it's got a future. The processes are healthy hydrologically, ecologically and so on. It displays mixed-age structures in the woodland vegetation or a diversity of habitats in response to variable ground conditions. It's a pleasant place to be. It's not just about variety. It's actually about its condition and the elements that give it diversity.

It is worth noting that when the medical metaphor is invoked, human beings tend to be regarded as the agents of disharmony and disease. The landscape architect as physician becomes less interested in people as the users of landscapes. This is something which John Vaughan came to recognise early in his career and he moved from a technical orientation to one which increasingly saw people as part of environmental processes:

The reason for monkeying around with the environment seems to be much more to do with the products that the environment delivers to people, rather than what the environment is, in itself, as an entity. And I think when you begin to contemplate what the environment delivers to people, you begin to face some really quite taxing questions, because you begin to have to balance out what people can demand from the environment before they begin to affect its structure in such a way that they prejudice the operation of the environment as an entity. Those questions have become, over my career, steadily more to the front of thinking. And obviously they're the driving forces behind current thinking about sustainability and Agenda 21, environmental capacity, and everyone is tinkering around with ways of trying to measure the interaction between people and the environment.

The 'Ecological Approach'

The Ecological Approach, as we saw in Chapter 8, was one which was premised on the idea that a landscape designed and managed on an ecological basis would be one which provided all kinds of benefits to people. Those who had faith in this approach expected psychological, physical, educational, social and spiritual gains to flow from the landscapes created, while the costs would reduce with time because such landscapes, it was held, would require diminishing maintenance inputs. It is clear from the history of some of these initiatives that some of this optimism was misplaced. The current generation of mid-career landscape architects are in a good position to evaluate the contribution that the Ecological Approach has made to contemporary theory and practice, and it was mentioned by several of the interviewees. We will look at the positive legacy first.

Phil Moss, now a principal with BDP in Manchester, obtained his first job after college with the landscape team at Warrington New Town, when their interest in the Dutch approach to landscape design was just developing. He described it as a very exciting time when the whole philosophy of design was open to intense debate:

> We debated long and very hard in the landscape group about this idea of creating housing and amenity within a quasi-natural environment and of course we went totally over the top and made housing developments full of oak trees and a lot of that's been now changed, but all the bits still

remain. I had a wonderful eight years there, because when I went there Risley Ordnance Factory was still Risley Ordnance Factory and it was still there with its rail lines and bunkers, and you go there now and there's 25,000 souls live there in a mixed environment. I was very fortunate to be allowed to build the forest park from what had been thirty ammunition bunkers and god-knows-what other things, and whilst a lot of the structured woodlands are based on oak–ash, I guess, there are all sorts of other things in there. I could still do my nice ornamental bits, which I liked.

I wondered how a landscape architect who had previously told me that he was an enthusiast for art and design had reacted to the scientifically dominated ecological approach. Moss told me that he had been caught up in the novelty of the approach, but also that he had still been allowed outlets for his creative urges:

> I think at the time we felt we were being terribly trendsetting. Nobody had really done this before. They probably had, but our knowledge was pretty limited. We debated it. We were committed to it, but not slavishly. I was never slavish. Some people got slavish: 'You can't plant that plant because it's not indigenous.' I was never in that camp. You were establishing the landscape infrastructure using those sound principles and there were good reasons for that; that's what would have been there if man hadn't have been on this earth. Because it's quasi-indigenous, the maintenance and management of it should be relatively straightforward in the long term – you've got to look at long term – but no, in the housing areas I still got my bedding plants in and my ornamental plants and my bamboo gardens and all the rest of it.

Moss had been back to Warrington shortly before I interviewed him and he felt that the design team's overall approach had been vindicated. I asked him whether he still believed in the Ecological Approach, or had he modified his view:

> It's bound to be modified because, hopefully, you continue your learning process as you go through life in your professional career. There is still a place on schemes for undertaking planting, large-scale planting that is very heavily based on

9.2

9.4

9.3

9.5

Figure 9.2 Figure 9.3, Figure 9.4 and Figure 9.5 The now mature landscape of Birchwood, Warrington. (Photographs taken in 1998.)

ecological design. The Channel Tunnel Terminal is a classic example for BDP. We implemented that terminal and we were trying to impose an enormous man-made structure on the Downs and we had to mitigate the adverse impacts in all sort of ways ... to try and put back what we destroyed and trying to create new areas to assist with making that development sit as comfortably as it could do within the environment. There's always a place for it, but it's always about picking horses for courses and not slavishly following one line or another.

Another enthusiast for the Ecological Approach was Neil Mattinson:

For me, the multidisciplinary approach we can take to projects and problem-solving today is so much stronger by embracing ecological principles, and . . . achieving landscape solutions which may well be ecologically based. Not every time. Quite often it's quite irrelevant. It depends upon the site, but certainly in general terms we believe that the ecological approach is extremely valid in landscape design, for a number of reasons.

One, it's the use of native indigenous plant species, at its most simplistic level. You're talking about what grows normally, naturally in any one system, country or wherever you happen to be. That has got to be right. For years we've fought with ornamental plantings, and you're often introducing plant material into alien soils, and it's a battle. It's the icing on the cake approach as opposed to fundamental long-term solution.

Mattinson was aware that ecological planting could look rather monotonous:

At the moment I feel that there's a little bit of a backlash been created. A lot of people view it as boring and mundane, and they think 'It's indigenous planting – what the heck, we can bulldoze that'. A lot of developers treat it as not significant landscape . . . because it's become so common, and it's so 'samey' from a visual point of view; what you've got now is private developers willing to chance their arm to take huge chunks of it out, forgetting of course that those are habitats for wildlife and flora, which for my mind has got a greater significance . . .

I think there are factions within the profession which certainly have become tired with it. I think not so much that they don't believe in it, but they're looking to find a way of re-inventing it almost . . . I think within the profession there are groups of people who want to take the native ecological approach and tweak it, and that's what we're looking to do, to actually give it a new relevance, if you like.

We will return to Mattinson's attempts to reinvigorate the Ecological Approach later in the chapter. First we must consider some of the harsher criticisms of the philosophy. Working in an inner city area, Salford's Perry Twigg could describe many of the drawbacks:

When I first started working in Salford in 1988 there were a lot of problems. Towards the end of the '70s there had been this move towards bringing ecology into the town. It was based on the works that had been carried out in a lot of the New Towns like Warrington, where they'd done a lot of woodland planting in the town. They were trying to introduce that into other urban areas, and when I first started at Salford that was the legacy . . . It was causing a lot of problems, although it looked good. It was very green and it probably attracted a lot of wildlife into these areas. The social and economic problems had been developing over the years and particularly in housing areas where ecological planting had been carried out, on either sides of footpaths and things were going wrong: people getting mugged, people getting burgled, the goods were being stored in these wooded areas and all sorts of things . . . basically people were complaining and then the Parks and Leisure section would come along and just hack these things down, and you were left with nothing on the ground, something that looks a complete mess.

Twigg went on to describe the contemporary approach to planting design, which has less to do with ecology and more to do with social requirements, particularly current fears about crime:

So now we actually design a lot more with maintenance in mind and it's probably a lot less ecologically based in urban areas . . . We are actually accredited to 'Secure by Design'. We've all been on training courses with Greater Manchester police, in terms of thinking that through in terms of the way we design and keeping the maintenance down, using maybe lower growing shrubs, a lot of evergreens and things like that. It doesn't really do much for the ecological side of things, but that's in the urban areas.

There is more scope for ecological planting in countryside and urban fringe areas:

We do actually do quite a lot of work on the countryside areas of Salford . . . We've done works reclaiming old reservoirs, derelict railway lines that have been closed and turned into linear walkways and where it's appropriate we carry out the ecological work as well.

Some of the problems with the Ecological Approach seem to have been the result of mistakes in the planting design. Even Milton Keynes, which is often held up as exemplary, is not immune from this criticism. At one stage of his career Peter Fischer worked for the Development Corporation and he told me:

At Milton Keynes you got the interpretation of the Dutch landscape, and I might sound disparaging, but the misinterpretation of it in some ways. Using fast-growing plant material without realising what you would have to do in a period of time to replace it . . .

. . . I could call it Dutch landscape but I don't think it was being done in the way that the Dutch really did it, because it wasn't being done in a properly considered ecological way. It was 'let's get instant landscape', and the intention was to get an instant effect rather than worry about how the ecological development of the landscape would function. And there were a lot of problems with the maintenance people about how it should be maintained.

Another criticism of the Ecological Approach is that it does not provide opportunities for interesting design, and can, if applied too rigorously, produce a monotonously uniform appearance. Fischer thought that this had happened at Milton Keynes:

It's essential that you get a variety of scale and a sense of spaciousness in an area, whereas at Milton Keynes open vistas and open skylines were too often enclosed or broken up with planting. Even if you go into the linear parks at Milton Keynes today, it's not that easy to get into a space where you really feel you've got a sense of spaciousness or real openness. When Milton Keynes started it was this blasted heath . . . well, not heath, but large field patterns, exposed landscape and it is very changed. I think it has lost something. I think it has become too regular. Partly it's the whole design concept of the city, but it lacks adequate spatial variety

and I think that's in part down to the design philosophy and how it was pursued, and I don't think the management approach to the landscape was ever the Dutch approach, in my view.

John Hopkins shares many of Fischer's misgivings, particularly in regard to the artless character of much ecological planting, but ironically he thinks that Milton Keynes was one of the places where they got the approach right!:

I think that that's perhaps one of the big mistakes of the ecological movement in this country through the '70s when we had Alan Ruff[3] and people like that working at Warrington. I think they conned a lot of people . . . what they did was they just said we can do good landscape for a lot less money. There was no art in it. It was just 'plant your native species and let them go'. And of course the New Town Development Corporations thought 'Yeah, that's cheap; we can afford that' and they tell us it's good. Well, you know, it wasn't good enough. I think Milton Keynes have got the balance right, in that it's ecologically based, there are open spaces, it works with the vegetation, it works with water, it works with geology, it works with the underlying soils, but it's high design. It's very, very good design. There's a lot of artwork incorporated into it . . . I don't think ecological design has to look rough and unkempt and uncared for. An orchard, a vineyard, they're ecologically sound and community sound landscape types. Meadows are ecologically sound and managed the right way they can look great as well.

Habitat creation

The Ecological Approach as practised in the New Towns in the 1970s was largely concerned with the creation of quasi-indigenous woodlands. There was a corresponding movement towards mixing wild-flower seeds in grass mixes, allowing meadow-like areas to be created. As landscape architects proved that such things could be done, they became more ambitious in the kinds of natural habitats they sought to simulate. Nigel Marshall described some of the work his team has been undertaking in East Sussex:

At Newhaven we've got a regeneration package; we've got an area of about 90 hectares which is a strategic gap between two settlements. It's an estuarine area. We are basically taking all the agriculture out and making new wetland habitats and areas of reed beds. Together with Eastbourne Park we will be doubling the area of reed beds in the county.

Levels of expertise vary and this sort of work is still seen as specialist, but the fact that it is being done opens up new possibilities for the landscape profession and broadens the palette for those designers who wish to work within an ecological ethos.

Some doubts and antagonisms

At the beginning of this chapter I mentioned that some landscape architects were not interested in, or

were even hostile to, an ecological approach to design. The criticisms are of three main types. First, there is the view that much so-called ecological design is superficial or tokenistic – just sprinkling wild-flower seed mixes or specifying native tree species, but not really reappraising humanity's relationship with the environment nor ensuring that the products of landscape architecture will be truly sustainable. Pauline Randall, for example, thinks that those landscape architects who tinker with their specifications like eco-consumers buying the latest brand of eco-friendly washing powder are missing the most important point, which is to create lasting landscapes:

I'm all for sustainability and in a very fundamental way. I suppose it's founded in a belief that Western society, or the world as a whole, is completely over-populated and that Western society is

Figure 9.6 Eastbourne Park from the air.

completely indulgent in its attitude towards our environment. I would rather see us investing our resources in very fundamental things – making sure we have a balance between nature and development, making sure that we create environments that will endure in our cities and that people enjoy, rather than repeatedly investing in new fashion statements. We've got a little park opposite our home which we have just had the centenary celebrations for. The layout has endured to this day and all it needs is for some railings to be replaced which were removed at the end of the war and the relaying of the paving. It really doesn't need anything else. The community use it, they love it, and I do believe that landscape architects should be able to provide that. They should be able to lay out spaces that stay that way for a good fifty years, not that are changed in five years' time because fashions change and someone has decided that everybody actually walks on the opposite diagonal because they didn't observe it properly to start with.

Then there is the view that ecology has an important place, but that it is a mistake to try to apply it in all circumstances. This was Peter McGuckin's position:

> I think if you asked me to design a nature reserve, ecology would be high on the list of priorities. It moves up and down the pecking order depending upon what is appropriate for the site. That's how it should be. You wouldn't say of Newcastle Quayside, which is a hard, urban landscape, that wildlife corridors were an important aspect of this project. There's hardly anywhere in it you can plant a tree, because the ground conditions are poor. The mistake actually would be to have ecology high up on the list of priorities, plant all these native species, then watch them die. So it might be further down the list for other practical reasons.

Finally, there are those who hold that other values, whether aesthetic or social, may be more important than ecological values. David Appleton, for example, believes that ecological rigour can be taken too far:

> As a practice we do quite a lot of ecological work . . . Even the simplest ditch nowadays, if you want to culvert it up, alter its course, would bring the

wrath of the Environment Agency down on your neck. I think I have no problem differentiating between designs that are weighted towards the needs of the users and designs which are actually looking at conserving a natural landscape. There are occasions when the two sit together quite happily, but I think that there are situations, for example in towns and cities, where you are actually designing for people, and their needs are actually paramount, and there is nothing wrong with that.

Rodney Beaumont acknowledged that ecological values were significant, while distancing himself from them. It was clear that the aesthetics of design mattered much more to him:

> Other people may get interest in creating or maintaining a sustainable landscape out there. I know that I don't want to design that landscape. I'm concerned that the designed landscape is not confused and devalued by words like 'conservation', words like 'recycling', words like 'biodiversity', words like 'organic'. The big worry I have about that is that people who talk like that really don't want to do anything. They don't want to change anything. I think part of what we do is about change and inspiration and that's really where I am sitting, debating and thinking at the moment, in my own situation.

These three main viewpoints are not mutually exclusive. One can find practitioners who believe that ecology is important in design,[4] and must be taken very seriously, but also that its significance varies depending upon the kind of project being considered; it plays a great part in broad scale rural projects, for example, but a much less important role in the design of urban parks and squares. Such people apply a form of calculus in which aesthetic and social values are prioritised for some sorts of projects, ecological values for others. Tom Robinson thinks in this kind of way. I asked him what role he saw for ecology in design:

> It's very important in the practice. As you know my partner is an environmental scientist. That is not to say that we will only do ecological design . . . because we do believe that there are certain spaces that lend themselves more obviously to mannered design. You can give them some slight environmental resource value by the size and the species

of trees you use or something minor like that, but we don't seek to squeeze an ecological design onto every site, because we think it would be inappropriate on so many occasions.

> . . . we believe a lot of what passes for ecological design is . . . shallow. Or conversely it's a highly managed, manicured, false environment for recreation purposes. I mean no problems, *per se*, with the latter if that's what people want to do, but real problems with the former, where simply by throwing down a wild-flower seed mix it's a wild meadow, or whatever, whilst knowing that the management after three years is going to be neglected and so you'll end up with absolutely nothing. Because Rachel[5] is an environmental scientist, we take ecological design very seriously and the sites have to . . . I wouldn't say pass a certain test before we'd agree to do that kind of work, but . . .

I asked him what factors would influence their decision to get involved in such work:

> Well the size of the site for instance, the function, the land use and obviously the management. It's pointless building something if the management intention isn't there to run it.

Robinson's approach fits fairly comfortably into the value schema I have been seeking to develop in this book. This accepts that aesthetic, social and ecological values all have their part to play in landscape design, but that they must be kept in balance, one with another. Such a way of conceptualising the value-structure of the profession does, it seems to me, fit the way in which landscape architects talk about their values. This is an idea explored further in Chapter 10.

Towards a new ecological aesthetic

In Chapter 8 I suggested that one of the most pressing issues that landscape architects needed to address was the impact of ecological thinking upon the aesthetics of landscape. It seems to me that this is an urgent task if landscape architecture is to acknowledge both aesthetics and ecology as fundamental sources of values without losing its coherence as a discipline. I found that this idea provoked a mixed reaction from my interviewees. John Hopkins, who, as we saw earlier, is a believer in the centrality of ecological values, was nevertheless sceptical about this favouring any particular style of design, and he cited Dan Kiley in support of this view:

> I think that in my design work I take the influences of romanticism, classicism and blend and mend. I think it was Dan Kiley who took the modern classical landscape to its ultimate form in this century. When he gave his lecture at the RIBA he said that he played a lot of golf. He's a golf fanatic. He'd love to design a golf course on a grid. And his argument is that the birds don't mind whether it's a straight line or not, as long as the relationship between the forest edge and the fairway is there, they don't care.

I find this dubious, for it seems to me that there will be those styles of design which maximise the value of a landscape for wildlife and those that do not.[6] To employ a *reductio ad absurdum*, a classically conceived urban plaza, mostly hard landscaped with perhaps a few ornamental trees in containers, can hardly be considered to be making any contribution whatsoever to the ecology of a city, and if it contains a formal water feature with fountains run off mains electricity it could be argued that its contribution to sustainable living is actually negative. On the other hand ecological design need not – and should not – be conducted in a deterministic way. The designs for the Earth Centre landscape discussed in Chapter 10 show that there is ample scope for the imagination.

Also encouraging was Neil Mattinson's interest in reinvigorating the Ecological Approach. He described a business park project he was working on near Cambridge:[7]

> We are preparing a master-plan scheme which will essentially set high-quality architecture, very high-quality architecture, in very naturalistic landscape, with soundly based ecological principles. Not just the wider landscape surrounding the site, but the internal site plots, if you like, whereas before we've all seen the sort of serried ranks of parking with beech hedging around it, or laurel hedging, or lots of avenues of trees, and we're trying an approach which allows a much more relaxed ecological design to be developed so those buildings sit within a wide landscape.
>
> We're not imposing an artificial landscape. We are in the sense that we're putting a building

footprint in there and we've got to assess the relationship between the building footprint and the wider landscape, so there's a transitional zone, but within that transitional zone we're looking to adopt ecological principles to the landscape design.

And the client is extremely interested in the approach. He's very wary. He's very concerned he's going to end up having a site looking as though it's unkempt and railwayesque in the sense of lupins everywhere and self-sown this, that and t'other. He's a little bit concerned because he's obviously going for blue-chip tenants, but the skill or the trick for us is to achieve that within what perhaps has to be quite a contrived, architecturally designed layout. It's got to be quite obvious that the landscape is meant to be like that and it isn't 'not-managed', and you can do that in all sorts of ways, just from hard detailing trim to the edges or perimeters, to a very high-quality maintenance regime; you accept that there will be mown grass, short grass, but very quickly you run that into another hierarchy of grass and so on and so forth, right through the whole structure.

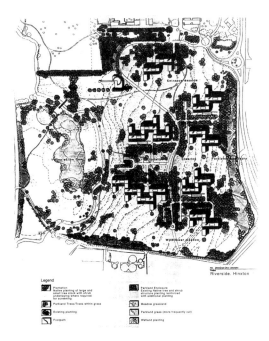

Legend

Plantation
Native planting of large and small tree stock with shrub underlaying where required for screening

Parkland Trees/Trees within grass

Existing planting

Footpath

Parkland Enclosure
Existing Native tree and shrub structure planting reinforced with additional planting

Meadow grassland

Parkland grass (more frequently cut)

Wetland planting

Riverside, Hinxton

Figure 9.7 Proposed landscape masterplan for a business park in Cambridgeshire by SGS Environment. This is the scheme referred to by Neil Mattinson during his interview.

I put it to Mattinson that landscape architecture with ecological principles to the fore had often produced dull design:

I disagree with that . . . that you can't make bold design statements with ecological approaches. I'm jolly sure you can. It's all about scale and massing. I think handled in the right manner you can make a very strong statement ecologically, with the ecological plant mix and grass mix, for instance . . . or waterbodies . . . and I've got no problem at all in actually, for instance, starting off with a water body that is naturalistic . . . it may well be man-made, but it actually relates to the wider landscape . . . why can't that water body then progress through a transitional form as it enters a built zone where there's obviously human intervention, and become stylised, but still with an ecological base to it.

You can still have the right plant material, the right water treatment. You know, what we want to avoid is pumps everywhere. Minimise the costs, get the water right, get the design of that water body right, get the shelving right, so it's self-supporting, so you don't end up with eutrophic condition . . . use the right plants, the right water depth. There's nothing wrong with it becoming stylised – that naturalistic water body could end up being a canal at one end. But what you're doing, you're pulling that ecological design approach in, rather than separating the two.

This is the direction in which landscape architecture should be going, but such thinking is still relatively rare and somewhat tentative.

Mixed feelings

I found more confusion and more mixed feelings about the place of ecological values in landscape architecture than I did about social or aesthetic values. This was not a surprise, because one might have predicted that the most recent source of values would be the least assimilated. But I also suspect that the failure on behalf of some practitioners to embrace ecology comes from unfamiliarity and fear. The recent history of the Ecological Approach has led some to conclude that ecology is anti-design, and as such a direct threat to other values which they hold dearly. I do not believe that this fear is justified, and, as the project described by Neil Mattinson indicates, the synergistic merging of design and ecological values may greatly enhance the final product.

Notes

1   Agenda 21 is a document produced by the United Nations Conference on Environment and Development held in Rio de Janeiro in 1992 which was intended to guide international action in the field of sustainable development well into the twenty-first century. Great onus for the implementation of Agenda 21 was placed upon local authorities which were each supposed to prepare their own Local Agendas by 1996. Of the 2,500 action items included in Agenda 21, over two-thirds related to local authorities.

2   A port on the north-east coast of England.

3   To the best of my knowledge Alan Ruff, who has for many years taught landscape architecture at Manchester University, was not employed at Warrington New Town, but he is closely associated with the 'Ecological Approach', having studied it in the Netherlands.

4   Having concluded my round of twenty-six interviews I have subsequently discovered several more designers of a strongly ecological persuasion! They include Luke Engleback of Battle McCarthy who has valiantly been seeking to introduce sound sustainable principles into the design of the Greenwich Peninsular redevelopment, and Andrew Grant and his team, whose work on the Earth Centre is described in Chapter 10.

5   Dr Rachel Penn, an ecologist, is the other partner in Robinson Penn.

6   Landscape ecologists tell us that there are very significant differences between straight edges and natural edges. For example, the presence of coves and lobes along an edge provide greater habitat diversity than along a straight edge, thereby encouraging higher species diversity. See Dramstad, Olson and Forman (1996) *Landscape Ecology Princiiples in Landscape Architecture and Land-Use Planning*, Island Press, Harvard.

7   This was Phase II of Hinxton Hall. Phase I was undertaken by Elizabeth Banks Associates.

10 Tri-valent design

Refocusing for the future

The opening chapter suggested that the values inherent in landscape architecture could be classified under three headings: aesthetic, social and ecological. The theoretical explorations undertaken in the even-numbered chapters have supported this view, while mapping some of the internal complexity of these value fields. In the odd-numbered chapters, the interviews with practitioners gave us further grounds for confidence in the appropriateness of this tripartite framework, while revealing some of the tensions which may exist between values in practice, as well as the extent to which practice can lag behind theory.

However, this book promised not only to give a descriptive overview of the ethical and aesthetic value systems inherent in landscape architecture but also to give some normative guidance to those who teach and practice. This, as the discussion of Berlin's value-pluralism in Chapter 1 indicates, has its limits. No one is in a position to say that we must all strive like Jellicoe to pursue landscape architecture as an art form, or that countless others who labour just to make things 'seemly' are mistaken. It is wrong-headed to attempt to compare an ecological landscape in Holland with a contemporary minimalist art-garden by Martha Schwartz, or at least to try to compare them against some common standard.

However, the framework suggested in Figure 1.3, p. 7 can form the basis for landscape criticism. We can say, for example, that a particular piece of design embodies strong aesthetic principles, that it works in harmony with the ecology of its site, but that it does not have a social dimension. Or that a design has been developed in a participatory manner with a local community, has been designed with sustainability in mind, yet lacks the quality of design detailing that would make it admirable in aesthetic terms.

Some of these possibilities have been explored in the bar charts in Figure 10.1. Similar charts could be used to evaluate approaches to particular projects or the outcomes of design interventions, but a word of caution is required. In the strictest sense of 'incommensurable', the values I have described as aesthetic, social and ecological cannot be weighed against one another. There is no common scale against which these values can be measured. Consequently the charts in Figure 10.1 do not have a vertical scale. However, this does not prevent us from talking meaningfully about high or low levels of aesthetic, social or environmental value, or for making critical comparisons between projects or designs. The diagrams in Figure 10.1 are to be understood in this limited sense. To admit that there are plural sources of values in landscape architecture is emphatically not to say that everything is relative and that one design is as good as any other.

Uni-valent, bi-valent and tri-valent design

On the top row we have three species of 'uni-valent' design. In (a) only aesthetic values are addressed. This could apply both to the inconspicuous and the assertive schools of landscape aesthetics. Accepting a plurality of values for the profession means that there is room for both approaches, although both may be constrained by the characteristics of the site.

In Chapter 2 it was suggested that the notion of

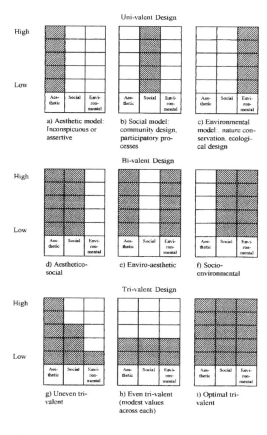

Figure 10.1 Some permutations of pluralistic design. Nine possibilities are shown, but many other combinations are implied.

'the genius of the place' remains a valid springboard for design, and this idea remains central to the value systems of most of the practitioners interviewed in the course of this study. In the majority of cases a respect for the particularities of places, their spatial, visual, textural and historical qualities, will lead gently towards more harmonious forms of design. Robert Camlin's design for Uppermill Cemetery (Case Study 4.1, pp. 68–69) demonstrates that a design can be sympathetic to its surroundings yet employ the most potent of symbolism. However, designs which respond to existing qualities with strategies of contrast are not to be disallowed.

If we accept that bi-valent or tri-valent design is richer than uni-valent design, social and ecological considerations will guide the aesthetics. Much more research needs to be done here. One of the 'most significant questions' mentioned in Chapter 1 concerned the relationship between aesthetics and ecology. This book is going to fall short of an answer, but we may hypothesise that the more aesthetically

sympathetic designs will turn out also to be the most satisfactory in social and ecological terms; at the present stage of knowledge this remains unproven.

Whenever designers or other professionals remark that 'the process is more important than the product' they may be invoking the community model depicted at (b), although the graph shows a rather extreme and hypothetical instance where no regard has been given to aesthetic or ecological matters. In reality much of the content of the participatory processes would be concerned with such issues. This is clear from the comments of the designers quoted in Chapter 7, who recognised that consultation is a two-way process in which the landscape architect not only listens to the needs and concerns of the users but is often involved in educating them and persuading them to adopt certain aesthetic or ecological objectives.

In (c) the only values addressed are environmental. Once again it is rather difficult to imagine such a pure example, although some nature conservation initiatives away from centres of population might come close to this model. Perhaps this is more readily conceived in North America where there are still extensive tracts of wilderness. In Western Europe landscapes are likely to be populated, so most projects correspondingly will have some social component.

In the second row are three bar charts which depict bi-valent approaches to design. These correspond to the areas of overlap between the circles in Figure 1.3, p. 7.

Functionalism is related to what I have called 'aesthetico-social design' at (d), but any design which pays attention to questions of style alongside matters of usefulness would fit into this category. Some of the contemporary park designs from Paris and Barcelona might be included here. It is an approach which is easily applied in urban situations where the natural processes that sustain the city are not always evident (and therefore easy to ignore).

The view that an ecological foundation to design automatically creates sound aesthetics is represented at (e). This category, the 'enviro-aesthetic', might also be applied to the work of Capability Brown and the English Landscape School, who were driven by aesthetic goals yet produced landscapes which we now recognise to have been sustainable, without the benefit of the science of ecology to assist them.

Meanwhile (f) represents the main thrust of the 'Ecological Approach', both in the Netherlands and the United Kingdom, a school of design which had both social and environmental ideals but, as we saw in Chapters 8 and 9, often failed to generate aesthetic interest.

The final chart at (i) suggests an ideal situation in which it has been possible to maximise all three values within a project. It is difficult to think of many actual projects which have come close to this ideal, though some of the more imaginative examples of the 'Ecological Approach' might be candidates.

It is easy to see that *in general* tri-valent design is better than bi-valent, which in turn is an improvement upon uni-valent, and this rescues the pluralistic approach to design values from charges of relativism. However, the maximised values represented in bar charts (a)–(f) mask some of the real difficulties that arise if one tries to compare values that have not been maximised with values that have. It is impossible, for example, to say that the project represented at (h), which has addressed all three areas of value but fallen well short of maximising any of them, is better than the project shown at (a) which has been aesthetically successful but has not addressed social or environmental issues at all.

Nevertheless, to the extent that designs can earn merit in each of these value fields, we should come to value most highly those designs which seem to succeed in aesthetic, social *and* ecological terms. This is the area I have called 'tri-valent' design.[1]

Finding examples of good tri-valent design is not easy. Many schemes which are recognisably 'good design' are nevertheless only good uni-valent or bi-valent design. For example the work on Newcastle's East Quayside described in Chapter 3 shows appropriate good taste and succeeds in harmonising disparate architectural styles while responding to the character of a unique historical setting. To the extent that it is also eminently practical and hard-wearing and answers the demands of its brief, it will probably succeed in social terms (although its creation was not the result of the kinds of collaborative processes described in Chapter 6). However, the third dimension of ecological sustainability seems to be absent, for the scheme is predominantly a hard landscape, utilising materials brought from a considerable distance, handling drainage in a conventional way and offering few advantages for wildlife. The same observation would apply to many urban landscape projects, whether they are exercises in modest aesthetic restraint or self-proclaiming pieces of art-landscape.

Similarly it is relatively easy to find examples of

work which address matters of ecology alongside matters of aesthetics. Peter Fischer's involvement in the planning applications for a golf course at Birch Grove, also mentioned in Chapter 3, fits this description, for not only was he concerned to minimise the visual impact of the development, he also sought to replant storm-damaged woodlands and enhance heathland habitats throughout the site. However, the scheme was essentially bi-valent as the brief came from a wealthy Hong Kong businessman who wanted a private golf course for his personal use, and therefore it did not have a strong social dimension.

Very often it is the social aspect which is the least well developed. With new developments, whether housing areas or business parks, the community of users may not exist beforehand. In such circumstances the sort of empathetic 'designer-knows-best' approach we encountered from some of the interviewees mentioned in Chapter 7 may be the best possible, but there is surely a tendency for designers to fall back upon this in situations where a more active engagement with local communities would be possible. There can be a tension between a designer's aesthetic ambitions and the requirement to involve others in making significant decisions.

It is instructive to look at some examples of projects which have emphasised community processes, such as the Groundwork Trust's 'Changing Places' projects described in Case Study 7.1 (see pp. 126–129). These illustrate very active community involvement and are underpinned by ecological considerations, yet their aesthetic impact is limited to making things 'seemly'. For landscape architects they are salutary because it seems possible to achieve fairly good results without professional design assistance. Although the Groundwork's philosophy of collaboration baulks at the idea of 'leadership', it would seem that an ability to motivate people is the essential skill needed for this kind of work, although it must be combined with an understanding of natural processes if it is to produce lasting results.

The two case studies which follow are intended to illuminate aspects of tri-valent design. Each contains elements of 'best practice' although each, to some degree, falls short of the ideal.

Burgess Park is an interesting example of a design expressly based upon considerations of ecology, community and art. The landscape design for the Earth Centre near Doncaster seeks to forge a new aesthetics based on an innovatory approach to sustainability.

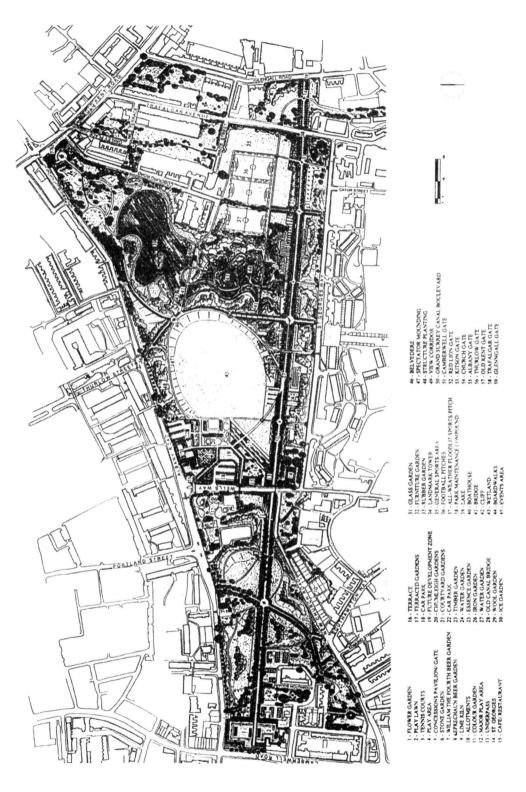

1 - FLOWER GARDEN
2 - PLAY LAWN
3 - TENNIS COURTS
4 - PLAY AREA
5 - CONCESSIONS PAVILION GATE
6 - STONE GARDEN
7 - WILLIAM THE FOURTH BEER GARDEN
8 - LEPRECHAUN BEER GARDEN
9 - LIME KILN
10 - ALLOTMENTS
11 - COLOUR GARDEN
12 - MAJOR PLAY AREA
13 - UNDERPASS
14 - ST GEORGES
15 - CAFE RESTAURANT
16 - TERRACE
17 - TERRACED GARDENS
18 - CAR PARK
19 - FUTURE DEVELOPMENT ZONE
20 - CHUMLEIGH GARDENS
21 - COURTYARD GARDENS
22 - CAR PARK
23 - TIMBER GARDEN
24 - WATER GARDEN
25 - ESSENCE GARDEN
26 - IRON GARDEN
27 - WATER GARDEN
28 - OLD CANAL BRIDGE
29 - WOOL GARDEN
30 - ICE GARDEN
31 - GLASS GARDEN
32 - FURNITURE GARDEN
33 - RUBBER GARDEN
34 - LANDMARK TOWER
35 - GENERAL SPORTS AREA
36 - FOOTBALL PITCHES
37 - ALL-WEATHER FLOODLIT SPORTS PITCH
38 - PARK MAINTENANCE COMPOUND
39 - LAKE
40 - BOATHOUSE
41 - BRIDGE
42 - CLIFF
43 - WETLAND
44 - BOARDWALKS
45 - EVENTS AREA
46 - BELVEDERE
47 - SPECTATOR MOUNDING
48 - STRUCTURE PLANTING
49 - VIEW CORRIDOR
50 - GRAND SURREY CANAL BOULEVARD
51 - CAMBERWELL GATE
52 - RED LION GATE
53 - KITSON GATE
54 - CHURCH GATE
55 - ALBANY GATE
56 - THURLOW GATE
57 - OLD KENT GATE
58 - TRAFALGAR GATE
59 - GLENGALL GATE

Figure 10.2 Masterplan for Burgess Park, London. (Courtesy of EDAW Ltd.)

Case study 10.1: Masterplan for Burgess Park, Southwark, London. Prepared by EDAW Ltd for Groundwork Southwark

History

The 54-hectare Burgess Park was one of two major parks proposed in the 1943 Abercrombie plan for London. Located in one of the capital's most deprived inner city areas, the park has remained incomplete despite major demolitions. In 1996 EDAW Ltd prepared a masterplan for the park on behalf of Groundwork Southwark (in association with the London Borough of Southwark, the Peckham Partnership and various community groups) which formed the basis of a bid for Millennium Commission funding. Unfortunately this bid was unsuccessful, but the Masterplan has been adopted by Groundwork as the basis for a park development programme which will now be pursued incrementally.

The Masterplan has been expressly developed around three themes: community, ecology and art (perceptive readers will notice the similarity to the title of this book!).

Community

The Masterplan Report states that the park should be 'of and for the community'. Local people should feel a sense of ownership and it must be meaningful to them. This has influenced the aesthetics of the design which is based upon ideas of local distinctiveness. The design draws out the specific history of the site. For example, the line of the Old Surrey Canal will be marked out and the wharfside uses will be 'remembered' as the inspiration for landscape forms, types, sculptures and furniture. In this way, and by involving the community in the detailed development of the designs, the intention is that all sections of the community will be able to read the landscape of Burgess Park and recognise it as their own.

The Park is to be developed as a social process, not merely as an aesthetic object. A varied programme of events – fairs, shows, open-air theatre, interpretative walks, etc. – will promote this process of engagement, while an improved system of paths and cycle routes, together with better signage and lighting, will encourage

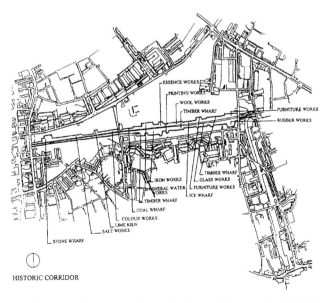

Figure 10.3 Plan showing the proposed 'historic corridor' in the Burgess Park proposals, which is based upon the line of the Old Surrey Canal. (Courtesy of EDAW Ltd.)

greater levels of use, which in turn will increase perceptions of safety for users.

Ecology

One of the principles expounded in the Masterplan Report is that the Park should promote the understanding of natural processes and human interventions. It will do this through physical demonstration – creating particular habitats, for example – as well as through interpretation and education.

The existing lake will be an important focus for this activity. It is proposed that the edges of lake be reformed to create an ecologically and visually interesting mixture of hard and soft margins. An extensive, ecologically diverse wetland of reeds, rushes, bog gardens and shallow pools is to be created as an extension to the lake habitat. Where possible, water features will collect rainwater, leading it down through channels and rills towards the wetlands and lake, thus making the natural process of drainage visible.

Delight

The Masterplan has a strong aesthetic developed from considerations of local distinctiveness. In addition to the historical references to the former street pattern and the life of the old canal already mentioned, the strong links which exist between this part of London and the County of Kent have formed the inspiration for a series of landscape forms and spaces which will be contemporary interpretations of Kentish landscape types such as hop-fields, oyster farms, pastures, hazel and chestnut coppices and orchards.

Figure 10.4 Sketch of the proposed wetland area at Burgess Park. (Courtesy of EDAW Ltd.)

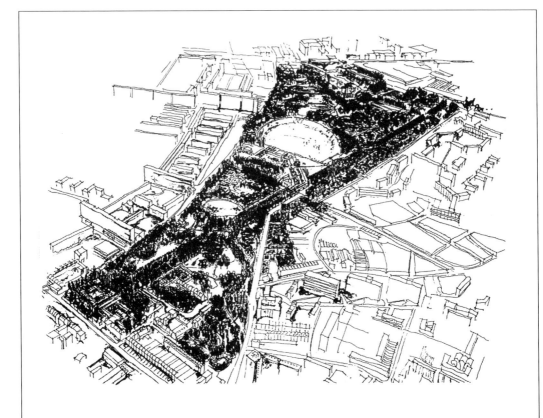

Figure 10.5 Aerial view of the Burgess Park proposals from the west. (Courtesy of EDAW Ltd.)

There will also be an extensive, evolutionary, community based arts programme for the Park (the community arts organisation Art-in-the-Park is already based there). Among the more imagin- ative proposals is the idea of an Avant-Garden Show to be held on an annual or bi-annual basis which is seem as the antithesis and antidote to the Chelsea Flower Show.

Case study 10.2: Landscape design for the Earth Centre, Doncaster. Landscape Architects: Grant Associates, Bath

Background

The Earth Centre, which is being built on a reclaimed colliery tip between Rotherham and Doncaster in South Yorkshire, is billed as the world's first visitor attraction based upon the theme of sustainable development. Its aim is to educate people about more sustainable ways of living in a stimulating and entertaining way. The landscape is as important as the buildings in this respect – in the words of its designer, Andrew Grant, it must 'exhilarate, inspire, engage, em- power and educate'.[2] It has been included here because it demonstrates that the new emphasis upon sustainability calls for an innovatory design aesthetics.

Ecology

Just as the buildings on site demonstrate the latest thinking in eco-friendly architecture, the land- scape of the site exemplifies the principles of sustainability. Buildings and landscape are presented as an integrated system in which the best practice in energy efficiency and water conservation are shown.

Central to this is a system which recycles water on site. The Water Works (designed by Alsop and Störmer) is both an exhibition space and a sewage treatment works. It houses the Living Machine which replicates and accelerates the natural purification processes of ponds and marshes. Treated effluent from the Living Machine is used for irrigating the site and maintaining water levels in the bog garden. Similarly, the landscape design conserves water by eschewing traditional drainage in favour of an above-ground system of swales and reed beds which lead to a new freshwater pond. Cleaned by the reed beds, this water sustains the ecology and the visual quality of the pond. Excavations beside the River Don have created new wetlands and damp hollows which create valuable new habitats for threatened species.

In many ways the designers of the Earth Centre landscape have turned conventional landscape architectural thinking upon its head. On many conventional projects immediacy of impact is an important concern, and it is common to find that advanced nursery stock – even semi-mature trees – have been bought in, sometimes from abroad, to fill this need. Such an approach is precluded by

Figure 10.6 Earth Centre, Doncaster. Sketch layout for the Water Conservation Garden. The large building in the centre is the Waterworks, with the terraced gardens to the left and the mounds of the woodland garden to the bottom right. (Courtesy of Grant Associates.)

the Earth Centre philosophy. The tree planting is largely confined to young native-grown material. Height has been provided in the short term by a 'forest' of temporary timber structures which will be clothed by quick-growing vines, hops and beans. Trees will be planted at the centre of these structures, to take advantage of the sheltered growing conditions.

Delight

The Earth Centre landscape has a distinctive aesthetic which proves that ecologically inspired design need not be dull nor confined to imitations of nature. There is a crispness and straightforwardness about much of the detailed design which owes something to modernist rationality. Land art, particularly the work of Isamu Noguchi, has been a direct influence upon the design of landform.

Because the proposed woodland areas will take time to grow, the designers have sought to make an immediate impression by the bold use of wild flowers, grasslands, cereals and horticultural crops. The planting design often presents familiar plants in an unfamiliar way. For example, rhubarb will be planted in large expanses and gooseberries (rather than shrub roses or berberis) will be planted as dense barrier shrubs. During the early years of the Centre, huge displays of sunflowers, lavender, irises, tulips and prairie flowers will capture the simple grandeur of flowering plants used *en masse*. Perhaps the bravest use of plant material is the decision to clothe the mound which shelters an arena in the Forest Garden with nettles – a plant which has a neglected potential for the manufacture of fabrics.

The landscape is coherent but diverse. As one moves from the lower levels of the site where the ponds and wetlands predominate one reaches the three cultivation terraces, the first dedicated to world gardens (such as the South East Asian Polyculture Garden and a Desert Garden), the second demonstrating the potential for organic gardening in the United Kingdom, and the last devoted to local Yorkshire traditions of gardening. On the drier slopes above the terraces woodlands have been planted. A second organisational

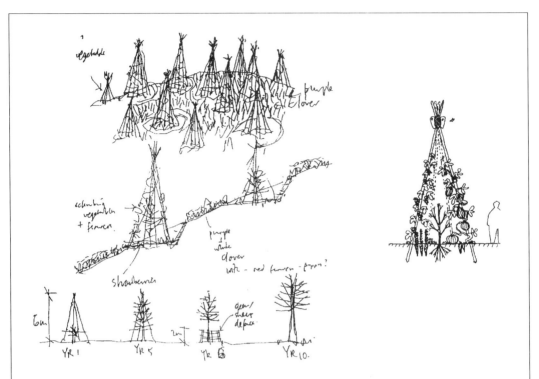

Figure 10.7 Earth Centre, Doncaster. Design development sketches for 'semi-temporary' tree shelters. (Courtesy of Grant Associates.)

Figure 10.8 Earth Centre, Doncaster: earth mounding and lattice domes.

Figure 10.9 Earth Centre, Doncaster: inside one of the lattice domes in the Woodland Garden.

principle places the more intensively managed, human-dominated landscapes between the Water Works and Future Works buildings to the west of the site. As one moves away the landscapes become wilder and less managed until one reaches the natural limestone scarp of Cadeby Rattles.

Community

If one were writing a school report for the Earth Centre, the appropriate comment for this section would be something like 'tries hard' or 'could do better'. The project differs from the previous case studies in that it is a national project driven by a very strong concept, rather than a local scheme tuned to the immediate needs of residents. Much of the site will be within a pay-boundary and

during construction considerations of safety and insurance liability dictate that the general public must be excluded.

The Centre is ground-breaking in its philosophy and design, and its pedagogical function in explaining and exemplifying sustainable technologies is central. But this means that, thus far, specialist expertise has been privileged over local knowledge, although the Centre runs an extensive programme of outreach activities which seeks to inform the local communities of Conisbrough and Mexborough (and nearby Doncaster and Rotherham) about the development of the site and where possible to involve local people. Locally responsive participatory design processes, however, have had a minor role to play in the

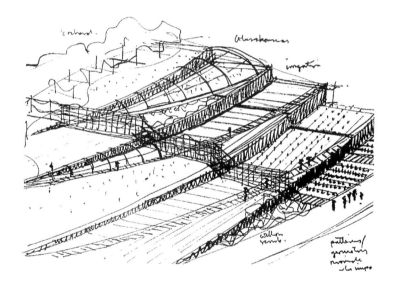

a)

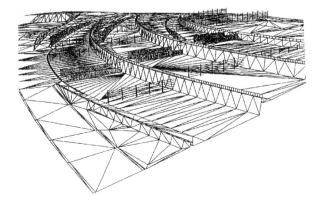

b)

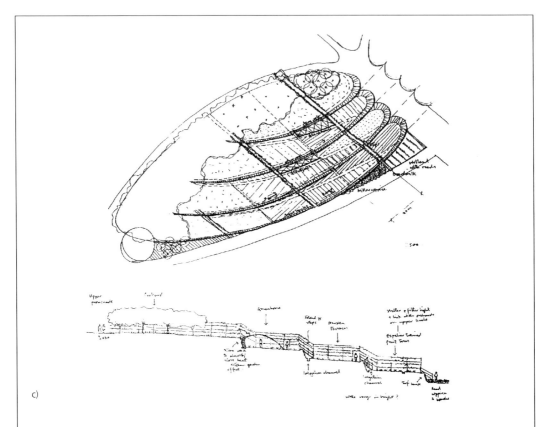

c)

Figure 10.10a, b and c Earth Centre, Doncaster. Design development drawings for the terraced gardens – the lowest terrace has world gardens, the next is devoted to organic gardening in the UK and the third is dedicated to Yorkshire gardening traditions. (Courtesy of Grant Associates.)

creation of the project, although, as it evolves, it seems certain that an engagement with the local community will be fostered, and that there will be opportunities for local participation in the more detailed aspects of the design.

Although the first phase of the Earth Centre is costing £44 million pounds, the project has had a battle to secure its funding and this has made it difficult to guarantee continuity of employment to local people. Regrettably over thirty locally employed rangers had to be laid off at one stage because the Millennium Commission, while happy to support capital costs and 'core staff', could not be persuaded to meet this aspect of the wages bill. However, the Centre's sustainable philosophy places great emphasis upon the importance of locally based activities, and there is an aspiration to assist in the regeneration of the area's economy which has suffered from the loss

of traditional heavy industries. The Earth Centre is a productive landscape. There has been an emphasis upon the creation of gardens that produce fruit, nuts, vegetables, herbs, flowers, medicines and dyes. Elsewhere on the site there will be biomass plantations of willow cultivars, and reeds will be grown in channels to be harvested for thatching and other crafts. Not only will local labour be needed for cultivation and harvesting, but staff foresee the growth of small-scale craft industries associated with the Centre. Moreover the presence of a major visitor attraction will support a range of service industries, for example in laundry, organic catering and even site security, which will provide opportunities for green-tinged entrepreneurship. It already seems that the Earth Centre has started to act as a catalyst for economic regeneration in the locality.

Any large-scale development can cause frictions with elements of the local community, and the Earth Centre is no different. This means that great care must be taken, for example, in questions of access. In planning the Centre care was taken not to close off any existing rights of way, although some customary paths had to be re-routed. By working with local ramblers to improve paths and waymarking, access to the non-pay areas associated with the site should be improved overall. Earth Centre development staff are very conscious of the need to build a positive relationship with the surrounding community and are committed to a range of liaison initiatives including an Earth Centre Friends Group, a Membership scheme (with discounts), a Youth Advisory Board and a Naturalists' Advisory Group.

The condition of practice

At times on my interview tour of Britain I have felt like a latter-day William Cobbett undertaking my own *Rural Rides*,[3] although my travels have been more urban or urban-fringe. After many hours spent on motorways or feeling my way through the gridlocked penumbras of sprawling cities like London, Birmingham or Manchester, it would be easy to write a gloomy prognosis. The message of Simon Rendel's Tranquil Area Maps (see Chapter 3) seemed to be confirmed, for everywhere I looked there were burgeoning housing estates and gaudy tin-shed retail parks, while mobile-phone relay masts have insidiously positioned themselves throughout the land. It is the lot of the landscape architect to be particularly sensitive to these incursions, and to compound our distress our vocation obliges us to seek out those places which are the most dispiriting.

Paradoxically it is the existence of so much ugliness, and the damage that has been done – and could still be done – to the ecosystems that support our existence, that makes the job of the landscape architect so worth while. Just as doctors are sanctioned by the existence of disease and lawyers by the perseverance of crime, so landscape architects are made necessary by the persistence of grot.

The profession in the UK has grown from 3,045 professional members in 1993[4] to 3,548 in 1997,[5] while the American Society of Landscape Architects has over 12,000 members.[6] In 1997 the Landscape Institute was awarded a Royal Charter, the real significance of which is that Her Majesty's Government has accepted that the LI is *the* expert body on questions of landscape. One does not have to be a royalist to feel pleased about this.

Occasionally we need to remind ourselves that this is a success story. As the pressures upon these densely populated islands continue to mount it would seem that the role of the landscape architect in Britain is guaranteed into the distant future. The job is always changing, shifting as society and government redefine priorities. When I was training in the late 1970s the enthusiasm was for country parks and the funding followed the enthusiasm. New Towns and coal-tip reclamation were also major sources of employment. The 1980s saw the emphasis move on the one hand to the edge-of-town business park and on the other to the inner city, where environmental improvement and urban regeneration were the rallying cries. Garden Festivals caught the public imagination. Groundwork Trusts emerged as a third-way option between the public and private sectors and pioneered new ways of working more closely with communities. The number of LI members employed by the Trusts has doubled since 1994. In the 1990s we have had urban development corporations and latterly the Millennium Commission and the Heritage Lottery Fund. As one source of funding has dried up, another has always seemed to bubble forth to take its place, but landscape architects, particularly those in private practice, can be forgiven if they are left feeling insecure by these ever-changing cycles. To stay in business they have to be adept at spotting future trends.

Landscape architecture can claim some very real successes. Land reclamation is perhaps the most substantial, but the contribution to urban redevelopment has also been enormous, while McHarg's advocacy of landscape planning has, in the course of a generation, led to the growth industries of environmental assessment and landscape appraisal. Yet landscape architects remain unsung heroes, and perhaps this, together with the unpredictable nature of the workload, accounts for the rather harassed and pessimistic demeanour of some of my interviewees. There is a widespread feeling that landscape architects lack profile and influence, that they are always responding to the agendas of others rather than setting their own. While the loss of the metropolitan county councils and their highly professional design teams was a serious set-back in the mid-1980s, the loss of the mandatory fee scale meanwhile put tremendous pressure upon private practices, leading sometimes to production-line design. Under such conditions it is difficult to invest time to create art, undertake lengthy public consultations or research and develop innovatory approaches to sustainable design. All the values explored in this book are put at risk by the ferocity of fee bidding.

Yet these values are all that the profession has to offer. If we abandon them we might as well accept the despised role of planting technicians that others have sometimes thrust upon us. In the competitive scramble for a share of the 1980s development bonanza, ecology, community and delight were sometimes jettisoned and the profession has not yet recovered from the harm that this caused. Only by remaining firmly on the high moral and aesthetic ground can the profession hope to thrive.

This book has been a warts-and-all presentation of the profession. It would have been relatively easy to have skewed my conclusions, for example by selecting only interviewees with impeccable ecological credentials. Rather than do this I tried to select an honestly representative cross-section of experienced people in practice.[7] It turns out, unsurprisingly, that some are more ecologically aware than others and are fully briefed about sustainability while some have little idea of what the latter means, that some are striving to be artists while others want nothing to do with the idea, and that some throw themselves into community participation while some run away from it as fast as they can. Whenever designers back away from one of the three main value areas, whether it be the aesthetic, the social or the ecological, they open up a split between theory and practice and deny themselves the opportunity to produce tri-valent design.

It is customary in concluding chapters to suggest remedies. My own prescriptions would be to counsel all landscape architects to look for opportunities to create art – or at least delight – in their projects, no matter how humble the sites they are working on

may appear to be; to include considerations of sustainability at all stages of the design process, from masterplan through to the specification of materials; and, where there is a community which will be affected by their designs, to allow sufficient time to get to know those people and to involve them in the process. But even as I say this, I recognise how often my own practice has fallen short of these ideals. This conclusion must not become a sermon. Everyone must find for themselves the ways in which to create beautiful, artistic, sustainable and socially useful designs.

Writing this book has been a personal odyssey. In place of the puzzlement I once felt about landscape architecture, I now feel that I have a very strong idea of what the profession stands for. The values are robust, though more complicated than I might have imagined. There is no *one* way to produce good landscape design; there are many right ways. Some, though, are better than others, and those which maximise social, ecological and aesthetic benefits are the best of all. One of the themes which emerged strongly was the advocacy by some of bolder, more assertive design. There is nothing wrong with bold design, but if it is to be more than uni-valent it should be ecologically based and socially meaningful as well. We certainly need some more examples of this sort. My hope is that this book will help to refocus the minds of landscape architects upon their mission, in all its urgency, while opening up to those outside the profession the range of benefits which this most comprehensive and aspirational of vocations can bestow.

Notes

1 I could be proved wrong, but I fear that this is not a name with which to fire the imagination. If anyone has a better one, I am open to suggestions.
2 A. Grant (1998) 'Life on Earth' *Landscape Design*, No. 270.
3 First published in 1830, William Cobbett's *Rural Rides* described the author's journeys through the lowland counties of southern England and contained his 'Economical and Political Observations relative to matters applicable to, and illustrated by, the State of those Counties respectively'.
4 Figure taken from *Landscape Architecture Europe*, Landscape Design Trust, 1993. Includes Fellows, Associates and Graduates.
5 Also includes Fellows, Associates and Graduates. Taken from The LI's employment survey in 1997 which also showed that 96.7% of these landscape architects were in employment, which seems like a healthy statistic!
6 From the ASLA website in July 1998.

Appendix

Practitioner profiles

The following people were kind enough to be interviewed for my research:

David Appleton Originally trained as a horticulturist, David Appleton found his way into landscape architecture by taking a technician's post with the Planning Department of Sheffield City Council and then enrolling for a postgraduate qualification in landscape design at Sheffield University. Upon graduation Appleton joined Greater Manchester Council in the heady days following local government reorganisation. Staff were young and motivated and, for once, the budgets they were given matched their aspirations. They also had the necessary political backing to turn their visions into reality. Appleton was given particular responsibilities for the strategic planning of the metropolitan area's river valleys – 'Literally we went away and created the first major greenspace network in the whole of the country.'

In 1978 Appleton established a private office which grew annually in the quantity and variety of commissions. Following the formation of the Appleton Group Partnership in 1991, the practice was able to operate across an even wider range of activities. Specific experience includes urban park design, industrial and commercial projects, landscape master-planning, environmental assessment, landfill and land reclamation schemes.

Elizabeth Banks is the principal of the North London practice which bears her name. Although the consultancy undertakes a wide range of work, it has a particular expertise in the restoration and management of historic gardens. During her time with Land Use Consultants, Banks devised a methodology for undertaking surveys of historic landscapes and prepared the *Inventory of Gardens and Designed Landscapes in Scotland* for the Countryside Commission of Scotland. In addition to her practice as a landscape architect, Banks also manages Hergest Croft Gardens, her family's 50-acre garden and arboretum which are open to the public and attract around 14,000 visitors per annum. Her book *Creating Period Gardens* was published by Phaidon in 1991.

Rodney Beaumont As a teenager Rodney Beaumont had aspirations towards becoming an architect, but at that time mathematics was seen as a prerequisite for most architecture courses and Beaumont confesses that he wasn't much of a mathematician. The alternative was to join Glasgow Corporation as an apprentice town planner. This led in turn to an interest in landscape architecture and further periods of study at Edinburgh College of Art and Manchester University. Emerging with a landscape qualification in 1970, Beaumont worked for brief spells with Lanarkshire County Council and Renfrew County Council before joining the Glasgow-based practice of William Gillespie and Partners in 1971, where he rose rapidly to the level of Partner. It was during the 1970s and 1980s that Gillespies became well known for their pioneering work in regenerating brownfield sites in urban conurbations. Beaumont recalls that there was a crusading spirit about being in practice during this period. At the time of the interview for this book Rodney Beaumont was running the Oxford office of William Gillespie and Partners. (No c.v. received – career details reconstructed from interview.)

Ivor Cunningham became interested in landscape design during his final year at the Architectural Association. Reacting against the arrogance and harsh intellectualism of modern architecture as it was then taught, Cunningham decided to study landscape architecture under Brian Hackett at what was then King's College, Newcastle. After further study in Holland, Cunningham went to work for Brenda Colvin and Sylvia Crowe who ran separate practices from shared premises close to London's Baker Street. In 1955 he was offered a position by the architect, Eric Lyons, and thus began an association with the Surrey-based practice that has endured for the whole of his professional career. In the days of disillusion with high-rise housing, the practice was notable for its pioneering work in producing high-density low-rise housing for the developers, SPAN. These projects were distinguished by the attention paid to matters of landscape and the quality of external spaces.

Nevil Farr Frustrated by his early years as an architect in Worcester, Nevil Farr discovered that landscape design could offer him more creative freedom and he enrolled upon the course at Cheltenham. He learnt much about the business as well as the art of landscape architecture from his four years with Derek Lovejoy and Partners in London. After a brief interlude in Milton Keynes, Farr went back to Lovejoy's and was then invited to establish a Liverpool office for the Donaldson Edwards Partnership in 1979. Although Farr has enjoyed design and the visual arts all his life, he confesses that what keeps him going is the excitement of practice, finding clients, bidding for work, winning work – 'keeping the whole thing afloat'. He now identifies strongly with Liverpool, the city in which he has lived and worked for the past twenty years.

Peter Fischer Born in Glasgow but raised in London, Peter Fischer became interested in landscape while studying for his undergraduate architecture degree at the University of Newcastle.

Rather than pursuing his architectural studies, he enrolled on the Diploma in Landscape Design, graduating in 1971. He explains that he was much more interested in site planning and the external aspects of architecture than he ever was with interiors. His first job was with Brian Clouston and Partners in Durham where he worked on reclamation projects and discovered a penchant for designing landform which he still possesses today. After two years in Canada and two more with Milton Keynes Development Corporation, he returned to London where he formed a practice with Gordon Bell in 1981.

In his current practice, Fischer undertakes many projects connected with the restoration of landfill sites, which offer him the opportunity to follow his interest in landform, but he has also been involved with a number of Townscape workshops for the Civic Trust Regeneration Unit. He finds this work difficult but fascinating, because of the human dynamics involved. As one of a team of consultants brought in to participate in intensive sessions with local government officers and representative groups, he says that the hardest thing is to 'knock all their heads together' and get them to co-operate.

Tim Gale was drawn to landscape architecture by early interests in natural history, painting and the study of maps. While studying landscape architecture at Leeds Polytechnic (now Leeds Metropolitan University) he was tutored by Alan Ruff who, at that time, was developing his interest in Dutch ecological landscapes. Shortly after graduating, Gale was employed by the City of Birmingham Architects Department where, to his great satisfaction, he found himself working on the landscape proposals for the National Exhibition Centre which was then in its early design stages. While working for Brian Clouston and Partners in the 1980s, Gale spent periods abroad in Hong Kong and Kuwait. In 1992 he formed a partnership with Tony Edwards which is based in central London.

James Hope discovered landscape architecture while studying horticulture in Edinburgh in the late 1940s, but worked for many years in commercial horticulture and landscape construction before working on Edinburgh University's landscape design programme in the early 1960s. For ten years he worked with Edinburgh University's Planning Research Unit with Professors Sir Robert Mathew and Percy Johnson-Marshall on urban and regional planning studies in Britain, Ireland and Portugal. Throughout his career Hope has been able to combine his practice as a landscape architect with academic interests. In addition to running the busy design practice, Landesign, which he formed in 1974, he has pursued an interest in environmental psychology which developed in the early 1970s when he began to investigate the perceptions of Edinburgh schoolchildren towards place and landscape. He is currently using Personal Construct Theory to develop improved methods of environmental assessment. A practical man as well as a scholar, he has somehow found the time to develop a number of simple, relatively inexpensive watering systems for indoor planting in offices and leisure centres, which are now in commercial production.

John Hopkins Following graduation from Thames Polytechnic (now the University of Greenwich) in 1978, John Hopkins embarked upon a world trip which would take him to Australia, India, Nepal, Malaysia and Kuala Lumpur, and later to New Zealand, the United States, China and Hong Kong. Along the way he found employment in local landscape architecture offices and developed a truly global perspective upon the profession. In the mid-1980s he undertook a Masters degree by research at Louisiana State University where his ideas about landscape architecture were much influenced by working with three professors, two of philosophy and one of environmental economics. Upon returning to England, Hopkins settled in the capital and at the time of our interview he was an Associate with EDAW. Shortly afterwards he moved to Landscape Design Associates.

Hopkins is a contributor to a recent book on the relationship between architecture and landscape edited by Jan Birksted of the University of East London.

Rebecca Hughes discovered landscape architecture while doing botanical fieldwork in South Wales for her undergraduate dissertation, where she saw the results of Sylvia Crowe's work on the design of forestry plantations for the Forestry Commission.

Realising that this was just the sort of work she would like to do, Hughes joined the postgraduate landscape design course at Newcastle University. Her earliest jobs were temporary positions in which her botanical knowledge was as important as her design training. She carried out ecological surveys and prepared management plans for the twelve National Trust properties on the Northumbrian coast, then visited Italy, Turkey and Greece, on behalf of Anthony Walker and Partners, to research Mediterranean plant materials for a botanical garden in Tripoli, Libya. In 1986 Hughes worked on an ethnobotanical research project in the rain forests of Papua New Guinea, gathering herbarium specimens of plants used for medicinal purposes by the communities of the Western Province.

Hughes has had a varied career, combining periods in local government, self-employed practice and teaching, but since 1993 has worked for Scottish Natural Heritage in Edinburgh, where she advises on the impact of novel, complex or contentious development proposals. She has played a leading role in the establishment of an inventory and computerised database of the landscape character of Scotland. Hughes was a member of the working party which produced *Guidelines for Landscape and Visual Impact Assessment* (Spon, 1995) on behalf of the Landscape Institute and the Institute of Environmental Assessment.

Margaret Jackson Although Margaret Jackson is a member of the Landscape Institute, she no longer works primarily as a landscape architect. She is a partner in Community Economic Development Consultants, Liverpool, and describes herself as a local economic development practitioner and consultant. Graduating initially in Geography, Jackson then completed a Diploma in Landscape Architecture at Manchester University while working as a landscape technician for Greater Manchester Metropolitan Council. Upon qualification she continued to work for the council and she has positive memories of a highly professional, well-funded and well-respected team of landscape architects who were undertaking large-scale reclamation work with a noticeably beneficial impact upon the city's environment. There followed less fulfilling positions in Liverpool's City Architecture Department and in private practice. Jackson's next position was as a landscape architect for the Liverpool Housing Trust. It was through working with housing associations that Jackson became involved in community development issues and in the late 1980s was invited to become the manager of the Eldonian Development Trust in the Vauxhall area of Liverpool. This has achieved international recognition as a model of good practice in community-led development initiatives. In 1991 Jackson won a German Marshall Scholarship and travelled extensively in the United States of America researching regeneration in low income neighbourhoods.

Ray Keeley After graduating in Geography and Geology, Ray Keeley completed his postgraduate studies in landscape architecture at the University of Newcastle in 1979. After a long period of settled employment in local government, first with Hamilton District Council in Lanarkshire, then with North Tyneside Council's Architect's Department, Keeley responded to the unsettled political and economic climate of the 1980s by accepting a voluntary redundancy package and venturing into self-employment. As well as undertaking commissions as a sole practitioner, he worked on a freelance basis for the City of Sunderland and for Groundwork North-East. At the time of our interview he had been working in this way for over six years, an existence which he found stimulating though at times precarious. Shortly after the interview Keeley took a position with St Edmundsbury Borough Council, returning to the relative security of local authority employment.

Heather Lloyd rebelled against parental hopes of a scientific career by enrolling upon an art foundation course at Cambridge College of Arts and Technology. While she enjoyed this thoroughly, she became increasingly disillusioned with what she saw as the shallowness of the world of textiles and fashion which she had thought to join. Acting upon a suggestion from her mother, she applied to study landscape architecture at Leeds Polytechnic (now Leeds Metropolitan University). Although Lloyd admits that she got into landscape architecture almost by accident, her enthusiasm for the profession is very evident. Her career, all within local government in the London area, has seen her rise from a lowly technician at the London Borough

of Bexley to Principal Project Planner at Westminster City Council. Lloyd believes in working closely with the public and her greatest satisfactions, as well as some of her most humbling defeats, have come from projects which involved high levels of community participation.

Peter McGuckin Upon graduating in landscape architecture in 1979, Peter McGuckin found employment with the local authority in his home city of Newcastle upon Tyne, where he rose to become a Senior Landscape Architect specialising in land reclamation. Moving into the private sector towards the end of the economically expansive 1980s, he was given responsibility for the landscape components of Tyne and Wear Development Corporation's Newcastle Business Park, a prestigious 25-hectare business park developed on the site of former shipyards and armaments factories which now provides office accommodation for several blue-chip companies including British Airways, IBM and AA Insurance Services. His close association with the redevelopment of industrial Tyneside continued when, with Bob Branson, he launched Branson McGuckin in 1992. One of their earliest and largest projects was Newcastle's East Quayside, another 'flagship' redevelopment by the Tyne and Wear Development Corporation.

Nigel Marshall has been Principal Landscape Architect within the Transport and Environment Department of East Sussex County Council since 1974. He leads the Landscape Group which provides a comprehensive service in landscape planning, design, implementation and management, together with a specialism in environmental presentation. Marshall holds a Diploma in Landscape Architecture from Thames Polytechnic (now the University of Greenwich), having trained while with the Greater London Council Parks Department.

His experience from seven years' working in London ranged from intensely urban situations to urban fringe and rural issues. Whilst with East Sussex he has sought to cultivate a rich diversity of work and skills within his team. He holds a strong belief in landscape planning from a base of landscape character assessment, which in turn directs the activities of landscape design and management. East Sussex has good reputation for landscape assessment, its work having been recognised by awards from the Landscape Institute and the Royal Town Planning Institute.

Neil Mattinson With an early career in local government, Neil Mattinson entered the private sector to work on the first International Garden Festival to be held in the UK, which took place in Liverpool in 1984. At the time of our interview he was an Associate Director with SGS Environment, a multidisciplinary environmental consultancy which was part of a large international company with interests in over 140 countries. Since then he has become a partner in the Peterborough-based practice, Landscape Design Associates. Mattinson's wide experience has encompassed landscape planning and environmental assessment, project management and master-planning. His main interests lie in the commercial, residential, leisure and recreational sectors, particularly the planning and design of projects in the urban/rural fringe.

Philip Moss But for a charismatic interviewer at Manchester Polytechnic, Philip Moss might not have become a landscape architect, but could have drifted into architecture, graphic design, industrial design or interior design, all of which interested him as a sixth-former. It is perhaps not surprising that Moss's career track ultimately delivered him to a large multidisciplinary practice where he now rubs shoulders with architects and engineers on a daily basis. As the director responsible for all BDP's UK landscape work he has been involved in numerous city-centre redevelopment schemes, business parks, urban renewal projects and transportation studies. Before joining BDP, Moss was a Landscape Group Leader with Warrington Development Corporation and was involved in the planning and implementation of all landscape work in the Birchwood and Bridgewater areas of the New Town.

Pauline Randall Graduating in the biological sciences from the University of London, Pauline Randall then took an MA in landscape architecture at the University of Sheffield. She gained early experience of river valley planning and land reclamation while working for Greater Manchester Council, which, together with her natural science

background, has contributed to the success of the practice, Randall Thorp, which she set up with her partner, Edward Thorp, in 1986.

In 1989 Randall successfully provided landscape planning and expert witness services for a new settlement project in Cambridge. She has regularly prepared and presented evidence at planning appeals and Local Plan or Unitary Development Plan inquiries. Her work has also included the quality control of landscape impact assessments for the Highways Agency. She became a Fellow of the Landscape Institute in 1995.

Simon Rendel was a disillusioned civil engineer with architectural tendencies when he met Peter Youngman, the eminent landscape architect, and realised that this was a profession which really interested him. After adding a postgraduate landscape qualification to his c.v. he went to work under David Randall at Berkshire County Council, where he found a mixture of planning and design work which thoroughly suited his abilities and inclinations. Upon moving to the Greater London Council he took on more managerial responsibilities which were not always so conducive. Rendel moved into the private sector in the mid-1980s and found it liberating in many ways, although he felt that commercial pressures often militated against quality in design. Some of his greatest satisfactions came in the mid-1990s when he developed the technique of Tranquil Area Mapping for the Countryside Commission and the Council for the Protection of Rural England. In 1995 he produced a map which showed that tranquil areas equivalent to the size of Wales had been lost in the last thirty-five years.

Sadly Simon Rendel died suddenly in 1997 not long after he had given the interview for this book.

Tom Robinson came into landscape architecture via an Oxford history degree and some vague yearnings to do something for the environment. But having stumbled across landscape architecture almost by accident, he soon realised that it was a profession which inspired him. Robinson has worked in both the public and private sectors, but clearly finds the latter more stimulating. In 1991 he went into partnership with an ecologist to form the environmental consultancy Robinson Penn. If some of the Romantic idealism which brought him into landscape architecture has faded, he remains nevertheless a devout believer in the importance of good environmental design and the value that this can bring to a wide range of development projects.

Dougal Thornton Bowing to parental pressure, Dougal Thornton studied geography at Aberdeen University rather than following his heart and going to art school. However, whilst at Aberdeen he discovered that it was possible to train at postgraduate level to become a landscape architect. It was a career which seemed to unite his geographical knowledge with his artistic inclinations, so he set off south of the border to get his Diploma in Landscape Design. At the time of our interview, Thornton had spent all of his career working in local government, either in the North East or in Central Scotland. He explained his loyalty to the public sector not so much in political terms, but by his belief that this was where he could produce work which would directly benefit ordinary people. Rather surprisingly Thornton finally broke with local authority life shortly after our interview and now runs his own practice in Stirling.

Cheryl Tolladay travelled the world for ten years before becoming interested in design while working as an *au pair* for an interior designer. Three years after her return to Britain she enrolled on a landscape architecture programme at Heriot-Watt University in Edinburgh. She recalls that there were several mature students on the course at that time, and that they were, if anything, even more idealistic and enthusiastic about landscape architecture than their younger classmates. Tolladay has not lost this zeal; indeed, she feels that in her present position as a Principal Landscape Architect in a Groundwork Trust in County Durham she is at

last able to do what she always thought landscape architects should be doing – improving terribly degraded environments.

John Vaughan As an undergraduate John Vaughan studied botany and zoology at the University of Newcastle, developing a particular interest in plant communities and habitat development. At the end of his course, when it looked as though he had a choice between teaching or going into research, someone suggested that he should investigate the university's Landscape Architecture course, which at that time purportedly had an emphasis towards ecological science. He was rather disillusioned to find that ecological thinking was not as prominent in design teaching as he had expected, and he had a further shock when he took his first professional position as a Landscape Assistant in Basildon New Town and discovered that landscape architects had to fight to get their ideas taken seriously.

Vaughan is not a person to duck challenges. The experience he gained over six years as a Senior Landscape Architect for Tyne and Wear County Council gave him the confidence to take on the role of Group Leader in the London Borough of Lambeth. In his current role as Project Director of the Great North Forest, political astuteness and persuasiveness are at least as important as technical know-how.

I am also grateful to the following landscape architects who agreed to be interviewed for my research, but who have not sent full c.v. details: Roger Kirk-Smith (ASH, Liverpool), Fiona Sim (London Borough of Newham), Perry Twigg (Salford Metropolitan Borough Council).

Index

Page numbers with the suffix *c* or *n* denote a caption or a note.